Error-Control Coding and Applications

Error–Control Coding and Applications

Djimitri Wiggert Ph.D.

The MITRE Corporation
Information and Surveillance Systems
McLean, Virginia

Artech House

Acknowledgements

This is an outgrowth of teaching I have done. In that regard, I wish to thank Dr. Neil J. Birch for his encouragement and for making available the opportunity to present the initial version of this material as an on-site course to personnel at the NASA Goddard Space Flight Center, Greenbelt, Maryland.

I am indebted to The MITRE Corporation, Washington Operations, and in particular to Mr. H.T. Grusin and Mr. J.D. Morrell for making available both stenographic and graphic arts support. Among the many who typed portions of the manuscript and its revisions, I would like to acknowledge major efforts by Mrs. Joanne Kuehni, Mrs. Carol Teachey, and Mrs. Frances Weyrauch.

Finally, many thanks to the staff at Artech House, particularly to Mr. Mark Walsh, Editor, and Ms. Jane Carey, Art Director, for their professional advice and assistance during the preparation of this work for publication.

ARTECH HOUSE, INC.
610 Washington Street
Dedham, Massachusetts 02026
Printed and bound in the United States of America

Library of Congress Card Catalog Number: 78-23237
Standard Book Number: 0-89006-066-5

To Barbara, Lara, Thea, Heidi and Kristian

TABLE of CONTENTS

Chapter 1

Introduction and Overview

1.1 General

In this book we shall examine error-control techniques* from the point of view of the user; that is, the individual who wishes to cope with errors in a specific instance of data transmission or data storage. In most cases, results will be presented without proof or derivation. However, there will usually be a discussion of *why* the result is useful and/or significant. Wherever it seems helpful to do so, plausibility arguments will be given. Examples will be introduced at many points along the way as illustrations of the theory. In fact, the same example may be brought through several stages by being utilized in conjunction with several different points of the theory.

A person who is considering the use of error control should consider the following questions:

1. How much improvement in performance is possible with error control?
2. How easily and at what cost can error control be implemented?
3. Is error control alone the best solution to a problem, or should it be supplemented (or even replaced) by another technique?

The first question requires as complete a knowledge as possible of the noise or error statistics of the unprotected transmission or storage system so that performance of various types of error control can be predicted. A measure of effectiveness used to help answer question 1 might be one of the following: decrease in error probability for fixed signal-to-noise ratio, decrease in transmitted power permitted for a fixed probability of error, or the length of the maximum correctable burst of errors.

*Techniques involving error detection as well as correction will be presented.

The second question addresses the engineering problems of cost, equipment and/or software complexity, speed required versus speed available, overall throughput rate, and trade-offs against other coding and non-coding error-control techniques. This question is, from the system engineering point of view, as important as the first. If adequate error protection through error-control coding can be obtained only by delaying final system output until it is no longer useful or by doubling the cost of the system without error control, for example, then certainly other methods should be considered.

The preceding leads us directly to the third question. The engineer should keep an open mind with regard to alternate techniques. For instance, it may prove less costly and sufficiently effective, compared with error control, to employ some form of space or frequency diversity or to take advantage of spectrum-spreading techniques (particularly if the latter are already being contemplated for their anti-jam and/or data security properties).

1.2 Overview of the Book

This introductory chapter will conclude in the next section with a presentation and discussion of a model of a digital communication (or storage) system. Chapter 2 addresses some terminology and analysis which connect communication waveforms and the discrete entities (digits) used in error-control coding.

Chapter 3 introduces the notions of linear algebra as the basis for decoding techniques for parity-check block codes, the most easily understood of all codes. The important relationship between distance and error-control properties is introduced in this chapter. An appendix which contains an elementary, detailed development of vectors and matrices makes the chapter self-contained as far as mathematical background is concerned. Chapter 4 develops what should be just enough of the results of abstract algebra (particularly groups and finite fields) and cyclic code theory to make possible an understanding and appreciation of the two classes of cyclic codes, the BCH and the Reed-Solomon codes, which are introduced and discussed in Chapter 5. The Bose-Chaudhuri-Hocquenghem (BCH) codes are the best block codes in general use for dealing with independent errors, while the Reed-Solomon codes enjoy a similar position for coping with bursts of errors.

The next four chapters (6 through 9) are devoted to convolutional codes — their properties, representation, and encoding — and to the three leading decoding techniques that have been developed. Threshold decoding, sequential decoding, and maximum-likelihood (Viterbi) decoding are all very effective techniques, each excelling under specific circumstances.

Burst-correcting techniques, including the use of error detection and retransmission, are the subject of Chapter 10. The book concludes in Chapter 11 with what is hoped will be a useful discussion of the trade-offs involved in selecting a coding scheme for each of several real-life situations in which the channel statistics are known, or at least strongly suspected, with emphasis on the engineering aspects of the problem.

1.3 Model of a Communication System

There are several useful models of a communication system, any of which can be used as a basis for discussion of communication and coding. A simple model which emphasizes the role of error control is shown in Figure 1-1. This model consists of a source, an error-control encoder, a noisy channel, an error-control decoder, and a sink or user, which are connected in cascade as shown. For this system, all information transferred between system blocks must be in digital form (usually 1's and 0's) in order for error control to be utilized in the manner shown. It is common practice to expand the source, channel, and sink blocks to produce the model shown in Figure 1-2. The dashed lines relate these new components of the model to those in Figure 1-1.

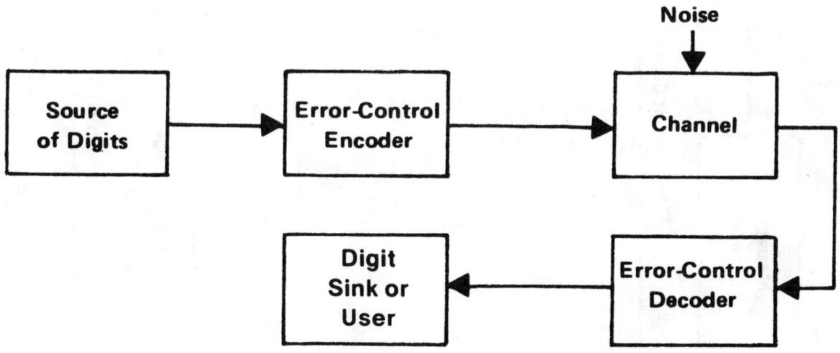

Figure 1-1/Simple Model of a Communication or Data Storage and Retrieval System

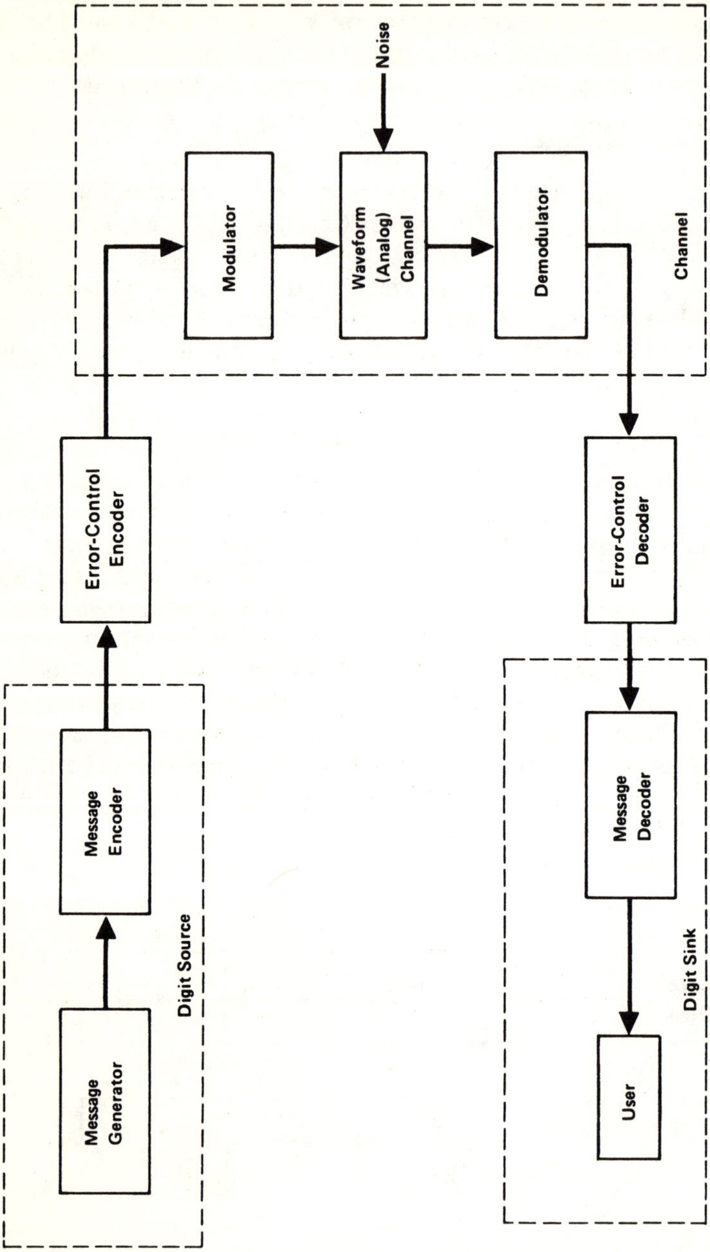

Figure 1-2/Expanded Model of Communication System

The message generator may have either a digital (discrete amplitude) or analog (continuous amplitude) output. To give an idea of the diversity of quantities which could be considered as messages, we mention the following as examples of digital messages:

- Final score of a football game
- Dow Jones closing average
- Amount of credit card purchase
- Number, kind, position, and velocity of vehicles spotted by an airborne observer.

An example of an analog message is the real-time record of the blood pressure of an orbiting astronaut.

Since the output of the message encoder must be suitable for input to the error-control encoder, this output must certainly be digital and is permitted to change only at specified times. Thus, if the message generator produces analog output, the message encoder must as a minimum possess analog-to-digital capability—for example, pulse code modulation (PCM). It is in the message encoder, too, that any redundancy in the message may profitably be removed. For example, the astronaut's blood pressure will be essentially constant for long periods of time. Thus it is wasteful of both time and bandwidth to transmit each and every value, either sampled or continuous. In this case, it may be best to transmit (e.g., by run-length encoding) only the changes which exceed some preset threshold. Finally, if the error-control encoder operates with a binary alphabet, it may be necessary to convert in the message encoder from some larger alphabet (e.g., number of PCM quantization levels) to a sequence of 0's and 1's.

From the discussion so far, it should already be clear that there is considerable variation in degree of detail which must be represented in any given situation and considerable latitude on the part of the person modeling the communication system. For example, one may also want to encrypt for communication security purposes. This encryption could take place at the analog message stage (e.g., spectrum scrambling) or at any of several points within the digital portion of the system.

Once the message has been digitized and redundancy removed (if desired) we re-introduce redundancy in the error-control encoder. This time, however, the redundancy is added at a fixed rate and in a known way which introduces structure to the error-control encoder output in the form of block, convolutional, or a combination of these codes. This output now passes into the channel. In most cases, this involves modulating the sequence of pulses onto a carrier. This is done by the block labeled "modulator."

The analog channel inevitably modifies the transmitted waveform. This could occur in a variety of ways, including adding noise and fading. Additive noise, such as that in a deep space channel, frequently has a Gaussian amplitude distribution and a frequency spectrum which is flat, at least over the signal bandwidth. Additive noise could also occur as impulse noise, which also has a broad frequency spectrum but strongly non-Gaussian amplitude statistics. Fading of signal strength is often adequately modeled by the Rayleigh distribution. One example of a mechanism causing fading is the multipath which frequently exists between an airborne or ground transmitter and a satellite. Fading results in bursts of errors in the input, and possibly the output, of the error-control decoder.

The function of the demodulator block of Figure 1-2 includes not only recovery of the modulating waveform (now corrupted by noise), but the generation of estimates of the digits transmitted. These estimates could simply be 0's and 1's (i.e., hard decisions). Alternatively, they could be quantized estimates (soft decisions) of these digits, with the demodulator either generating values between or beyond the values corresponding to 0 and 1 or generating 0's and 1's plus a rough measure of the reliability of each digit estimate.

The error-control decoder then operates on these estimates of the transmitted digits to produce its estimate of the transmitted encoded message sequence. This decoder could be a table look-up based on a calculation of the most likely transmitted block code word, or it could be a sequential decoder, to cite only two possibilities. The estimate of the encoded transmitted message sequence is now presented to the message decoder so that it can in turn generate its estimate of the transmitted message.

It should be emphasized that the communication system model just presented is neither unique nor necessarily the most suitable one to use in all situations.* As an illustration of the type of complex system one might encounter in practice, consider Figure 1-3. Here we have multiplexing of data, multiple levels of error control,

*For another approach to a model, see Fano [24].

encryption for security, and spectrum spreading for anti-jam, anti-multipath, multiple access, and/or additional security. Such a system typifies a modern civil government, large business, or military communication system carrying a mix of voice, data and facsimile. (For an analysis of the architecture and functioning of another model of such a system, see the paper by Glenn [1a]). The MUX (multiplex) and DEMUX functions could be carried out to place several telephone conversations (MUX1) or voice and data streams (MUX2) on a single channel by either time-or frequency-division multiplexing. The multiple levels of error-control coding could be a concatenated scheme using a Viterbi (convolutional) inner code (ERROR CONTROL CODER/DECODER 2) and a Reed-Solomon (block) outer code (ERROR CONTROL CODER/DECODER 1) in which symbols of the Reed-Solomon code become the binary digit stream entering and leaving the Viterbi coder/decoder combination. Here each coder/decoder pair is matched to the channel which it serves. Thus, the convolutional code could be coping with random-error CHANNEL 2, making CHANNEL 1 a generally noiseless channel with occasional bursts of Viterbi decoder output errors. This latter channel is amenable to error control by the burst-error oriented Reed-Solomon code.

Encryption, long a part of the military communication picture, has become increasingly common in the civilian sector as well, as corporations and police departments strive to protect themselves against unwanted electronic eavesdropping.

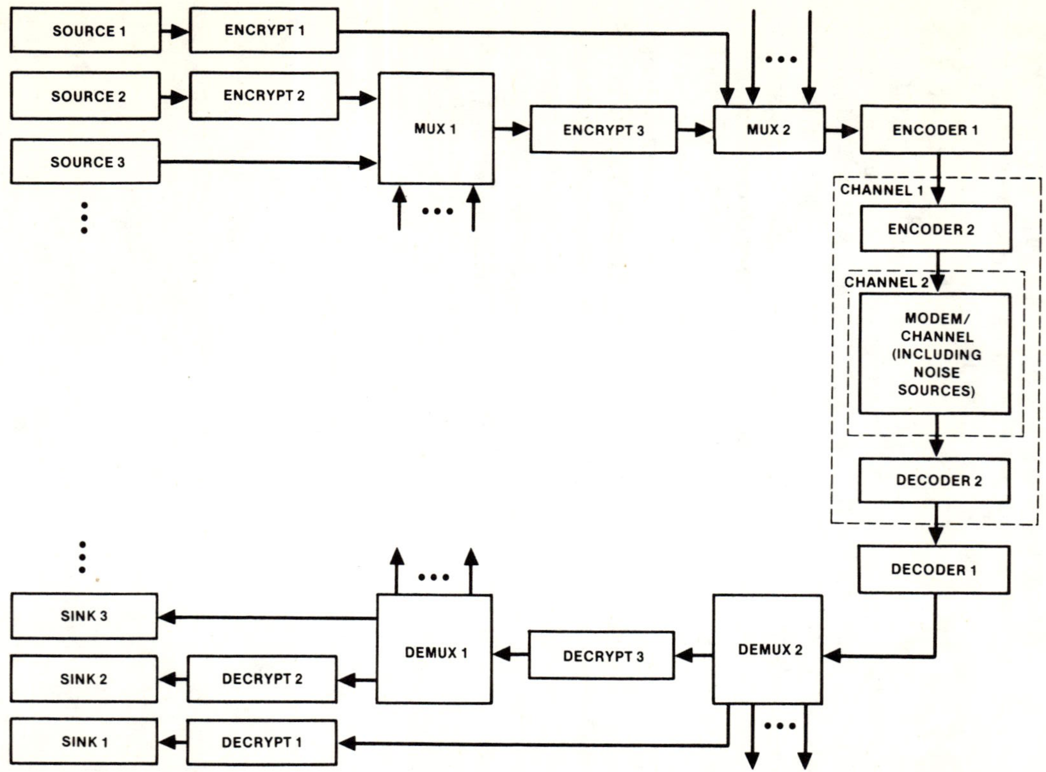

Figure 1-3/A Possible "Real-Life" Communication/Data-Transmission System

Chapter 2

Communication Theory Considerations

2.1 Introduction

It is the purpose of this chapter to relate error control and digital communication, in which operations for the most part are performed on discrete values of variables, and the world of waveforms, which are basically analog. By analog we mean here the attribute of being able to assume any of a continuum of values which cover either a finite or an infinite range. Clearly, channel noise is an analog waveform although its effects can be represented digitally in terms of the output of a demodulator. One of our prime concerns in this chapter will be to demonstrate one way in which the analog output of a demodulator can be converted to digital form with the help of one or more decision thresholds. Another concern will be the consideration of the minimum ratio of signal energy to noise power density for which demodulation and synchronization are possible. We will not, however, present a tutorial on modulation and demodulation or discuss the pro's and con's of various modulation/demodulation schemes.

2.2 Binary Antipodal Signaling

As a simple illustration of the way in which analog information (plus noise) can be converted to digital form, we consider a modulation scheme in which binary information is transmitted by means of antipodal waveforms; that is, if a 1 corresponds to the waveform f(t), then a 0 corresponds to [–f(t)]. We shall assume that f(t) has duration T and energy $\mathcal{E}$:

$$\int_0^T f^2(t)\, dt = \mathcal{E} \tag{2-1}$$

Finally, we shall assume stationary, white, Gaussian noise with sample function n(t) of one-sided power density N_o watts/Hz. That is, all of the noise power appears in the positive frequencies with the power spectrum as shown in Figure 2-1.*

Figure 2-1/Single-Sided White Noise Spectrum

We shall assume that we have optimum** demodulation of our received waveform. This is shown in texts on signal theory to be achieved by the use of a filter matched to the signal f(t). That is, the filter has impulse response h(t) = f(T−t). Thus, if we use this filter and sample its output at time t = T as follows:

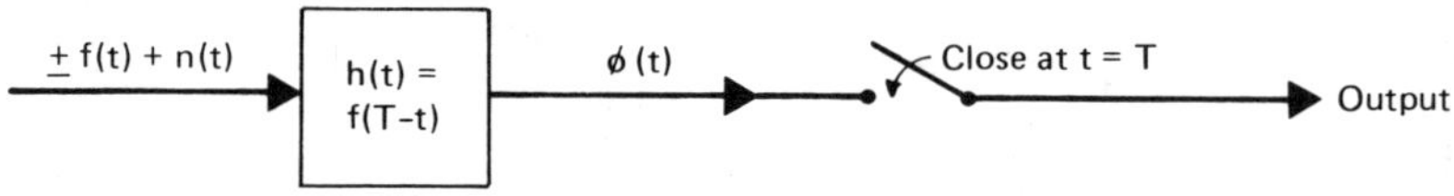

then the (voltage) value designated by Output will be characterized by having the largest possible ratio of signal energy to noise power density, in this case given by $\mathcal{E}/N_o$, where $\mathcal{E}$ is the energy in ± f(t).

Let filter output waveform $\phi(t)$ consist of components $\phi_s(t)$ and $\phi_n(t)$, due to signal and noise, respectively:

$$\phi(t) = \phi_s(t) + \phi_n(t) \qquad (2\text{-}2)$$

*The reader who is unfamiliar with any of the notions and terminology used here can find excellent treatments of this material in Chapters 3 and 4 of Wozencraft and Jacobs [1], Chapters 4 and 9 of Carlson [2], or Chapters 2 and 4 of Hancock [3], among many texts on the subject.

**In the sense of maximizing the ratio of signal energy to noise power density at the demodulator output.

Since the matched filter is a linear system, superposition of inputs corresponds to superposition of outputs. Since the filter output is the convolution of the filter's impulse response with the input waveform, we have

$$[\pm f(t) + n(t)] * h(t) = \phi_s(t) + \phi_n(t) \quad (2\text{-}3)$$

or at time t = T

$$\int_o^T [\pm f(T-\tau) + n(T-\tau)]\, f(T-\tau)\, d\tau = \phi_s(T) + \phi_n(T) \quad (2\text{-}4)$$

This expression consists of both deterministic and random components. That is, the matched filter output is a random variable. By virtue of linearity we have

$$\pm \int_o^T f^2 (T-\tau) d\tau = \phi_s(T) \quad (2\text{-}5a)$$

$$\int_o^T n(T-\tau) f(T-\tau) d\tau = \phi_n(T) \quad (2\text{-}5b)$$

With the change of variable $\tau' = T-\tau$, equation (2-5a) becomes

$$\pm \int_o^T f^2 (\tau')\, d\tau' = \pm\, \mathcal{E} = \phi_s \quad (2\text{-}6)$$

the signal energy. Equation (2-5b) obviously can not be evaluated explicitly. However, for our purposes, this is not a problem, since it turns out that all we really need is a statistical description of the filter output. In particular, we want the mean and variance and, if possible, the probability density of the output.

The mean is easily found. Using the symbol E to denote expected value, we have

$$\begin{aligned} E[\phi_s(T) + \phi_n(T)] &= E\left\{\int_o^T [\pm f^2 (T-\tau) + f(T-\tau)n(T-\tau)]\, d\tau\right\} \\ &= \pm \int_o^T E[f^2 (T-\tau)]\, d\tau \\ &\quad + \int_o^T E[f(T-\tau)n(T-\tau)]\, d\tau \end{aligned} \quad (2\text{-}7)$$

The first integral on the right has actually been evaluated in the preceding paragraph; it is $\mathcal{E}$. The second integral on the right can be written

$$\int_0^T f(T-\tau)E[n(T-\tau)]\,d\tau$$

Its value is zero since we specified the noise to have zero mean. Thus, the mean of the matched filter output is $\pm\mathcal{E}$.

The calculation of the variance of the output is nearly as simple as that of the mean. We have (dropping the argument T)

$$\mathrm{var}(\phi_s + \phi_n) = E[(\phi_s + \phi_n - \mathcal{E})^2] \tag{2-8}$$

Collecting the deterministic portion of this gives us

$$E[(\phi_s - \mathcal{E})^2] + E[\phi_n{}^2] + 2E[\phi_s - \mathcal{E})]$$

Since $\phi_s = \mathcal{E}$, the first and third expected values are trivially zero. This leaves

$$E[\phi_n{}^2] = E[(\int_0^T n(T-\tau)f(T-\tau)d\tau)^2] \tag{2-9}$$

which may be written

$$E[\phi_n{}^2] = E[\int_0^T ds \int_0^T n(T-\tau)n(T-s)f(T-\tau)f(T-s)d\tau]$$

$$= \int_0^T ds \int_0^T d\tau\; f(T-\tau)f(T-s)E[n(T-\tau)n(T-s)] \tag{2-10}$$

The expected value $E[n(T-\tau)n(T-s)]$ is simply the autocorrelation function $R_{nn}(\tau,s)$ of the noise. Assuming that the noise process is stationary, it can be shown that

$$E[n(T-\tau)n(T-s)] = (N_o/2)\delta(\tau-s) \tag{2-11}$$

for the noise power density of Figure 2-1, where $\delta(\tau-s)$ is the usual impulse or Dirac delta "function." Substitution of equation (2-11) into equation (2-10) yields, after some manipulation,

$$E[\phi_n{}^2] = \mathcal{E}N_o/2$$

so that var $(\phi_s + \phi_n)$ is also $\mathcal{E}N_o/2$.

Since the filter input was Gaussian, linearity (again!) tells us that the output must also be Gaussian with a mean of $\pm\ \mathcal{E}$, depending on the signal sent, and variance $\mathcal{E} N_o/2$. The probability density function is thus one of the two curves shown in Figure 2-2.

The next question is: How do we use this information to decide whether a 0 or 1 was sent? For example, suppose we had matched filter output V_1 as shown in Figure 2-2 on the next page. Intuitively we would choose +f(t) as the transmitted signal. Decision theory (which we will not discuss at all here*) tells us that for 0 and 1 equally probable at the transmitter, the optimum decision (in the sense of minimizing the probability of error) is obtained as follows:

(1) Define decision regions R_o and R_1 as the regions

$$\phi_s + \phi_n < 0 \text{ and } \phi_s + \phi_n \geqslant 0, \text{ respectively.}$$

(2) Choose 0 as the transmitted symbol if $\phi_s + \phi_n$ is in R_o.
Choose 1 as the transmitted symbol if $\phi_s + \phi_n$ is in R_1.

Finally, what is the probability of error associated with our decision? In words, it is the probability of announcing that one symbol was sent when actually the other was sent. In terms of Figure 2-2, it is the probability that we are associating our filter output with the wrong density function. This, in turn, is equal to the area under the tail of the incorrect density function curve. Following our decision rule of the preceding paragraph, in the case of the received value V_1, we would announce that a 1 had been sent. If, in fact, a 0 had been sent, our probability of error would be the area of the shaded region of Figure 2-2 as shown on the next page.

*The interested reader can find excellent treatments in Wozencraft and Jacobs [1] or Carlson [2] among others.

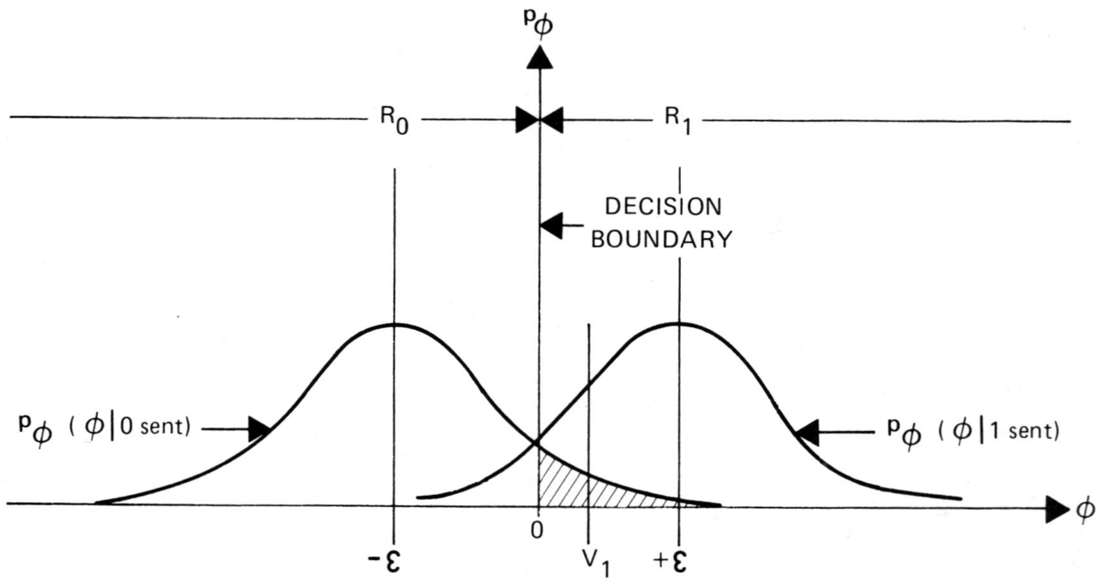

Figure 2-2/Probability Density Functions, Decision Regions, and Error Probability for Binary Signaling (0 and 1 Equally Likely).

This area is given by the analytical expression for the probability of error given that 0 was transmitted:

$$P(e|0) = \int_0^{\infty} p_{\phi}(\phi|0)\, d\phi$$

$$= \int_0^{\infty} \frac{1}{\sqrt{2\pi}\ \sqrt{\mathcal{E}N_o/2}} \exp\left[-\frac{(\phi + \mathcal{E})^2}{\mathcal{E}N_o}\right] d\phi \qquad \text{(2-12a)}$$

Similarly,

$$P(e|1) = \int_{-\infty}^{0} \frac{1}{\sqrt{2\pi}\ \sqrt{\mathcal{E}N_o/2}} \exp\left[-\frac{(\phi - \mathcal{E})^2}{\mathcal{E}N_o}\right] d\phi \qquad \text{(2-12b)}$$

Thus, the total probability of error is

$$P(e) = P(0)\, P(e|0) + P(1)\, P(e|1)$$

A channel defined physically by symbol energy $\mathcal{E}$, noise power density N_o, and the decision process just described is usually represented mathematically by the *binary symmetric channel* (BSC) shown in Figure 2-3(a), with transition probability p equal to either of the integrals in Equations (2-12a) and (2-12b). Note, however, that the input probabilities P(0) and P(1) need not be equal. Note also that transitions are independent from one digit to the next; that is, the channel is memoryless. Any change in these channel input probabilities will cause the decision boundary (now at $\phi = 0$) to shift either right or left. It can be shown that for the situation considered, the decision boundary is located in the optimum position.

More generally, the number of inputs, number of outputs, and transition probabilities may take on any desired set of values in any combination. This generalization of the BSC is called the *discrete memoryless channel* (DMC). A two-input, three-output channel with arbitrary transition probabilities is shown in Figure 2-3(b). A practical example of a DMC is a channel with binary inputs and, say, 3-bit (or 8-level) quantization at the output. Such a channel model is applicable to some convolutional decoding schemes which have been implemented and which are discussed later in this book.

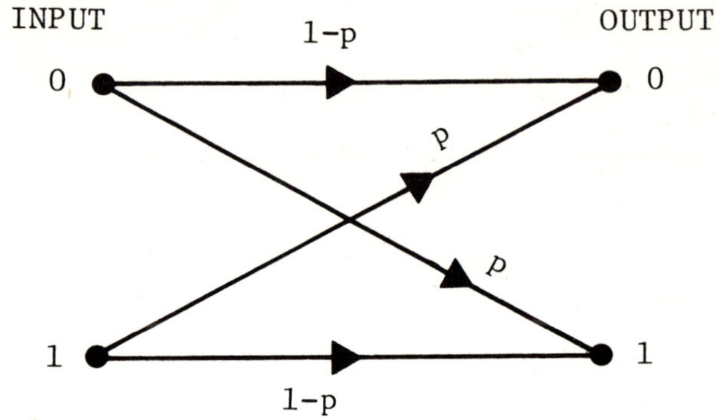

(a) Binary Symmetric Channel

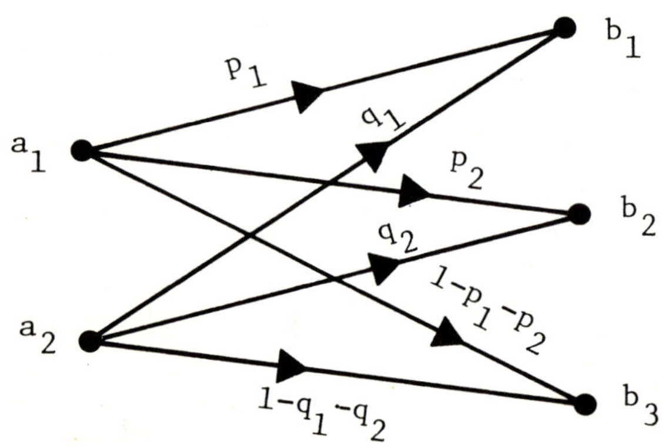

(b) Example of General Discrete Memoryless Channel

Figure 2-3/Models of Discrete Channels

2.3 Some Important Terminology

It is important to note the distinction between the concepts of bit, symbol or digit, and chip. In this book we will use *bit* in two ways: to denote the unit of information using base 2 when taking logarithms (as in $I = -\log_2 P_i$ bits for a message of probability P_i); and to denote a 0 or 1 value of data (or information*). The terms *symbol* and *digit* are more general and are used to denote either information or redundant digits (0's and 1's in most cases), as in the expression "channel symbol". Finally, *chip* arises most often in conjunction with systems using band-spreading (usually, though not necessarily, via pseudo-noise (PN) sequences) for protection against jamming or interference. Writers use the phrase "number of chips per bit" when they mean number of chips per data bit or per channel symbol.

To illustrate, the energy per symbol E_s (identical to $\mathcal{E}$ as used in Section 2.2) will usually refer to channel symbol. To obtain energy per bit from this value, therefore, compute $E_B = (n/k)E_s$, where the code being used has rate $R = k/n$. As an important consequence of this relationship, note that the use of redundant digits for error control does *not* result in reduced energy per bit. There is a price, of course, and it is paid in terms of complexity, increased bandwidth (by the factor n/k), and/or increased cost.

2.4 Demodulator Limit on Coding Gain

We alluded earlier in the chapter to the potential difficulties in trying to use error-control coding in conjunction with an E_B/N_o which is below some critical threshold value. We now address this problem more specifically. This question received considerable attention, especially in the context of a space channel or satellite relay channel, in both analytical and simulation studies between 1967 and 1971**.

*This is in contrast with the usage frequently encountered in the literature on communication systems, in which "bit" is used indiscriminately to denote not only information or data but also any 0 or 1, regardless of its actual significance.

**See for example, Cahn [4], Heller [5], and Cahn, Huth, and Moore [6].

The situation usually modeled, analyzed and/or simulated builds on the discussion of binary antipodal signaling (i.e., biphase modulation) of a convolutionally encoded data stream. A typical system might be the one shown in Figure 2-4, in which the more complete model of Figure 1-3 has been specialized to biphase modulation and convolutional coding, and the encryption and multiplexing have been eliminated in the interest of simplicity. The portions of the system of special interest here are the three blocks pertaining to the insertion of reference bits, phase recovery, and ambiguity resolution. The need for phase recovery arises because this is a coherent system, one which depends upon knowledge of the carrier phase. Degradation of the received signal can result from oscillator drift, phase jitter, and relative motion of the transmitting and receiving terminals and/or relay satellite.

Since it is not our purpose here to go into the principles of Costas or phase-lock loop operation*, we shall simply summarize as typical the results given in Cahn, Huth, and Moore [6] for simulations of the system shown in Figure 2-4. This simulation was parameterized by the ratio of the loop bandwidth B_L to the channel symbol rate R_t. Probability of bit error at the demodulator output was evaluated as a function of the ratio E_B/N_o of energy per bit to noise power density. The standard of comparison was ideal coherent demodulation of the binary PSK signal plus noise. For $B_L = R_t/120$, a degradation from the ideal of about 0.4 dB was observed at an E_B/N_o of about -1 dB, corresponding to $P_B = 0.1$. When $B_L = R_t/12$, performance began to degrade at about $E_B/N_o = 5$ dB and deviated from the ideal by 0.5 dB at $E_B/N_o \approx 3$ dB, $P_B \approx 0.03$. As B_L increased beyond $R_t/12$, degradation was rapid and severe.

It is clear that there is indeed a limit on the usability of coding to compensate for errors due to low E_B/N_o. That is, for any modulation and coding combination there exists a value, or range of values, of E_B/N_o below which the demodulator output P_B is sufficiently degraded that the error-control scheme would be hard put to restore a tolerable (10^{-5} or better) output data bit error rate.

*Excellent treatments are provided in Viterbi [7] and in Gardner [8], among others.

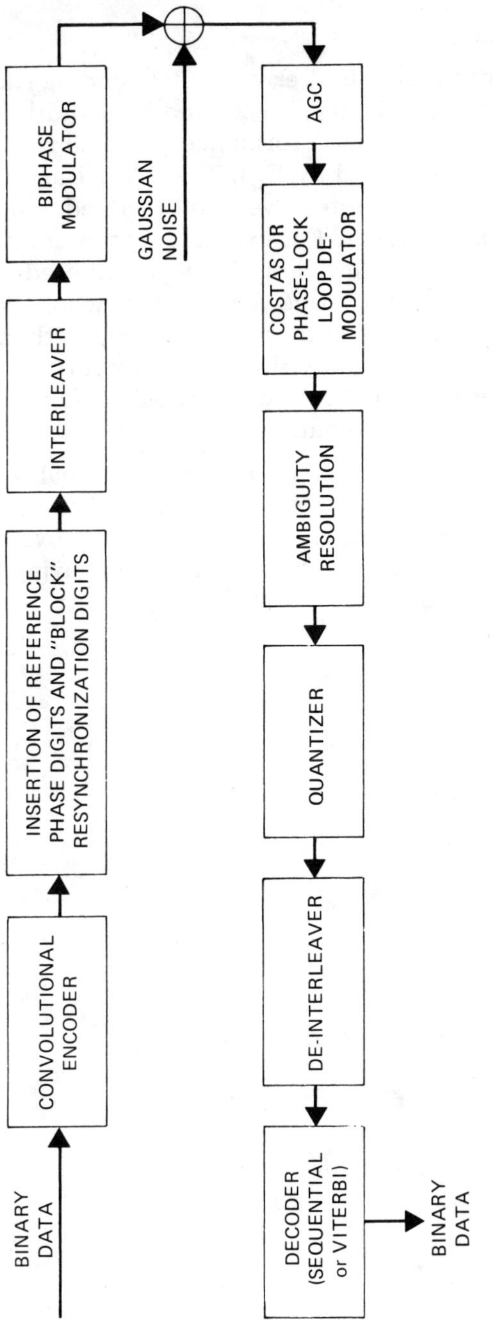

Figure 2-4/Model of System Featuring Biphase Modulation and Convolutional Coding

2.5 Conclusion

In summary, we observe that error-control coding trades a combination of cost, complexity, speed, and bandwidth for some combination of improved performance (P_B) and reduced transmitter power (as expressed by E_B). The relative amount of each of these six system attributes given up or gained depends on the overall constraints present. For example, communication from a deep-space probe would probably be power limited because of weight limitations on the space vehicle. This would call for a simple encoder and transmitter there and consequently a more complex, expensive, and probably slower (non-real-time) decoder on earth to compensate for the very low signal-to-noise ratio characteristic of the deep space channel.

The trade-off between error probability and signal-to-noise ratio for a block code and a number of constraint lengths of a convolutional code is shown in Figure 2-5. Curve A is provided as a reference to show the gains in performance and/or savings in transmitter power possible through the use of error-control coding.

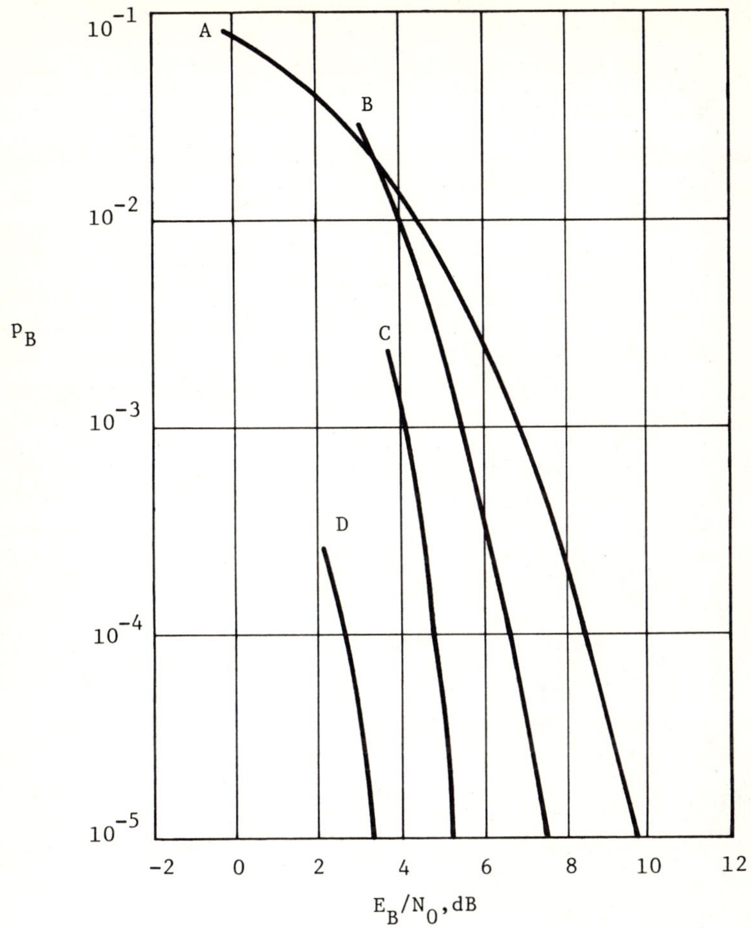

KEY

A: COHERENT PSK (UNCODED)

B: (24, 12) BCH, A (23, 12) BCH CODE AUGMENTED WITH AN OVERALL PARITY CHECK

C: R = 1/2, K = 32 CONVOLUTIONAL CODE WITH SEQUENTIAL DECODING

D: SAME AS C, EXCEPT K = 48

Figure 2-5/Typical Performance Gains Possible with Block and Convolutional Codes

Chapter 3

Introduction to Parity-Check Codes

3.1 Introduction

In studying the construction and properties of error-detecting and error-correcting codes, we shall make extensive use of the notions associated with the theory of vector spaces because many readers are probably already familiar with them from previous work in linear algebra or linear system analysis.* Furthermore, the vector space approach leads easily and naturally into the important and commonly used representation of a code in terms of its generator and parity-check matrices. This approach will be complemented by an approach utilized by Gallager [9] which, while using vectors and matrices, cleverly avoids the need to define and discuss vector spaces.

Following some mathematical preliminaries on groups and vector spaces, this chapter will discuss encoding and decoding of block codes only, and only in terms of their generator and parity-check matrices.

3.2 Why Study Abstract Algebra?

In order to understand and use any but the simplest parity-check code, it is necessary to develop a background in the concepts and operations of abstract algebra. While the words "abstract algebra" may imply to many an engineer the idea of something totally unrelated to reality, let it be stated here and now that this is not the

*For those who desire it, an introduction to vectors and matrices and to the operations performed by and upon them, is presented in the appendix to this chapter.

case. Abstract algebra enables us to identify the fundamental properties of such familiar mathematical systems as the real numbers†, the rational numbers*, and the set of all integers, as well as less familiar systems with a finite number of elements, such as the set 0, 1 with "binary arithmetic"**. Basic similarities and differences also become apparent. For example, we shall see that 0, 1 and its arithmetic as just defined are mathematically far more like the reals than they are like the integers. Examples of the kinds of systems to be discussed include a group, a field, and a vector space. The reals, rationals, and the set 0, 1 with binary arithmetic are examples of a field, while the integers using only addition are an example of a group. Since systems with a finite number of elements are used extensively in coding theory, it is a good idea to become comfortable with them as early as possible. For this reason, illustrative examples and exercises will emphasize groups, fields, and vector spaces having a finite number of elements.

3.3 Properties of Mathematical Systems

Every mathematical system consists of one or more *elements* and at least one *operation* on any two of these elements, while the same element may be used twice with respect to the operation. The elements might be a certain few or all of the integers, rationals, reals, or complex numbers, or they might be literals (a, b, x, y, etc.). An operation could be ordinary addition or multiplication, or addition modulo some number m in which the result is the remainder left after dividing the ordinary arithmetic sum by m.

†All numbers (integers, fractions, decimals) we use in day-to-day arithmetic, as well as numbers like π, e, $\sqrt{2}$, etc.

*All numbers expressible in the form p/q, where p and q may be any integers (whole numbers) as long as q $\neq$ 0.

**Rules of binary arithmetic are: (addition) 0+0=1+1=0,0+1=1+0=1; (multiplication) 0×0=0×1=1×0=0, 1×1=1.

All mathematical systems must satisfy a small set of requirements. These requirements are:

(G1) *Closure* under the specified system operation(s); i.e., if a and b are elements and x is an operation of system S, then $a \times b$ is also an element of S. (Note that $a \times b$ need not be equal to $b \times a$.)

(G2) Inclusion of an *identity* element i with respect to the operation x, whose effect is to leave any element unchanged. That is, $a \times i = i \times a = a$ for any a in S.

(G3) The existence for every element in S of an *inverse* a^{-1} (in S) with respect to the operation x, such that $a \times a^{-1} = a^{-1} \times a = i$.

(G4) An *associative law*; that is, if a, b, and c are in S, then $(a \times b) \times c = a \times b \times c = a \times (b \times c)$ so that $a \times b \times c$ has an unambiguous meaning.

3.4 Groups

If the above properties (G1) through (G4) are the only requirements on S, then S is called a *group*. If $a \times b = b \times a$ for all a and b in S, then the group is said to be *commutative* (or *abelian*) with respect to, or under, the operation x.

Example 3-1. The set S_I of all positive and negative integers and 0, with the operation of ordinary addition, is a group. That is, the group operation x is now the familiar operation "+". Clearly the sum of any two elements of S_I is again an element of S_I (e.g., $1 + 2 = 3$, which is in S_I; similarly, $2 + (-4) = 2$). The identity element is 0, since $0 + a = a + 0 = a$ for any number a in S_I. Finally, the inverse a^{-1} of any element a is $(-a)$, since $a + (-a) = 0$, the identity element. Note that this group is commutative, since the order of the elements in any sum $a+b$ has no effect on the result.

Example 3-2. The simplest example of a group is the single element 0 under ordinary +: 0+0=0, verifying closure, identity, and inverse; the associative law is trivially shown.

Example 3-3. Perhaps the next simplest example of a finite group consists of the elements 0 and 1 and the operation $\oplus$, which denotes addition modulo 2. That is, $1 \oplus 1 = 0$, because $1+1=2$, and $2 \div 2 = 1$ with remainder $= 0$. The complete addition table may be written

$\oplus$	0	1
0	0	1
1	1	0

where the entries in the first row and first column are the addends, and the entry of the intersection of any given row and column is the modulo-2 sum of the entries heading that row and column. This table clearly shows the closure property and the fact that 0 is the identity element under $\oplus$. What is the inverse of each element? That is, what value for a^{-1} satisfies $a \oplus a^{-1} = 0$ for $a=0$ and for $a=1$? A look at the table shows that each element is its own inverse: $0 \oplus 0 = 1 \oplus 1 = 0$.

3.5 Fields and Vector Spaces

The group, defined and discussed in the preceding section, is of interest to us in its own right. It is also a necessary concept in defining two more complicated but more useful systems: *field* and *vector space.*

A *field* is a set of at least two elements and two operations, indicated here by + and ×, which satisfies the following properties:

(F1) It is a commutative group under one operation (say +).

(F2) It is a commutative group under the other operation × except that 0 (the identity under +) has no inverse under ×.

(F3) A *distributive law* holds which is defined by $a \times (b + c) = (a \times b) + (a \times c)$.

Note that property (F3) is a statement of linearity. The utility of this property will be illustrated in conjunction with Examples 3-8 and 3-9 below.

Example 3-4. The set of all positive and negative integers and 0, with the operations of ordinary addition + and ordinary multiplication × , is not a field. While it is a commutative group under + (see Example 3-1), is closed under ×, and has 1 as the identity element under ×, only 1 and −1 have inverses under × (themselves). The distributive law given by Property (F3) is satisfied for any set of integers and/or 0; for example, $2 \times (3 + (-1)) = 2 \times 2 = 4$, and $2 \times 3 + 2 \times (-1) = 4$.

Example 3-5. A very familiar example of a field is the set of rational numbers under ordinary addition and multiplication.

Example 3-6. The set 0, 1 is a field under $\oplus$ (as defined in Example 3-3) and ordinary multiplication. In this case we have a *finite* (or Galois*) field. Property (F1) has been verified in Example 3-2. All parts of property (F2) along with (F3) can be verified from the following multiplication table:

×	0	1
0	0	0
1	0	1

The notation GF (q) is used to denote the finite field of q elements.

Before defining a vector space, we shall first define a vector in the sense in which it is used in algebra and coding theory and in which it will be used here. We use the terminology "vector v having n components over a field F." This means simply that, for any integer $n \geqslant 1$, **

$$\mathrm{v} = (v_1, v_2, v_3, \ldots, v_n) \tag{3-1}$$

is an n-tuple in which each v_i is an element of a field F. For example, v = (1, 0, 1) could be a vector over the real numbers,

*After the French mathematician who first postulated the existence of finite fields and studied many of their properties.

**We shall see that for block codes, n is finite; for convolutional codes, it is infinite in theory but finite, though very large, in practice. We will not become enmeshed here in details of convergence in infinite-dimensional spaces (i.e., n infinite).

or it could just as well be a vector over the finite field GF(2) having only the elements 0 and 1. Two operations are defined for vectors. For $v_1 = (a_1, a_2, \ldots, a_n)$ and $v_2 = (b_1, b_2, \ldots, b_n)$, these operations are:

(V1) Addition of two vectors, defined by

$$v_1 + v_2 = (a_1 + b_1, a_2 + b_2, \ldots, a_n + b_n) \tag{3-2}$$

(V2) Multiplication by a scalar; that is, by an element of F.

Scalar multiplication is defined by

$$cv_1 = (ca_1, ca_2, \ldots, ca_n) \tag{3-3}$$

where c and all of the a_i's are elements of F, and multiplication is the "x" operation defined for F.

In particular, Operation (V2) tells us that the negative $-v_1$ of v_1 is $(-1) \times v_1$ and is given by

$$-v_1 = (-a_1, -a_2, \ldots, -a_n)$$

Finally, the scalar product (or dot product) of two vectors is defined as

$$v_1 \cdot v_2 = a_1 b_1 + a_2 b_2 + \ldots + a_n b_n \tag{3-4}$$

the result of which is once more a scalar. This operation will be of only limited use in our work here.

Example 3-7. Suppose $v_1 = (2, 0, 1)$ and $v_2 = (1, 1, 2)$ with vector components taken from the field F consisting of the elements 0, 1, and 2 with modulo-3 arithmetic. That is, addition and multiplication, respectively, are defined by

+	0	1	2
0	0	1	2
1	1	2	0
2	2	0	1

x	0	1	2
0	0	0	0
1	0	1	2
2	0	2	1

Then properties (V1) and (V2) for vectors are both illustrated by the following sum:

$$\begin{aligned} 2\mathbf{v}_1 + \mathbf{v}_2 &= 2 \times (2, 0, 1) + (1, 1, 2) \\ &= (2 \times 2, 2 \times 0, 2 \times 1) + (1, 1, 2) \\ &= (1, 0, 2) + (1, 1, 2) \\ &= (1 + 1, 0 + 1, 2 + 2) \\ &= (2, 1, 1) \end{aligned}$$

The scalar product of $\mathbf{v}_1$ and $\mathbf{v}_2$ is

$$\begin{aligned} \mathbf{v}_1 \cdot \mathbf{v}_2 &= 2 \times 1 + 0 \times 1 + 1 \times 2 \\ &= 2 + 0 + 2 \\ &= 1 \end{aligned}$$

We can now define a *vector space* (v.s.) *over a field F:* It is a commutative group under + (with components from F, and + as defined in F) for which addition of elements (vectors) is defined by Property (V1). It is closed under the operation of scalar multiplication defined by Property (V2). Furthermore, the two distributive laws

$$a(\mathbf{v}_1 + \mathbf{v}_2) = a\mathbf{v}_1 + a\mathbf{v}_2$$

$$(a + b)\mathbf{v}_1 = a\mathbf{v}_1 + b\mathbf{v}_1$$

and the associative law

$$a(b\mathbf{v}_1) = (ab)\mathbf{v}_1$$

all hold, where a and b are scalars. The additive identity is $\mathbf{0} = (0, 0, \ldots, 0)$, and the additive inverse $\mathbf{v}^-$ of vector $\mathbf{v}$ is

$$\mathbf{v}^- = (a_1^-, a_2^-, \ldots, a_n^-)$$

where a_i^- is the additive inverse of a_i in F. (3-5)

The importance of the distributive laws and the associative law is that they define and thus permit "moving a scalar (or vector) across the parenthesis" in situations where the product of a vector and a scalar are involved. These three laws will now be illustrated by examples. Let

$v_1 = (-1, 4)$, $v_2 = (2, 3)$, $a = 3$, and $b = -2$. Then

Example 3-8.

$$\begin{aligned} a\,(v_1 + v_2) &= 3 \times [(-1, 4) + (2, 3)] \\ &= 3 \times (1, 7) = (+3, 21) \end{aligned}$$

$$\begin{aligned} av_1 + av_2 &= 3 \times (-1, 4) + 3 \times (2, 3) \\ &= (-3, 12) + (6, 9) = (3, 21) \end{aligned}$$

Example 3-9.

$$\begin{aligned} (a + b)\,v_1 &= (3-2) \times (-1, 4) = 1 \times (-1, 4) = (-1, 4) \\ av_1 + bv_1 &= 3 \times (-1, 4) + (-2) \times (-1, 4) \\ &= (-3, 12) + (2, -8) = (-1, 4) \end{aligned}$$

Example 3-10.

$$\begin{aligned} a(bv_1) &= 3 \times [(-2) \times (-1, 4)] = 3 \times (2, -8) \\ &= (6, -24) \end{aligned}$$

$$\begin{aligned} (ab)\,v_1 &= [3\,(-2)] \times (-1, 4) = (-6) \times (-1, 4) \\ &= (6, -24) \end{aligned}$$

To the reader who says "That's obvious," we can only point out that these operations are "obvious" only for the familiar case in which v_1 and v_2 are replaced by scalars, giving ordinary field operations throughout. The extension of these notions to non-scalar quantities certainly seems natural enough but, as you may have learned by experience, intuition is helpful but not always sufficient or even correct. In the case of any new system such as the v.s. here, all properties must be defined anew — in this case, in terms of the more familiar field over which the v.s. is defined.

Example 3-11. The set of all triples (a_1, a_2, a_3) over the field F defined in Example 3-7 is a v.s. V_1. Since each component can assume any of 3 values, there are $3^3 = 27$ distinct vectors in V_1.

Example 3-12. The set of those triples defined in Example 3-11 having one component (say a_3) held equal to 0 is also a v.s. (call it V'_1), in this case with $3^2 = 9$ elements or vectors. These are: (0, 0, 0), (0, 1, 0), (0, 2, 0), (1, 0, 0), (1, 1, 0), (1, 2, 0), (2, 0, 0), (2, 1, 0), (2, 2, 0).

The elements of the v.s. V_1 of Example 3-11 can be constructed from those just listed for V'_1 by letting the last component of each vector assume the values 1 and 2 as well as 0. We say that V'_1 is a *proper subspace* of V_1. That is, V'_1, as noted, is itself a v.s., and its vectors constitute only a fraction of all the vectors in V_1.

Listing all of the elements of a v.s. is an exhaustive (and possibly exhausting) method of describing the space. The obvious question is: Isn't there a better way of doing this? The answer is a definite yes. A closer look at the nine vectors just listed above shows the following properties:

Some are simply multiples of others; for example, (0, 2, 0) = 2 × (0, 1, 0), and (1, 2, 0) = 2 × (2, 1, 0). (Remember that our v.s. is over GF (3)). Thus, the vector on the right-hand side of each of these two equalities could be used to generate the one on the left side. The same scalar-multiple relationship holds for (1, 0, 0) and (2, 0, 0), and for (1, 1, 0) and (2, 2, 0). Thus, at least four vectors could be omitted from the original list of nine without causing any loss in the ability to represent the entire v.s. Furthermore, (0, 0, 0) is not needed in our compact list of vectors since it can be generated as the sum of any vector v_1 and its additive inverse v_1^- [e.g., (1, 1, 0) and (2, 2, 0)]. This leaves four out of the original nine vectors of V'_1: (0, 1, 0), (1, 1,0), (2, 1, 0), and (1, 0, 0). Of these, notice that

$$(2, 1, 0) = 2 \times (1, 0, 0) + (0, 1, 0)$$

and $$(1, 1, 0) = (1, 0, 0) + (0, 1, 0)$$

That is, (2, 1, 0) and (1, 1, 0) can each be written as a sum of scalar multiples, or *linear combination*, of (1, 0, 0) and (0, 1, 0). Thus, we have shown that all nine elements can be generated by operating on (1, 0, 0) and (0, 1, 0), neither of which can be produced from the other. These two vectors are an example of a pair of *linearly independent* vectors. In general, a set of vectors $v_1, v_2, \ldots, v_m$ is linearly independent if no vector, say v_i, in the set is expressible as a linear combination

$$v_i = a_1 v_1 + a_2 v_2 + \ldots + a_{i-1} v_{i-1} + a_{i+1} v_{i+1} + \ldots + a_m v_m$$

of other vectors in the set. Furthermore, since the entire nine-element v.s. can be generated by taking linear combinations of (1, 0, 0) and (0, 1, 0) and no others, these two vectors are said to form a *basis* for the subspace. More generally, a basis is a set of linearly independent vectors from which all vectors of a v.s. can be generated as linear combinations. Thus, (1, 0, 0) and (1, 1, 0) are also a basis for V_1'. Figure 3-1 shows these two bases.

We have just shown by example and some labor that a v.s. can be completely represented by a rather small subset of its elements, and we have demonstrated a cumbersone way of determining such a subset. A compact way of writing down such a basis is as rows of a matrix:

$$A_1 = \begin{bmatrix} 1 & 0 & 0 \\ 0 & 1 & 0 \end{bmatrix} \qquad \text{or} \qquad A_2 = \begin{bmatrix} 1 & 0 & 0 \\ 1 & 1 & 0 \end{bmatrix}$$

3.6 Linear Codes

Be definition, a *linear code* is a vector space, with each code word a vector. Thus, matrix representation of a code is an ideal way to describe the code compactly and completely. A matrix whose rows are a basis for the v.s. whose vectors make up the code is called a *generator matrix* for the code.

Since it is often useful to be able to determine a basis (i.e., to construct a generator matrix), given a set of vectors which constitutes a code, a systematic and efficient procedure is presented in the appendix to this chapter. Example A3-4 illustrates the technique using the vector space of Example 3-12. The number of non-zero rows remaining after the matrix reduction described in this appendix is the number of linearly independent vectors in the corresponding v.s. This number is called the *dimension* of the v.s. If k is the dimension of a v.s. and *n* is the number of components

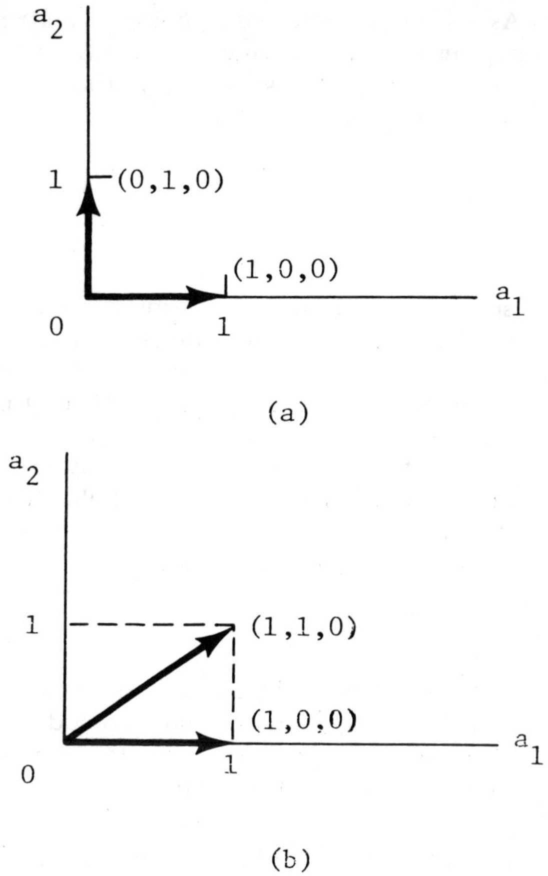

Figure 3-1/Two Bases for the Subspace V_1' of Examples 3-11 and 3-12

in a vector, then $k \leqslant n$. A matrix consisting only of these non-zero rows, in this case the matrix

$$G = \begin{bmatrix} 1 & 0 & 0 \\ 0 & 1 & 0 \end{bmatrix}$$

is a generator matrix, as derived earlier, for the code whose code words constitute the v.s.

Example 3-13. As another example of a generator matrix, consider the following, this time with elements taken from the field consisting of the elements 0 and 1, with binary arithmetic as defined and discussed earlier in this chapter.

$$G_1 = \begin{bmatrix} 1 & 1 & 0 & 0 & 1 \\ 0 & 1 & 1 & 1 & 1 \\ 0 & 0 & 1 & 0 & 1 \end{bmatrix}$$

The v.s. V_1 corresponding to G_1 has dimension k= 3, with n= 5. How many code words are there in the code generated by G_1? That is, how many vectors are in the v.s. for which the rows of G_1 are a basis? As obvious lower and upper bounds on this number, we have, respectively, $3 = k$ and $32 = 2^n$. To determine the actual number, we recall that the v.s. is generated by forming all linear combinations (with coefficients from the field over which the vectors are defined) of the basis vectors. For basis vectors v_1, v_2, and v_3, we can write an arbitrary vector v of V_1 as:

$$v = a_1 v_1 + a_2 v_2 + a_3 v_3$$

Since each a_i can assume either of 2 values, there are $2^3 = 8$ possible combinations of a_1, a_2, and a_3; that is, 8 code words are generated by G_1. In general, observe that since there are k rows in a generator matrix, there are then 2^k and q^k code words when G_1 has elements from GF(2) and GF (q), respectively.

An interesting alternative way of looking at the generator matrix (and one which eliminates the need to discuss vector spaces) has been neatly presented by Gallager [9]. We shall consider it now because it provides added insight into the significance of the generator matrix. We first transform G_1 to

$$G_1' = \left[\begin{array}{ccc|cc} 1 & 0 & 0 & 1 & 1 \\ 0 & 1 & 0 & 1 & 0 \\ 0 & 0 & 1 & 0 & 1 \end{array}\right] = [I_3 \,|\, P] \tag{3-6}$$

by adding the third row of G_1 to the second row and then adding the newly calculated second row to the first row. Here I_3 (in general, I_k) is the 3 x 3 (or k x k) identity matrix, and P is a k x (n–k) matrix whose properties will become apparent shortly. Now define a row vector **u** (which can be thought of as a *message*) by

$$\mathbf{u} = (u_1, u_2, u_3)$$

and let the row vector **x** be defined by

$$\mathbf{x} = \mathbf{u}\, G_1{}'$$

Writing out this last equation in full gives

$$(x_1, x_2, x_3, x_4, x_5) = (u_1, u_2, u_3, u_1 + u_2, u_1 + u_3) \tag{3-7}$$

Notice that the first k (=3) components of **x** are identically equal to the k components of **u**, while the remaining n–k (=5–3) components of **x** are linear combinations of components of **u**. Thus, the effect of $G_1{}'$ on **u** has been to reproduce **u** and then append to it a number of additional digits. These additional digits are called *check digits*, or parity checks in the case of GF(2); they represent redundant information about the original vector **u**. In fact, it is useful here to write **x** as

$$\mathbf{x} = (u_1, u_2, u_3, c_1, c_2) \tag{3-8}$$

In general, $(u_1, \ldots, u_k, c_1, \ldots, c_{n-k})$, is a form which calls attention to the nature of the various digits of **x** which we have just been discussing. The vector **x** is thus the code word corresponding to message **u**.

For a generator matrix (such as $G_1{}'$) in which the left-hand portion is I_k, the corresponding code is called a *systematic* code because the k digits of **u** appear unchanged as the first k digits of **x**. Thus, the specific choice of **u** determines uniquely the code word **x**. This statement holds true even if $G_1{}'$ is replaced by G_1. In this case, however, we find $x_1 = u_1, x_2 = u_1 + u_2, x_3 = u_1 + u_3, x_4 = u_2, x_5 = u_1 + u_2 + u_3$, so that the code is now *non-systematic.*

A code in which a k -component message **u** is represented by an n-component code word **x** is commonly referred to as an *(n, k) code*. In terms of the generator matrix, n is the number of columns and k the number of rows. Finally, in terms of the corresponding vector space, n is the number of components in any vector and k is the dimension of the space.

One final useful and important relationship between the check digits (c's) and the message digits (u's) will now be developed. This relationship involves the well-known *parity-check matrix* H. Let g_{ij} be the element in the i-th row and j-th column of a generator matrix G. Inspection of equations (3-7) and (3-8) shows that for the (5, 3) systematic code which we have been considering, the following relationships hold:

$$c_1 = x_4 = u_1 + u_2 \qquad c_2 = x_5 = u_1 + u_3 \tag{3-9}$$

which may be rewritten, in view of equation (3-7) and the properties of modulo-2 addition, as

$$x_1 + x_2 + x_4 = 0 \qquad x_1 + x_3 + x_5 = 0 \tag{3-10}$$

Equations (3-10) have the matrix form

$$[x_1 \; x_2 \; x_3 \; x_4 \; x_5] \begin{bmatrix} 1 & 1 \\ 1 & 0 \\ 0 & 1 \\ \hdashline 1 & 0 \\ 0 & 1 \end{bmatrix} = [0 \quad 0] \tag{3-11}$$

from which we see that the top three rows of the 5x2 matrix are P as defined by equation (3-6), and the bottom two rows are simply I_2.

What code vectors x satisfy equation (3-11)? To answer this question, we first write out the vector equation in scalar form:

$$\begin{aligned} x_1 + x_2 + x_4 &= 0 \\ x_1 + x_3 + x_5 &= 0 \end{aligned} \tag{3-12}$$

This is a system of two equations in five unknowns, so the solution contains three arbitrary parameters. For the system of equations as written, it is convenient to let these parameters be simply x_1, x_2, and x_3, giving

$$\begin{aligned} x_4 &= x_1 + x_2 \\ x_5 &= x_1 + x_3 \end{aligned} \tag{3-13}$$

There are 2^3 possible sets of values x_1, x_2, x_3, where **u** = (x_1, x_2, x_3), so that there are also 2^3 code vectors, found most easily from equation (3-13). For example, if $x_1 = 1$, $x_2 = 1$, and $x_3 = 0$, then $x_4 = 1 + 1 = 0$, $x_5 = 1 + 0 = 1$, so (1, 1, 0, 0, 1) is a code vector. All vectors found in this way will, of course, be generated by matrix $G_1{}'$ of equation (3-6). The vector just found is, in fact, the sum of the first two rows of $G_1{}'$.

It is not difficult to generalize the example just concluded (bearing in mind our assumption of a systematic code, however) so that $x_i = u_i$ for i = 1, 2, . . . , k . We have G given by

$$G = \begin{bmatrix} 1 & 0 & \ldots & 0 & g_{1,k+1} & g_{1,k+2} & \cdots & g_{1,n} \\ 0 & 1 & \ldots & 0 & g_{2,k+1} & g_{2,k+2} & \cdots & g_{2,n} \\ \cdot & \cdot & & \cdot & \cdot & \cdot & & \cdot \\ \cdot & \cdot & & \cdot & \cdot & \cdot & & \cdot \\ \cdot & \cdot & & \cdot & \cdot & \cdot & & \cdot \\ 0 & 0 & \ldots & 1 & g_{k,k+1} & g_{k,k+2} & \cdots & g_{k,n} \end{bmatrix} = [I_k \; P] \qquad (3\text{-}14)$$

Then the check-digit portions of the equation **x** = **u**G become

$$\begin{aligned} c_1 &= x_{k+1} = g_{1,k+1} x_1 + g_{2,k+1} x_2 + \ldots + g_{k,k+1} x_k \\ c_2 &= x_{k+2} = g_{1,k+2} x_1 + g_{2,k+2} x_2 + \ldots + g_{k,k+2} x_k \\ &\cdot \qquad \cdot \qquad \cdot \qquad \cdot \qquad \cdot \\ c_{n-k} &= x_n = g_{1,n} x_1 + g_{2,n} x_2 + \ldots + g_{k,n} x_k \end{aligned} \qquad (3\text{-}15)$$

Taking a typical check digit $c_j = x_{k+j}$ and re-writing its equation as

$$\sum_{i=1}^{k} g_{i,k+j}\, x_i - x_{k+j} = 0 \qquad j = 1, 2, \ldots, n-k \qquad (3\text{-}16)$$

the reader can verify that equations (3-16) are equivalent to the matrix equation

$$(x_1\ x_2\ \ldots\ x_n)\begin{bmatrix} g_{1,k+1} & \cdots & g_{1,n} \\ g_{2,k+1} & \cdots & g_{2,n} \\ \cdot & & \\ \cdot & & \\ \cdot & & \\ g_{k,k+1} & \cdots & g \\ -1 & \ldots & 0 \\ \cdot & & \\ \cdot & & \\ \cdot & & \\ 0 & \ldots & -1 \end{bmatrix} = (0\ \ldots\ 0) \tag{3-17}$$

$$\text{or}\quad \mathbf{x}\begin{bmatrix} P \\ -I_{n-k} \end{bmatrix} = \mathbf{0} \tag{3-18}$$

where P is the same matrix as in equation (3-14) and **0** is a row vector with n–k components. We usually write the symbol H for the matrix

$$\begin{bmatrix} P \\ -I_{n-k} \end{bmatrix}$$

and call H the *check matrix.* In the usual case of coefficients (or matrix elements) from GF(2), the minus signs in equations (3-16), (3-17), and (3-18) become plus signs and

$$H = \begin{bmatrix} P \\ I_{n-k} \end{bmatrix}$$

is the *parity-check matrix.*

3.7 The Concept of Distance

Since the need for creating codes in the first place stems from the desire to transmit (or store and retrieve) data accurately in the presence of errors, there must be found ways of recovering at least the correct information digits in the presence of errors regardless of the information positions within the code word or, in fact, even if the information digits do not appear explicitly, as in a non-systematic code. This problem will be addressed in a later section for simple block codes. Before actually beginning this subject of *decoding*, however, the notion of *distance* between sequences will be discussed as a necessary prerequisite. More precisely, *decoding metric* is the functional form while distance is the value assumed by the metric in any particular case. Examples of decoding metric are Hamming distance and *a posteriori* probability.

In general terms, the distance between two sequences of digits is a measure of the degree to which these sequences differ. In the discussions in this book, a sequence will usually be a code word or a corrupted version of a code word. We shall work almost exclusively with the *Hamming distance*, which is the number of positions in which the two sequences differ. This is the most widely used *metric* or measure of distance for binary sequences. Thus, $v_1 = 10111$ and $v_2 = 01101$ having a Hamming distance of 3; we write $d(v_1, v_2) = 3$. Another way of looking at Hamming distance is that it is the number of 1's in the difference (or mod 2, position-by-position sum) of the two vectors, that is, the *weight* of the difference vector. In the example of this paragraph, $v_1 - v_2 = 11010$, which has weight 3. We write $w(v_1 - v_2) = 3$ and have the general result

$$d(v_i, v_j) = w(v_i - v_j) \qquad (3\text{-}19)$$

The minimum weight of any code word is the most commonly used measure of a code's effectiveness. Since a linear code is a vector space, the difference, or sum, of any two code words (but not other sequences in general) is also a code word. For this reason, the minimum distance between any two code words can be determined by finding the minimum weight of any word in the code. Since it is true that the greater the Hamming distance between code words, the more difficult it is to change one into the other, it follows that codes with the largest possible minimum distance should be, and are, much sought after. It is not our purpose in this book to supply details as to how such codes are developed. We will, however, describe and/or tabulate distance properties of good codes, as well as giving the codes themselves in some cases.

3.8 Basic Results in Word Error Probability

Suppose we transmit 0's and 1's through the binary symmetric channel (BSC) derived in Chapter 2 and shown in Figure 2-3(a). This channel treats 0's and 1's exactly alike. In order to have any practical significance, transition probability p must obviously be less than 1/2. For $p < 1/2$, any symbol which passes through the channel is more likely to come out unchanged than it is to be transformed into the other value. A channel which acts on each symbol independently of all past and future symbols is called a *memoryless* channel. For any memoryless channel, the probability of a particular output sequence, given a particular code word transmitted, is equal to the probability of the sequence of errors introduced by the channel. This sequence of errors is assumed to be independent of the word transmitted. That is, suppose that code word **x** is sent and sequence **y** is received. The difference between **x** and **y** is the error vector **e**, also made up of 0's and 1's and given by

$$\mathbf{e} = \mathbf{y} - \mathbf{x} \tag{3-20a}$$

which becomes

$$\mathbf{e} = \mathbf{y} + \mathbf{x} \tag{3-20b}$$

in GF(2).

Let us try to determine the most likely error sequences, in order of decreasing probability. Since each symbol is affected independently of all others, the probability of any error sequence is simply the product of the probabilities of the individual symbols which constitute it. Thus, if $\mathbf{e} = (e_1, e_2, \ldots, e_n)$, then

$$P(\mathbf{e}) = P(e_1)\,P(e_2)\ldots P(e_n) = \prod_{i=1}^{n} P(e_i) \tag{3.21}$$

where the notation Π means "product of." A 1 in an error vector means that the position in the transmitted word will be changed, giving an error there in the received vector.

Now let us apply equation (3-21) to several error vectors. For transition probability p, a symbol is received correctly with probability $1 - p$. Therefore, a transmitted vector consisting of n independent symbols will be received correctly with probability $(1 - p)^n$. Any vector containing exactly one error has probability

$p(1-p)^{n-1}$. Similarly, a pair of errors will occur in a specific pair of positions in the vector with probability $p^2(1-p)^{n-2}$. In general, the probability of a particular n-component vector (or n-symbol sequence) containing b errors is $p^b(1-p)^{n-b}$. The important point here is that since $p < 1/2$, any sequence with no errors is most probable and, in particular, is more probable than any sequence with one error, which in turn is more probable than any two-error sequence, and so on. That is,

$$P(\text{no errors}) > P(1 \text{ error}) > P(2 \text{ errors}) > \ldots > P(n \text{ errors}). \tag{3-22}$$

Now consider the probability of all possible single-error sequences. Since a single error can occur in any of n positions, the probability of a sequence with exactly one error somewhere is $np(1-p)^{n-1}$. It is easy to reason that two errors among n symbols can occur in exactly $n(n-1)/2$ ways, so that the probability of two errors occurring in some way is

$$\frac{n(n-1)}{2}p^2(1-p)^{n-2}$$

In general, the total probability of all b-error sequences is

$$P(b \text{ errors}) = \binom{n}{b} p^b (1-p)^{n-b} \tag{3-23}$$

where the symbol $\binom{n}{b}$ denotes the number of ways in which n objects may be chosen b at a time without regard to their order. The value of $\binom{n}{b}$ is given by

$$\binom{n}{b} = \frac{n(n-1)(n-2)\cdots(n-b+1)}{b!} = \frac{n!}{b!(n-b)!}$$

Here, as usual, the factorial notation (!) is defined by

$$b! = b(b-1)(b-2)\cdots 3 \cdot 2 \cdot 1.$$

3.9 Decoding Procedures*

We shall conclude this chapter on parity-check codes with a discussion of decoding procedures for discrete memoryless channels, with particular emphasis on the BSC. Consider first the probability of error P_e for a single channel symbol. The probability of a channel symbol error, conditional on symbol y being received, is $P(e|y)$. Without loss of generality, suppose $y=0$ for a BSC. Then a decision error has been made on y if $x = 1$ was sent. Applying Bayes rule**, we can write

$$\begin{aligned} P\,(e|0 \text{ received}) &= P\,(1 \text{ sent}|0 \text{ received}) \\ &= \frac{P\,(0 \text{ received}|1 \text{ sent})\; P\,(1 \text{ sent})}{P\,(0 \text{ received})} \end{aligned} \tag{3-24}$$

Now, P (0 received|1 sent) is just the channel transition probability p. Thus, setting P (0 sent) = P_0 and P (1 sent) = P_1, we have

$$\begin{aligned} P\,(0 \text{ received}) &= P\,(0 \text{ received}, 0 \text{ sent}) + P\,(0 \text{ received}, 1 \text{ sent}) \\ &= P\,(0 \text{ received}|0 \text{ sent})\,P_0 + P\,(0 \text{ received}|1 \text{ sent})\,P_1 \\ &= (1-p)\,P_0 + pP_1 \end{aligned}$$

so that

$$P\,(e|0 \text{ received}) = \frac{pP_1}{(1-p)\,P_0 + pP_1} \tag{3-25}$$

Note that if $P_0 = P_1$ (i.e., 0 and 1 equally likely to be sent), then equation (3-25) reduces to P (e|0 received) = p.

With block codes, it is appropriate to consider the probability of decoding a block (received vector) incorrectly; that is, deciding on the wrong transmitted code word rather than the probability of a single bit error. The mathematical reasoning and formalism used in obtaining equation (3-25) are still value, however, with symbols replaced by vectors in the derivation.

*More complete and general discussions of decoding rules than the one given here can be found in Abramson [10] and Gallager [9].

**Bayes rule for events A and B is: $P(B|A)\,P(A) = P(A|B)\,P(B)$. For other forms of the rule see, for example, Wozencraft and Jacobs [1] pp. 75 and 115.

Now consider transmitted vectors (code words) $\mathbf{x} = (x_1, x_2, \ldots, x_n)$ and received vectors $\mathbf{y} = (y_1, y_2, \ldots, y_n)$, and suppose we receive a particular sequence $\mathbf{y}_R$. If $\mathbf{x}_k$ was actually sent, then the probability of correct decoding is

$$P_c = P\,(\mathbf{x}_k \text{ announced} | \mathbf{y}_R \text{ received}).$$

We can reach a decision as to what was sent on the basis of either of the following comparisons.

In the first comparison, compute $P\,(\mathbf{x}_i \text{ sent} | \mathbf{y}_R)$ for each code word $\mathbf{x}_i$ and announce that $\mathbf{x}_k$ was sent if

$$P\,(\mathbf{x}_k \text{ sent} | \mathbf{y}_R) > P\,(\mathbf{x}_i \text{ sent} | \mathbf{y}_R) \tag{3-26}$$

for all $i \neq k$. (In case of a tie, we could still agree to announce $\mathbf{x}_k$.)

Clearly, this rule maximizes P_c and thus minimizes the probability of decoding error P_e, where

$$P_e = 1 - P_c$$

Thus, not surprisingly, this rule is called *minimum-error-probability decoding.*

How do we compute the probabilities used in equation (3-26)? In the interest of compactness and without loss of clarity, we can write $P\,(\mathbf{x}_i \mid \mathbf{y}_r)$ for $P\,(\mathbf{x}_i \text{ sent} \mid \mathbf{y}_R)$. Then, again applying Bayes rule, we have

$$P\,(\mathbf{x}_i | \mathbf{y}_R) = \frac{P\,(\mathbf{y}_R | \mathbf{x}_i)\, P\,(\mathbf{x}_i)}{P\,(\mathbf{y}_R)} \tag{3-27}$$

so that for a given received vector $\mathbf{y}_R$ we announce that $\mathbf{x}_k$ was sent if, for all $i \neq k$,

$$P\,(\mathbf{y}_R | \mathbf{x}_k)\, P\,(\mathbf{x}_k) \geqslant P\,(\mathbf{y}_R | \mathbf{x}_i)\, P\,(\mathbf{x}_i) \tag{3-28}$$

As we showed in Section 3.8, the assumption of a memoryless channel leads to

$$P(\mathbf{y}_R|\mathbf{x}_i) = \prod_{j=1}^{n} P(y_{Rj}|x_{ij})$$

where y_{Rj} and x_{ij} are the j-th components of vectors $\mathbf{y}_R$ and $\mathbf{x}_i$, respectively. $P(\mathbf{x}_i)$ is just the probability of sending the code word $\mathbf{x}_i$. Thus, to implement equation (3-28), we announce that $\mathbf{x}_k$ was sent if

$$\prod_{j=1}^{n} P(y_{Rj}|x_{kj})\, P(\mathbf{x}_k) \geqslant \prod_{j=1}^{n} P(y_{Rj}|x_{ij})\, P(\mathbf{x}_i) \tag{3-29}$$

for all $i \neq k$.

Equation (3-29) shows that input message (or code word) probabilities must be known in order to carry out minimum-error-probability decoding. When these probabilities are unknown, we can still decode in a reasonable way if we use *maximum likelihood* (ML) decoding. The ML decoding rule is:

Given received vector $\mathbf{y}_R$, compute $P(\mathbf{y}_R|\mathbf{x}_i)$ for each code word $\mathbf{x}_i$. Then announce $\mathbf{x}_k$ sent if

$$P(\mathbf{y}_R|\mathbf{x}_k) \geqslant P(\mathbf{y}_R|\mathbf{x}_i) \tag{3-30}$$

for all $i \neq k$.

Comparison of equations (3-28) and (3-30) shows that the two decoding rules are equivalent if all code words $\mathbf{x}_i$ are equally probable.

The following three examples are intended to illustrate and contrast the decoding rules of equations (3-28) and (3-30) and to show the impact of input message probabilities on the resulting decisions. All three examples assume a memoryless BSC with crossover probability $p=0.1$ (which, as you may know, represents an extremely noisy channel); input code words $\mathbf{x}_1 = 000$ and $\mathbf{x}_2 = 111$; and received sequence $\mathbf{y}_R = 001$.

Example 3-14. With the conditions given in the preceding paragraph, let $P(\mathbf{x}_1) = P(\mathbf{x}_2) = 1/2$. Then we find

$$P(\mathbf{y}_R|\mathbf{x}_1) = (0.9)^2 \ (0.1) = 0.081$$
$$p(\mathbf{y}_R|\mathbf{x}_2) = (0.1)^2 \ (0.9) = 0.009$$

and so by the ML decoding rule we announce $\mathbf{x}_1$ sent if $\mathbf{y}_R$ is received. In view of the equal input (code word) probabilities, we know that the minimum-error-probability rule leads to the same decision.

Example 3-15. Now let $P(\mathbf{x}_1) = 0.1$, $P(\mathbf{x}_2) = 0.9$. As in Example 3-14, we have $P(\mathbf{y}_R|\mathbf{x}_1) = 0.081$, $P(\mathbf{y}_R|\mathbf{x}_2) = 0.009$, so that the ML decoding rule gives the same decision ($\mathbf{x}_1$ sent) as in Example 3-14. Equation (3-28) for the minimum-error-probability rule becomes

$$P(\mathbf{y}_R|\mathbf{x}_1)\,P(\mathbf{x}_1) = (0.081)\ (0.1) = 0.0081$$
$$P(\mathbf{y}_R|\mathbf{x}_2)\,P(\mathbf{x}_2) = (0.009)\ (0.9) = 0.0081$$

giving a toss-up. We can arbitrarily announce either $\mathbf{x}_1$ or $\mathbf{x}_2$ as the transmitted code word.

Example 3-16. Finally, let $P(\mathbf{x}_1) = 0.01$, $P(\mathbf{x}_2) = 0.99$. The ML decision is obviously still unchanged, but note what happens in the minimum-error probability case:

$$P(\mathbf{y}_R|\mathbf{x}_1)\,P(\mathbf{x}_1) = (0.081)\ (0.01) = 0.00081$$
$$P(\mathbf{y}_R|\mathbf{x}_2)\,P(\mathbf{x}_2) = (0.009)\ (0.99) = 0.00891$$

Therefore we must announce that $\mathbf{x}_2$ was sent, even though this implies two channel errors out of three digits transmitted. The reason, of course, is that now $\mathbf{x}_1$ is very much less likely than $\mathbf{x}_2$ to have been transmitted.

The ML decoding procedure just described can be implemented by computing for the received vector $\mathbf{y}_R$ the 2^k values of $P(\mathbf{y}_R|\mathbf{x})$ and picking out the largest one. This effort grows exponentially with code length n for constant code rate k/n. On the other hand, values of $P(\mathbf{y}_R|\mathbf{x})$ could be computed beforehand and stored for speedy look-up. But there are 2^n

values of $\mathbf{y}_R$ for each of 2^k values of $\mathbf{x}$, giving 2^{n+k} entries $P(\mathbf{y}_R | \mathbf{x})$ in storage. Some improvement in these astronomical* storage requirements is possible with a decoding table to be described below.

Assume we have an (n, k) binary code, and suppose we construct a table of binary n-tuples in the following way:

1. Write down the 2^k code words as column headings.
2. Choose an n-tuple of smallest possible weight which is not in the code.
3. Add this n-tuple to each code word, giving a second row below the row of code words.
4. Choose another n-tuple, again of smallest possible weight, which does not appear in the table constructed up to this point.
5. Add this n-tuple to each code word, generating another row in the table.
6. Repeat steps 4 and 5 until the entire set of 2^n n-tuples appears in the table, arranged into 2^k columns with a code word heading each column.

The table constructed in this way (called the *standard array*) can be used for ML decoding; that is, whenever an n-tuple is received, it is located in the table and decoded as the code word heading the column in which it was found. A simple example of this procedure is provided below.

Example 3-17. Suppose n=4, k=2, and our code words are 0000, 0101, 1011, and 1110. This is a systematic code in which the first two digits are information and the last two are checks formed as follows: the first check digit is a repetition of the first information digit, and the second check digit is the sum of the two information digits. Arrange the code words in a row (row 1 of the table below). Pick a minimum-weight vector not in the code, say 1000,

*For example, even the modest set of values n=24, k=12 gives $2^{36} = (512)^4 \approx 6.25 \times 10^{10}$ stored values.

and add it to each code word (row 2). Pick another minimum-weight vector 0100 not appearing in either of the first two rows and add it to each code word (row 3). Note that row 3 also contains 0001. Thus, the only remaining vector of weight 1 is 0010, which we use to generate row 4. Since $2^4 = 16$, we have generated all possible 4-tuples in our table.

0000	0101	1011	1110
1000	1101	0011	0110
0100	0001	1111	1010
0010	0111	1001	1100

Now let us use the table of Example 3-17 to decode. Any received vector will be decoded into the code word which heads the column in which that particular vector appears. This procedure thus decodes into the nearest code word, which is a maximum-likelihood procedure. Therefore, any received vector containing two or more errors will certainly be decoded into the wrong code word, as will a vector produced by error vector 0001. If, for example, 0001 were the actual error vector and 0000 had been transmitted, we would decode to 0101 as the transmitted vector, thus giving an error. On the other hand, if error vector 1000 actually occurred when 1011 was transmitted, then received vector 0011 would be correctly decoded. Suppose the error vector was 1100, and 1110 was sent. Then 0010 would be received, which would be decoded into 0000.

The construction of the decoding table shows that this decoding technique requires storage which grows exponentially with code length n. The decoding computation is trivial, (a one-step table look-up.)

As the final result in this discussion of the decoding of block codes, we make use of the standard array just described by combining it with a trivial computation to achieve a significant reduction in storage requirements at the decoder with no appreciable decrease in speed. To do this we need to introduce the notion of the *syndrome* of a vector. For received vector $\mathbf{y}$ and transmitted code word $\mathbf{x}$, the syndrome is simply

$$s = \mathbf{y}\,H = (\mathbf{x} + \mathbf{e})\,H = \mathbf{e}\,H$$

since $\mathbf{x}\,H = \mathbf{0}$. That is, the syndrome is actually the result of applying the parity-check equations to the error vector.

This in itself is not much help, but the following result* makes the syndrome a very useful quantity. Two vectors, $\mathbf{y}_1$ and $\mathbf{y}_2$ are in the same row of the standard array if and only if their syndromes are equal. Thus, if we receive a vector through a noisy channel and compute its syndrome, we now know, assuming the error-correcting capability of the code has not been exceeded, the identity of the error (or noise) vector. Once we know this, we simply add this noise vector (modulo 2) to the received vector and obtain the transmitted code word.

The key to the reduction of storage requirements is that instead of storing the entire row of the standard array, we need store only the first element of that row (i.e., the error vector) along with its (unique) syndrome. Even the modest array of Example 3-17 is appreciably reduced in size. Whereas the original array consists of $2^4 = 16$ entries (12 vectors plus the 4 code words), the new storage consists of the code words plus 3 error vectors plus 2 syndromes, for a total of 10 entries.

Peterson and Weldon [11] cite the case of a (100, 80) code, for which the standard array has 2^{100} entries whereas the storage for syndrome decoding requires about $2^{n-k} = 2^{20}$ entries (still a very large number).

We shall encounter the concept of the syndrome again in conjunction with threshold decoding of convolutional codes.

3.10 Errors vs. Erasures

Up to this point, the only type of corruption of transmitted data which we have discussed is the *error*. An error actually represents two unknown quantities in general: location and symbol value. In the binary case this simplifies to location alone. An *erasure*, on the other hand, has a known location but a completely unknown value. An erasure could arise, for example, if the demodulator output failed to pass some confidence level, giving rise to considerable uncertainty as to the value of the symbol or binary digit. The position in the code word would then be flagged at the decoder input as an erasure.

*See, for example, Peterson and Weldon [11] for a proof.

Chapter A3

Introduction to Matrices

A3.1 Definitions and Notation

A matrix is a rectangular array of entries or elements; these may be elements of a field, a ring, or any of several other algebraic systems. Since our main interest here is in elements of a field, usually finite, we shall restrict descriptions and examples to matrices whose elements are field elements. The operations such as addition and multiplication defined for simpler algebraic structures may also be defined for matrices; furthermore, because of their greater complexity, matrices have other operations defined.

"Row" and "column" are used with their everyday meanings to indicate a particular subset of the elements of a matrix. A matrix is usually denoted by a capital Roman letter, with any of its elements denoted by the corresponding subscripted lower-case letter. The subscripts are ordered; that is, the first indicates the row and the second, the column in which that element is located in a particular matrix. Thus $a_{2,4}$ is the element from the second row and fourth column of matrix A, with A often written as:

$$A = \begin{bmatrix} a_{1,1} & a_{1,2} & a_{1,3} & \cdots & a_{1,n} \\ a_{2,1} & a_{2,2} & a_{2,3} & \cdots & a_{2,n} \\ \cdot & \cdot & \cdot & & \cdot \\ \cdot & \cdot & \cdot & & \cdot \\ \cdot & \cdot & \cdot & & \cdot \\ a_{m,1} & a_{m,2} & a_{m,3} & \cdots & a_{m,n} \end{bmatrix} \qquad \text{(A3-1)}$$

Square brackets and large parentheses are the two most common ways of enclosing all of the elements of a matrix. Another way of denoting a matrix is by enclosing a general element in parentheses. Thus, illustrating in sequence the three forms of matrix notation just described, we can write:

$$A = \begin{bmatrix} 1 & 2 \\ 3 & 4 \end{bmatrix} = \begin{pmatrix} 1 & 2 \\ 3 & 4 \end{pmatrix} = (a_{i,j})$$

A matrix having m rows and n columns is called an m × n matrix. If m = n, the matrix is *square*. The elements $a_{i,i}$ in any matrix constitute the *main diagonal* of the matrix.

A notion which will be used quite often is that of the *transpose* of a matrix. We write A^T for the transpose of any matrix A, and define A^T by $(a_{i,j})^T = (a_{j,i})$. That is, A^T is formed from A by letting the i-th row of A become the i-th *column* of A^T. This automatically also makes columns of A into the same numbered rows of A^T. Thus, if

$$A = \begin{bmatrix} 1 & 2 & 3 \\ 4 & 5 & 6 \end{bmatrix} ,$$

then

$$A^T = \begin{bmatrix} 1 & 4 \\ 2 & 5 \\ 3 & 6 \end{bmatrix} .$$

In particular, the transpose of a row vector is a column vector, and vice versa. This property will be used extensively in subsequent chapters in the formulation of linear codes and their properties.

Finally, if we write

$$A = \begin{bmatrix} \alpha_1 \\ \alpha_2 \end{bmatrix}$$

with

$$\alpha_1 = (1, 2, 3) \ , \ \alpha_2 = (4, 5, 6)$$

then $\alpha_1^T = \begin{bmatrix} 1 \\ 2 \\ 3 \end{bmatrix}$, $\alpha_2^T = \begin{bmatrix} 4 \\ 5 \\ 6 \end{bmatrix}$

and A^T may be written

$$A^T = \begin{bmatrix} \alpha_1^T & \alpha_2^T \end{bmatrix}.$$

A3.2 Elementary Operations on Matrices

Addition of two or more matrices can be carried out if, and only if, the matrices have the same number of rows and the same number of columns. In this case, matrix addition is defined in terms of the addition of corresponding elements, using the operations of the field of which the elements are members. That is, if matrices A and B are both m x n with elements from the same field F, then the sum of A and B exists and is given by

$$A + B = (a_{i,j})+(b_{i,j}) = \begin{bmatrix} a_{1,1} & a_{1,2} & \cdots & a_{1,n} \\ a_{2,1} & a_{2,2} & \cdots & a_{2,n} \\ \cdot & & & \\ \cdot & & & \\ \cdot & & & \\ a_{m,1} & a_{m,2} & \cdots & a_{m,n} \end{bmatrix} + \begin{bmatrix} b_{1,1} & b_{1,2} & \cdots & b_{1,n} \\ b_{2,1} & b_{2,2} & \cdots & b_{2,n} \\ \cdot & & & \\ \cdot & & & \\ \cdot & & & \\ b_{m,1} & b_{m,2} & \cdots & b_{m,n} \end{bmatrix}$$

$$= \begin{bmatrix} a_{1,1}+b_{1,1} & a_{1,2}+b_{1,2} & \cdots & a_{1,n}+b_{1,n} \\ a_{2,1}+b_{2,1} & a_{2,2}+b_{2,2} & \cdots & a_{2,n}+b_{2,n} \\ \cdot & \cdot & & \cdot \\ \cdot & \cdot & & \cdot \\ \cdot & \cdot & & \cdot \\ a_{m,1}+b_{m,1} & a_{m,2}+b_{m,2} & \cdots & a_{m,n}+b_{m,n} \end{bmatrix} \qquad \text{(A3-2)}$$

with each sum $a_{i,j} + b_{i,j}$ formed in F.

From earlier work with fields, we might guess that if subtraction is defined for the field elements, then it is also defined for the corresponding matrices. This turns out to be the case. Note in passing that the additive identity matrix is the one whose elements are all zeroes; it will be denoted by Φ.

Multiplication of any matrix by a field element (scalar) is defined exactly as it was in the case of a vector:

$$cA = (ca_{i,j}) = \begin{bmatrix} ca_{1,1} & ca_{1,2} & \cdots & ca_{1,n} \\ ca_{2,1} & ca_{2,2} & \cdots & ca_{2,n} \\ \cdot & \cdot & & \cdot \\ \cdot & \cdot & & \cdot \\ \cdot & \cdot & & \cdot \\ ca_{m,1} & ca_{m,2} & \cdots & ca_{m,n} \end{bmatrix} \qquad \text{(A3-3)}$$

Another kind of multiplication is defined for matrices; this is the product of two matrices. It is necessary that the number of columns in the first (left-hand) factor be equal to the number of rows in the second (right-hand) factor. That is, if the first matrix is $m \times n$, then the second must be $n \times p$; the product is then an $m \times p$ matrix.

If $c_{i,j}$ is the general element of the product $C = AB$, then $c_{i,j}$ is defined by

$$c_{i,j} = \sum_{\ell=1}^{n} a_{i,\ell} \; b_{\ell,j} \qquad \begin{matrix} i = 1, \ldots, m \\ j = 1, \ldots, p \end{matrix} \qquad \text{(A3-4)}$$

That is, once the i-th row of the first factor and the j-th column of the second factor have been chosen, the operation proceeds by forming the product of the first element in the i-th row of the first factor and the first element in the j-th column of the second factor, adding the product of the second element in the i-th row and the second element in the j-th column, adding the product of corresponding third elements, etc., and continuing through all pairs of corresponding elements in the i-th row of the first factor and the j-th column of the second factor. This rule is illustrated by

$$AB = \begin{bmatrix} \cdot & & \cdot \\ \cdot & & \cdot \\ \cdot & & \cdot \\ a_{i,1} & \cdots & a_{i,n} \\ \cdot & & \cdot \\ \cdot & & \cdot \\ \cdot & & \cdot \end{bmatrix} \begin{bmatrix} \cdots & b_{1,j} & \cdots \\ \cdot & \cdot & \cdot \\ \cdot & \cdot & \cdot \\ \cdot & \cdot & \cdot \\ \cdots & b_{n,j} & \cdots \end{bmatrix} = \begin{bmatrix} c_{1,1} & \cdots & c_{1,j} & \cdots & c_{1,n} \\ \cdot & & \cdot & & \cdot \\ \cdot & & \cdot & & \cdot \\ \cdot & & \cdot & & \cdot \\ c_{i,1} & \cdots & (a_{i,1}\ b_{1,j} + a_{i,2}\ b_{2,j} + \cdots + a_{i,n}\ b_{n,j}) & \cdots & c_{i,n} \\ \cdot & & \cdot & & \\ \cdot & & \cdot & & \\ \cdot & & \cdot & & \\ c_{m,1} & \cdots & c_{m,j} & \cdots & c_{m,n} \end{bmatrix} = C$$

Another view of matrix multiplication is that it is accomplished by forming the scalar product of the row vector which constitutes the i-th row of the first factor and the transpose of the column vector which is the j-th column of the second factor. Thus, if we set

$$\alpha_i = (a_{i,1}\ a_{i,2}\ \ldots\ a_{i,n})$$

and

$$\beta_j = \begin{bmatrix} b_{1,j} \\ b_{2,j} \\ \cdot \\ \cdot \\ \cdot \\ b_{n,j} \end{bmatrix}$$

then we can write

$$A = \begin{bmatrix} \alpha_1 \\ \alpha_2 \\ \cdot \\ \cdot \\ \cdot \\ \alpha_m \end{bmatrix}, \quad B = \begin{bmatrix} \beta_1 & \beta_2 & \ldots & \beta_p \end{bmatrix}$$

and

$$AB = \begin{bmatrix} \alpha_1 \cdot \beta_1^T & \alpha_1 \cdot \beta_2^T & \ldots & \alpha_1 \cdot \beta_p^T \\ \alpha_2 \cdot \beta_1^T & \alpha_2 \cdot \beta_2^T & \ldots & \alpha_2 \cdot \beta_p^T \\ \cdot & \cdot & & \cdot \\ \cdot & \cdot & & \cdot \\ \cdot & \cdot & & \cdot \\ \alpha_m \cdot \beta_1^T & \alpha_m \cdot \beta_2^T & \ldots & \alpha_m \cdot \beta_p^T \end{bmatrix} \tag{A3-5}$$

with $\alpha_i \cdot \beta_j^T$ denoting the usual scalar product.

Example A3-1. Let

$$A = \begin{bmatrix} 4 & 2 \\ -1 & 1 \end{bmatrix}, \quad B = \begin{bmatrix} 1 & 0 & -9 \\ 7 & -2 & 5 \end{bmatrix}, \quad C = \begin{bmatrix} -3 & 5 \\ 1 & -2 \end{bmatrix}$$

where the integer elements of matrices A, B, and C can be regarded as coming from the (infinite) field of rational numbers. Then A + B and B + C are not defined, but

$$A + C = \begin{bmatrix} 4 + (-3) & 2 + 5 \\ -1 + 1 & 1 + (-2) \end{bmatrix} = \begin{bmatrix} 1 & 7 \\ 0 & -1 \end{bmatrix}$$

The matrix 2B is given by

$$2\begin{bmatrix} 1 & 0 & -9 \\ 7 & -2 & 5 \end{bmatrix} = \begin{bmatrix} (2)(1) & (2)(0) & (2)(-9) \\ (2)(7) & (2)(-2) & (2)(5) \end{bmatrix}$$

$$= \begin{bmatrix} 2 & 0 & -18 \\ 14 & -4 & 10 \end{bmatrix}$$

The product AB is defined since (number of columns in A) = (number of rows in B):

$$P = AB = \begin{bmatrix} 4 & 2 \\ -1 & 1 \end{bmatrix} \begin{bmatrix} 1 & 0 & -9 \\ 7 & -2 & 5 \end{bmatrix}$$

$$= \begin{bmatrix} (4)\,(1) + (2)\,(7) & (4)\,(0) + (2)\,(-2) & (4)\,(-9) + (2)\,(5) \\ (-1)\,(1) + (1)\,(7) & (-1)\,(0) + (1)\,(-2) & (-1)\,(-9) + (1)\,(5) \end{bmatrix}$$

$$= \begin{bmatrix} 18 & -4 & -26 \\ 6 & -2 & 14 \end{bmatrix} \tag{A3-6}$$

The product BA is not defined, however, since B has three columns compared with two rows in A. As an illustration of the vector dot product concept, consider the element

$$p_{2,3} = \alpha_2 \cdot \beta_3^T = (-1, 1) \cdot (-9,5) = (-1)\,(-9) + (1)\,(5) = 14$$

We are also in a position to discover an important property of matrices. Let us first compute

$$AC = \begin{bmatrix} 4 & 2 \\ -1 & 1 \end{bmatrix} \begin{bmatrix} -3 & 5 \\ 1 & -2 \end{bmatrix} = \begin{bmatrix} -10 & 16 \\ 4 & -7 \end{bmatrix} \tag{A3-7}$$

Now find

$$CA = \begin{bmatrix} -3 & 5 \\ 1 & -2 \end{bmatrix} \begin{bmatrix} 4 & 2 \\ -1 & 1 \end{bmatrix} = \begin{bmatrix} -17 & -1 \\ 6 & 0 \end{bmatrix} \qquad \text{(A3-8)}$$

Obviously, $AC \neq CA$, illustrating the property that matrix multiplication is not in general commutative.

There is a multiplicative identity I. It is a square matrix having all 1's on its main diagonal and 0's elsewhere. We usually write I_k for the k x k identity matrix. Not every non-zero square matrix A has a multiplicative inverse A^{-1} which satisfies

$$AA^{-1} = A^{-1}A = I.$$

For example, suppose that $A = \begin{bmatrix} 1 & 0 \\ 2 & 0 \end{bmatrix}$, and let

$$A^{-1} = B = \begin{bmatrix} b_{1,1} & b_{1,2} \\ b_{2,1} & b_{2,2} \end{bmatrix} \qquad \text{(A3-9)}$$

Then, since B must satisfy AB = I, or

$$\begin{bmatrix} b_{1,1} & b_{1,2} \\ 2b_{1,1} & b_{2,2} \end{bmatrix} = \begin{bmatrix} 1 & 0 \\ 0 & 1 \end{bmatrix},$$

we have the simultaneous scalar equations

$$\begin{aligned} b_{1,1} &= 1 & b_{1,2} &= 0 \\ 2b_{1,1} &= 0 & 2b_{1,2} &= 1 \end{aligned} \qquad \text{(A3-10)}$$

a system which obviously has no solution. Thus, there is no matrix B which satisfies AB = I for the given A.

A3.3 Calculation of the Inverse

The technique applied at the end of Section A3.2 is not the best way to calculate the inverse of a matrix, also called *inverting a matrix*, especially for matrices larger than 2 by 2. The preferred method, and one which is also used with some digital computer matrix inversion programs, consists of transforming the given matrix into the identity matrix and at the same time applying to an identity matrix the same operations that are applied to the given matrix. When this series of operations is complete, the identity will have been transformed to the inverse of the original matrix. A clever way of doing this is to define

$M = [A \mid I]$ and operate on rows of M until we have

$M' = [I \mid A^{-1}]$. Before illustrating this technique, it will be helpful to define an *elementary row transformation* of a matrix as any of the following three operations on the rows of a matrix:

R1 — the interchange of two rows

R2 — multiplication of a row by a non-zero scalar*

R3 — addition to a row of a non-zero scalar multiple of another row.

Example A3.2 Let A be defined over the real numbers as follows:

$$A = \begin{bmatrix} 1 & 2 & 1 \\ 2 & 1 & 2 \\ 0 & 1 & 1 \end{bmatrix}$$

Then operation R1 applied to rows 1 and 3 gives

$$A_1 = \begin{bmatrix} 0 & 1 & 1 \\ 2 & 1 & 2 \\ 1 & 2 & 1 \end{bmatrix} \quad ;$$

R2 applied to row 1 of A, for the scalar equal to 4, gives

$$A_2 = \begin{bmatrix} 4 & 8 & 4 \\ 2 & 1 & 2 \\ 0 & 1 & 1 \end{bmatrix}$$

*Here, as with vectors, the term *scalar* refers to a field element.

Finally, operating on A with R3 by adding (–1) times row 3 to row 1 gives

$$A_3 = \begin{bmatrix} 1 & 1 & 0 \\ 2 & 1 & 2 \\ 0 & 1 & 1 \end{bmatrix}$$

An important observation about these row transformations is this: each row transformation of matrix A can be obtained by left-multiplying* A by the matrix obtained by applying the corresponding row transformation to I_3. Thus,

$$A_1 = U_1 \ A \qquad \text{(A3-11)}$$

where
$$U_1 = \begin{bmatrix} 0 & 0 & 1 \\ 0 & 1 & 0 \\ 1 & 0 & 0 \end{bmatrix}$$

was obtained by applying transformation R1 to rows 1 and 3 of I_3. (The reader may want to verify equation (A3-11) by carrying out the indicated matrix multiplication.)

Similarly,

$$A_2 = V_1 \ A \quad \text{for } V_1 = \begin{bmatrix} 4 & 0 & 0 \\ 0 & 1 & 0 \\ 0 & 0 & 1 \end{bmatrix}$$

(where row 1 of I_3 was multiplied by 4 to get V_1);

and

$$A_3 = W_1 \ A \quad \text{for } W_1 = \begin{bmatrix} 1 & 0 & -1 \\ 0 & 1 & 0 \\ 0 & 0 & 1 \end{bmatrix}$$

(row 3 of I_3 subtracted from row 1 to get W_1).

*Left- (or pre-) multiplying matrix A by matrix P means forming the product PA.

Let P be the product of all transformation matrices which, when applied in succession to a k x k matrix A, produce I_k*:

$$PA = I_k \tag{A3-12}$$

Then, for M as defined earlier in this discussion,

$$PM = [PA \,|\, PI_k] = [I_k \,|\, P] \tag{A3-13}$$

Equation (A3-13) follows from equation (A3-12) and from the fact that multiplication by the identity matrix leaves any matrix unchanged. Post-multiplying both members of equation (A3-12) by A^{-1} gives

$$(PA)A^{-1} = I_k\, A^{-1} \tag{A3-14}$$

By the associative law of multiplication, the left-hand side of equation (A3-14) is just P, so that this equation reduces to

$$P = A^{-1}$$

which is the result promised earlier. We have therefore shown how to find the inverse (when it exists) of a matrix by the use of row transformations, which is an easy technique to understand and to carry out. A simple example should be useful at this point.

Example A3-3.

Let $A = \begin{bmatrix} 4 & 1 \\ 2 & 1 \end{bmatrix}$. Then $M = \begin{bmatrix} 4 & 1 & 1 & 0 \\ 2 & 1 & 0 & 1 \end{bmatrix}$.

*It is not always possible to find such a matrix P, in which case A is called *singular*.

Assume that all computation is in the field of rational numbers. The following row operations are applied in succession to M and the matrices derived from it:

Subtract row 2 from row 1.
Multiply row 1 (of matrix obtained in preceding step) by ½.
Subtract twice row 1 from row 2.

The matrices which result are:

$$\begin{bmatrix} 2 & 0 & 1 & -1 \\ 2 & 1 & 0 & 1 \end{bmatrix}, \quad \begin{bmatrix} 1 & 0 & \tfrac{1}{2} & -\tfrac{1}{2} \\ 2 & 1 & 0 & 1 \end{bmatrix},$$

$$\begin{bmatrix} 1 & 0 & \tfrac{1}{2} & -\tfrac{1}{2} \\ 0 & 1 & -1 & 2 \end{bmatrix} = \begin{bmatrix} I_2 & A^{-1} \end{bmatrix}$$

Thus,

$$A^{-1} = \begin{bmatrix} \tfrac{1}{2} & -\tfrac{1}{2} \\ -1 & 2 \end{bmatrix}$$

The relationships $AA^{-1} = A^{-1}A = I$ can be checked by the reader.

A3.4 Reduction to Triangular Form

The sequence of steps used in transforming the matrix of Example A3-3 was not chosen at random, although for very small matrices like A in this example, the sequence is not so important. There is a definite procedure to be followed in reducing a matrix to the identity matrix, or, more generally, to triangular form.

First, recall the following definition: the set of elements $a_{i,i}$ of the m x n matrix A is called the *main diagonal* of A, whether A is square or not. With this definition in mind, we define the upper triangular form of a matrix (so-called for reasons which should be clear from its properties):

1. Every element on the main diagonal is 0 or 1.
2. Every element below the main diagonal is 0.
3. If an element on the main diagonal is 1, all other elements in that column are 0.

To put a matrix in this form, the following procedure, which uses only row transformations, is applied to the i-th row, for i = 1, 2, . . . , m in succession:

Step 1. If $a_{i,i} = 0$, interchange the i-th and k-th rows (i.e., apply row transformation R1 defined in Section A3.2) for any $k > i$, so that the new $a_{i,i} \neq 0$. If this is impossible, repeat Step 1 for row i + 1.

Step 2. If $0 \neq a_{i,i} \neq 1$, multiply all elements of row i by $a_{i,i}^{-1}$ (i.e., apply transformation R2).

Step 3. For $\ell \neq i$, add $-a_{\ell,i}$ times the i-th row to the ℓ-th row (i.e., apply transformation R3).

Step 1 places a non-zero element on the main diagonal if that is possible for the row in question; otherwise, a 0 is placed. Step 2 scales a non-zero $a_{i,i}$ to 1. Step 3 places zeroes in all positions above and below a non-zero $a_{i,i}$. This procedure is best understood with the help of an example.

Example A3-4. Consider the matrix

$$B = \begin{bmatrix} 0 & 1 & 1 & 2 \\ 1 & 4 & 3 & 6 \\ 0 & 3 & 1 & 0 \end{bmatrix}$$

Set i = 1 and observe that $b_{1,1} = 0$, while $b_{2,1} \neq 0$. Therefore, (Step 1) exchange rows 1 and 2 of B, giving

$$B_1 = \begin{bmatrix} 1 & 4 & 3 & 6 \\ 0 & 1 & 1 & 2 \\ 0 & 3 & 1 & 0 \end{bmatrix} .$$

For B_1, Step 2 is unnecessary because the new $b_{1,1}$ is already equal to 1, while Step 3 is unnecessary since $b_{2,1} = b_{3,1} = 0$. Now set i = 2 and look at the second row of B_1. Since $b_{2,2} = 1$, Steps 1 and 2 are unnecessary. Step 3, however, must be carried out for $\ell = 1$ and $\ell = 3$. Thus, $b_{1,2} = 4$, so we add (–4) times row 2 to row 1, giving

$$B_2 = \begin{bmatrix} 1 & 0 & -1 & -2 \\ 0 & 1 & 1 & 2 \\ 0 & 3 & 1 & 0 \end{bmatrix} .$$

Similarly, $b_{3,2}$ is changed to 0 by adding (–3) times row 2 of B_2 to row 3:

$$B_3 = \begin{bmatrix} 1 & 0 & -1 & -2 \\ 0 & 1 & 1 & 2 \\ 0 & 0 & -2 & -6 \end{bmatrix}$$

In B_3, $b_{3,3} \neq 0$, so Step 1 is unnecessary. Since $b_{3,3} \neq 1$, Step 2, with $b_{3,3}{}^{-1} = -½$, gives

$$B_4 = \begin{bmatrix} 1 & 0 & -1 & -2 \\ 0 & 1 & 1 & 2 \\ 0 & 0 & 1 & 3 \end{bmatrix}$$

Finally, Step 3 applied to B_4 for $i = 3$, $\ell = 1$ and 2, gives

$$B_5 = \begin{bmatrix} 1 & 0 & 0 & 1 \\ 0 & 1 & 0 & -1 \\ 0 & 0 & 1 & 3 \end{bmatrix}$$

which is in upper triangular form.

A nonsquare matrix was intentionally chosen for this example to show how the idea of the main diagonal applies in such a situation. Notice that once all elements but one in a column have been made equal to 0, further row operations made according to the triangularization procedure will have no effect on elements in columns numbered less than the current value of i.

In the procedure just illustrated, any row which is a linear combination of others will ultimately become all 0's. Of what use is this to us? The number of non-zero rows remaining after triangularization is the number of linearly independent rows and hence the dimension of the v.s. spanned by the rows of the matrix. The next example, based on the code used in Example 3-12, illustrates the statements made in this paragraph and the preceding one.

Example A3-5. The details of this example are shown in Figure A3-1 on the next page. In this case, each row of the original matrix has been identified by means of a number enclosed in a circle. Operations on the rows are indicated throughout by using the numbers *originally* assigned to the rows. Thus, ⑦ – 2 x ④ means that twice the fourth row of the original matrix is subtracted from the seventh row. In the third stage of Figure A3-1, parentheses are used to help identify operations on the matrix of the preceding stage. Each stage represents more than one of the steps of the triangularization process. Note that the final stage shows only two non-zero rows, clearly indicating that the entire code can be generated from the vectors (1, 0, 0) and (0, 1, 0).

NOTE: All circled numbers refer to rows of first matrix. All computations are in GF(3), for which addition and multiplication tables appear in Section 3.5.

Row				Operation				Operation			
①	0	0	0	④	1	0	0	④	1	0	0
②	0	1	0	②	0	1	0	②	0	1	0
③	0	2	0	③	0	2	0	③ − 2 × ②	0	0	0
④	1	0	0	⑤ − ④	0	1	0	(⑤ −④) − ②	0	0	0
⑤	1	1	0	⑥ − ④	0	2	0	(⑥ −④)− 2 × ②	0	0	0
⑥	1	2	0	⑦ −2 × ④	0	0	0	⑦ − 2 × ④	0	0	0
⑦	2	0	0	⑧ −2 × ④	0	1	0	(⑧ − 2 × ④)− ②	0	0	0
⑧	2	1	0	⑨ −2 × ④	0	2	0	(⑨ − 2 × ④)− 2 × ②	0	0	0
⑨	2	2	0	①	0	0	0	①	0	0	0

Figure A3-1/Matrix Reduction for Code of Example 3-12.

Chapter 4
Abstract Algebra and Cyclic Codes

4.1 Introduction

In this chapter, we shall present the minimum amount of the theory of finite fields and of cyclic codes to make possible an understanding of the properties of cyclic codes in general and (for work in later chapters) of BCH, Reed-Solomon, and Zierler codes in particular. The work of the present chapter builds on the material on finite fields introduced in Chapter 3. We shall state results without proof, as before, but will motivate and illustrate these results to an extent which should render them useful and meaningful to the reader.

4.2 Properties of Polynomials Over a Field

The Euclid Division Algorithm, stated in Theorem 4-1 below, is of importance to us because of what it tells us about the remainder when one polynomial is divided by another. The result holds regardless of the degrees of the polynomials involved. We shall use the notation deg [f(x)] to denote the degree of the polynomial f(x).

Theorem 4-1.

Let a(x) and b(x) be polynomials of at least the first degree with coefficients in some field F. Then there exist unique polynomials q(x) and r(x), also with coefficients in F, such that

$$a(x) = q(x)\, b(x) + r(x) \tag{4-1}$$

where q(x) may be of any degree but the degree of r(x) is less than the degree of b(x). Note that the more familiar "division problem" form of equation (4-1) is $a(x)/b(x) = q(x) + r(x)/b(x)$. Note also that deg [q(x)] + deg [b(x)] = deg [a(x)] unless deg [b(x)] > deg [a(x)], in which case q(x)=0. Of particular interest to us is the case F = GF(q). Nonetheless, as an aid to initial understanding, our first example will use F = the rationals.

Example 4-1. Let $a(x) = x^3 + 1$, $b(x) = x^2 + 1$, F = rational numbers. Then, by the following procedure (or by long division of polynominals), we get

$$x^3 + 1 = x(x^2 + 1) - x + 1 = x \cdot b(x) + (-x + 1)$$

so that $q(x) = x$, $r(x) = x + 1$.

Example 4-2. Let $a(x) = x^3 + 1$ and $b(x) = x^2 + 1$, but let F = GF(2). Then $x^3 + 1 = x(x^2 + 1) + x + 1$
so that $q(x) = x$, $r(x) = x + 1$.

Example 4-3. Let $a(x) = x^2 + 1$, $b(x) = x^3 + 1$, F = GF(2). Since deg [b(x)] > deg [a(x)], q(x) must be 0. This forces $r(x) = x^2 + 1$.

Just as we defined arithmetic modulo some prime number in Chapter 3, we now define operations modulo an irreducible polynomial with coefficients from some field F. Consider a polynomial a(x), either given or the result of one or more operations with other polynomials, and another polynomial p(x). Then by *a(x) modulo p(x)* we mean the remainder r(x) which results when we divide a(x) by p(x), and we write

$$a(x) = r(x) \bmod p(x) \tag{4-2}$$

to mean $a(x) = q(x)p(x) + r(x)$

where, as before, r(x) has degree less than the degree of p(x).

Example 4-4. (a) For the conditions of Example 4-2, we have

$$x^3 + 1 = x + 1 \bmod (x^2 + 1)$$

(b) If p(x) = a(x), then clearly r(x) = 0; thus, for example,

$$x^3 + 1 = 0 \bmod (x^3 + 1)$$

We now define a polynomial a(x) to be *reducible* over a field ***F*** if there exist two polynomials b(x) and c(x), both of degree one or greater with coefficients in ***F***, such that

$$a(x) = b(x)c(x)$$

Note that another term for "reducible" might be "factorable". Note also that this definition excludes simply factoring out a field element to give $a(x) = k\, a_1(x)$, where k is an element of ***F***. A polynomial is called *irreducible* if it is not reducible. Irreducible polynomials will be of prime importance in the subsequent study of cyclic codes.

Example 4-5. Consider $a(x) = x^2 + 1$. If ***F*** is the rationals or reals, a(x) is certainly irreducible. If ***F*** is the field of complex numbers, however, we have

$$x^2 + 1 = (x + j1)\,(x - j1)$$

where $j = \sqrt{-1}$. Finally, if ***F*** = GF(2), $x^2 + 1 = (x + 1)^2$.

It will be helpful in later discussions to have available the notion of a *monic* polynomial as a polynomial in which the highest-degree team has a coefficient of unity. Furthermore, we say that an element α is a root of a(x) with coefficients in ***F*** if $a(\alpha) = 0$. Note that α may not be an element of ***F***. Thus, in Example 4-5, $\alpha = \pm\, j1$ is not in the reals, so that $x^2 + 1$ has no real roots.

The following theorem is often taken as an axiom in introductory algebra courses. It can, however, be derived from more fundamental principles and is therefore a theorem.

Theorem 4-2.

An element α is a root of a(x) if and only if $(x-\alpha)$ is a factor of a(x). There are no more than n distinct roots for a(x) of degree n. (As discussed in the preceding paragraph, α may or may not be an element of the coefficient field of a(x).)

4.3 Some Properties of Galois Fields

We need just a bit more algebraic theory before we can begin to discuss cyclic codes. This theory has to do specifically with finite, or Galois, fields.

First consider a family (for want of a mathematically more precise word at this time) of polynomials with coefficients from a *finite* field GF(q). Bearing in mind that operations on the coefficients take place in GF(q), let the operations on these polynomials be the following:

Operation PA. Polynomial addition; i.e., term-by-term

Operation PMR. Multiplication of polynomials followed by reduction modulo some n-th degree polynomial p(x) which is irreducible over GF(q).

The result of applying the foregoing definitions of polynomials and operations is this key result: The set of polynomials generated in this way constitutes a field of q^n elements which we can designate $GF(q^n)$ and which has the set of all possible polynomials resulting from Operation PMR as just one of at least two representations.

Example 4-6. Suppose $p(x) = x^2 + x + 1$, which is irreducible over GF(2). Consider the following two polynomials over GF(2): $x + 1$ and $x^2 + 1$. Then, taking all results mod $(x^2 + x + 1)$, we have

$$(x^2 + 1) + (x + 1) = (x^2 + x + 1) + 1 = 1$$

$$(x + 1)(x^2 + 1) = x^3 + x^2 + x + 1 = x(x^2 + x + 1) + 1 = 1$$

Note in this example that an alternate approach to the first sum yields $x^2 + x + (1 + 1) = x^2 + x$. Is this at odds with the result obtained the first time? No, because all results must be of degree less than the degree of p(x). Thus, reduction of $x^2 + x$ modulo $(x^2 + x + 1)$ yields, as above,

$$x^2 + x = x^2 + x + 1 + 1 = 1$$

In this case, q = n = 2, and the elements of $GF(2^2)$ may be represented as 1, x, x + 1, and 0.

Now define the *multiplicative order* of an element α of GF(q) to be the smallest integer μ (of the set of natural numbers, not from GF(q)) such that

$$\alpha^{\mu} = 1 \text{ (in GF(q))}. \qquad (4\text{-}4)$$

If μ = q-1, then α is called a *primitive element* of GF(q). In this case, it can be shown that the successive powers of α generate all non-zero elements of GF(q). In addition, it can be shown that every Galois field contains at least one primitive element.

Example 4-7. Consider the field $GF(2^2)$ just defined and discussed in Example 4-6. Note that now q = 4. The element $\alpha_1 = x$ is a primitive element (with $\mu = 3$) of $GF(2^2)$, since

$$x^2 = x + 1$$

$$x^3 = x(x + 1) = x^2 + x = 1 \ (\text{mod } x^2 + x + 1)$$

Similarly, $\alpha_2 = x + 1$ is a primitive element, since $(x + 1)^2 = x^2 + 1 = x$, and $(x + 1)^3 = (x + 1)\, x = 1$. Is $\alpha_3 = 1$ a primitive element of GF(4)? No, because its powers fail to generate the other nonzero field elements.

Another important concept is that of *minimal polynomial.* For our purposes, the following definition will suffice. The minimal polynomial $m_\alpha(x)$ over GF(q) of the element α, which may or may not be in GF(q), is the monic polynomial of lowest degree such that $m_\alpha(\alpha) = 0$.

Example 4-8. To avoid confusion, we shall use y instead of x as the indeterminate in this continuation of Examples 4-6 and 4-7. We then ask the question: What is the minimal polynomial of each of the non-zero elements (1, x, x+1) of $GF(2^2)$ represented there? For $\alpha_3 = 1$, clearly $m_{\alpha 3}(\alpha_3) = y + 1$, since $\alpha_3 + 1 = 0$. For $\alpha_1 = x$, the possibilities for $m_{\alpha_1}(y)$ are: y, y + 1, y^2, $y^2 + 1$, $y^2 + y$, and $y^2 + y + 1$. Clearly, y and y + 1 are not zero when $\alpha_1 = x$ is substituted for y. Similarly, no second-degree polynomial, except $y^2 + y + 1$, is equal to zero when x is substituted for y. Thus $m_{\alpha_1}(y) = y^2 + y + 1$. Finally, substitution of y = x + 1 into each of the six polynomials y, . . . , $y^2 + y + 1$ in turn, shows that $m_{\alpha_2}(y) = y^2 + y + 1$; that is, $(x + 1)^2 + (x + 1) + 1 = (x^2 + 1) + (x + 1) + 1 = x^2 + x + 1 = 0$, and none of the other polynomials is 0 for y = x + 1.

We can use these results to display two alternate representations of $GF(2^2)$:

Elements of $GF(2^2)$ as Powers of Primitive Element $\alpha_1 = x$	Elements of $GF(2^2)$ as Powers of Primitive Element $\alpha_2 = x + 1$
0	0
$1 = \alpha_1^3$	$1 = \alpha_2^3$
$x + 1 = a_1^2$	$x = a_2^2$
$x = \alpha_1$	$x + 1 = \alpha_2$

In view of its usefulness in the construction of cyclic codes, one last property of a Galois field will be stated. Given a prime number p, a polynomial f(t) over GF(p), and α an element of $GF(p^n)$ and a root of f(t) = 0, then for each $m \geqslant 0$ it is true that $f(\alpha^{pm}) = 0$. For example, if p=2, n=4, and α is a root of $f(t) = t^2+t+1=0$, then the following are also roots of f(t) =0: $\alpha^p = \alpha^2$, $\alpha^{p^2} = \alpha^4$, and $\alpha^{p^3} = \alpha^8$.

4.4 Introduction to Cyclic Codes

In most discussions of cyclic codes, it is customary to reverse the usual order in which the components of a code word are listed. This results in vectors of the form

$$\mathbf{x} = (x_{n-1}, x_{n-2}, \ldots, x_0) \qquad (4\text{-}5)$$

For cyclic codes, a notation which is preferable because of its usefulness in illustrating and deriving important properties is the polynomial form

$$x_{n-1}\, t^{n-1} + x_{n-2}\, t^{n-2} + \cdots + x_1\, t + x_0 \qquad (4\text{-}6)$$

which is in one-to-one correspondence with the vector **x** of equation (4-5).

We have been talking about cyclic codes without having as yet defined them. This definition will now be given: A cyclic code is a linear code with the special property that if a vector is a code word, so are all cyclic (end-around) shifts of this vector. To show that constructing a cyclic code is not a trivial matter, consider the following example.

Example 4-9. Consider the (3,2) linear code with generator matrix

$$G_1 = \begin{bmatrix} 1 & 1 & 0 \\ 0 & 0 & 1 \end{bmatrix}$$

Does G_1 generate a cyclic code? The rows of G_1 certainly are not cyclic shifts of each other. The third (and only other) non-zero vector of the code is 111, which is only a cyclic shift of itself. How about $G_2 = \begin{bmatrix} 1 & 0 & 0 \\ 0 & 1 & 0 \end{bmatrix}$? Either row of G_2 is a shift of the other, but the other shift, 001, can not be constructed from G_2. The only untried form for a generator matrix is

$$G_3 = \begin{bmatrix} 1 & 1 & 0 \\ 0 & 1 & 1 \end{bmatrix}$$

The sum of the row vectors in G_3 is 101, which, together with the rows of G_3, yields a set of cyclic shifts of a single vector. (In all cases, the vector 000 satisfies the cyclic property.)

To understand why G_3 succeeded where G_1 and G_2 failed in generating a cyclic code, we must look at the results of the cyclic property on the code polynomials. These polynomials are tabulated here:

G_1	G_2	G_3
$t^2 + t$	t^2	$t^2 + t$
1	t	$t + 1$

A look at G_2 and G_3 and their corresponding code polynomials suggests that a single shift of a vector to the left corresponds to multiplying its corresponding polynomial by t. If this is true, then for G_3 we should get 101 (the leftward cyclic shift of 110) to correspond to $t^3 + t^2$. But this last polynomial has degree greater than n−1=2. What can be done? It turns out that all polynomials must be reduced modulo t^n-1 (t^n+1 over GF(2)).

Thus, to deal with $t^3 + t^2$, we can write (since n=3)

$$t^3 + t^2 = (t^3 + 1) + (t^2 + 1) = t^2 + 1 \mod (t^3 + 1),$$

and $t^2 + 1$ corresponds to the vector 101. The next shift would give

$$t^3 + t = (t^3 + 1) + (t + 1) = t + 1 \mod (t^3 + 1)$$

which brings us back to the second row of G_3. Finally, consider $t^2 + t + 1$ (which is not in the code generated by G_3). The leftward shift of vector 111 corresponds to

$$(t^3 + t^2 + t) + 1 + 1 = t^2 + t + 1 \mod (t^3 + 1)$$

Note that this method of reducing modulo $t^n + 1$ is much easier than long division of the given polynomial by $t^n + 1$.

Let us continue to concentrate on the cyclic code defined by matrix G_3. Clearly the lowest degree polynomial which occurs is t + 1. In general, we call the monic polynomial of lowest degree which is a codeword the *generator polynomial g(t)* of the cyclic code. It is easy to show (see problems) that all polynomial multiples of g(t), reduced modulo t^n-1, are code words of the same cyclic code, that g(t) must divide t^n-1, and that the degree of g(t) is n–k.

Example 4-10. We have already shown that the multiples of g(t), mod t^n-1, are code words for the code defined by G_3. Does $g(t) = t+1$ divide $t^n-1 = t^2+1$? Obviously, yes, since $t^2 + 1 = (t+1)^2$ over GF(2). It is also clear that the degree of g(t) is n–k=3–2=1.

With the properties just specified for g(t), along with the correspondence stated at the start of this section between a code vector and its polynomial representation, we have sufficient information to write down the generator matrix for a cyclic code, given its generator polynomial. Since G for an (n, k) code must have exactly k linearly independent rows, we take for these rows the vector corresponding to g(t), along with its first k–1 linear shifts.

This gives a matrix G with k rows and (n–k+1) + (k–1) = n columns, since the degree n–k polynomial g(t) has n–k+1 terms, some possibly 0. Consequently we have, for $g(t) = g_{n-k}\, t^{n-k} + g_{n-k-1}\, t^{n-k-1} + \ldots + g_1 t + g_0$:

$$G = \begin{bmatrix} g_{n-k} & g_{n-k-1} & \cdots & g_1 & g_0 & & & \\ & g_{n-k} & g_{n-k-1} & \cdots & g_1 & g_0 & & \\ & & g_{n-k} & g_{n-k-1} & \cdots & g_1 & g_0 & \\ & & & \ddots & & & & \\ & & & & g_{n-k} & g_{n-k-1} & \cdots & g_1 \; g_0 \end{bmatrix} \qquad (4\text{-}7)$$

where the blank areas have all zeroes as entries. For a code over GF(2), $g_{n-k} = g_0 = 1$.

Example 4-11. Let n = 7, k = 4. Then g(t) is of degree n–k=3. Suppose $g(t) = t^3 + t + 1$ over GF(2). Then G has four rows and seven columns and is given by

$$G = \begin{bmatrix} 1 & 0 & 1 & 1 & 0 & 0 & 0 \\ 0 & 1 & 0 & 1 & 1 & 0 & 0 \\ 0 & 0 & 1 & 0 & 1 & 1 & 0 \\ 0 & 0 & 0 & 1 & 0 & 1 & 1 \end{bmatrix}$$

Any generator matrix for a cyclic code constructed in the manner of Example 4-11 can be transformed by row operations into a matrix for a systematic code. (See Section A3.4 in the appendix to Chapter 3.)

Example 4-12. The matrix of example 4-11 becomes successively

$$\begin{bmatrix} 1011000 \\ 0101100 \\ 0010110 \\ 0011101 \end{bmatrix}, \quad \begin{bmatrix} 1011000 \\ 0101100 \\ 0111010 \\ 0110001 \end{bmatrix}, \quad \begin{bmatrix} 1011000 \\ 1110100 \\ 1100010 \\ 0110001 \end{bmatrix}$$

The final matrix represents the same code in systematic form with the last four digits as information digits.

4.5 Implementation of Cyclic Codes

One of the attractive features of cyclic codes is the ease with which encoding can be implemented through the use of linear shift registers. The shift register implements either the degree -(n–k) generator polynomial g(t) or the degree–k check polynomial h(t), and the number of stages in the shift register is equal to the degree of the polynomial being implemented. Thus, the choice of implementation is frequently made on the basis of whether n–k or k is the smaller number.

For binary codes, coefficient values of 0 and 1 are implemented by an open and a short circuit, respectively. For codes over GF(q) with $q > 2$, the circuitry becomes slightly more complicated because multiplication of elements of GF(q) must be performed. An alternative to hard-wired logic would be a programmable microprocessor.

We shall illustrate the encoding process with the (7,4) cyclic code of Examples 4-11 and 4-12. This code has $g(t) = t^3 + t + 1$ and $h(t) = (t^n - 1)/g(t) = t^4 + t^2 + t + 1$. Extension to other codes should be obvious. In our shift register diagrams the contents of each stage appear at the output of that stage. We assume that the shift register stages have all been set to zero prior to the start of a new encoding operation.

The shift register of Figure 4-1 will perform encoding based on g(t) and will produce a systematic code. Initially, the gate is enabled and switch S is in position 1. This allows the four information digits to go simultaneously to the modulator or channel and into the shift register. After this has taken place, the gate is disabled, and S moves to position 2. Three more shifts are required to finish computing the three check digits, after which they are shifted out to the modulator or channel. This implementation exploits the fact that the information portion of the code word can be written, using the Euclid division algorithm, as $x_{n-1}t^{n-1} + x_{n-2}t^{n-2} + \ldots + x_{n-k}t^{n-k} = q(t)g(t) + r(t)$. Here r(t) must be of degree at least one less than n–k, the degree of g(t). In view of the cyclic nature of the code, q(t)g(t) is a code word and so, therefore, is $x_{n-1}t^{n-1} + \ldots + x_{n-k}t^{n-k} - r(t)$. But since the coefficients $x_{n-1}, \ldots, x_{n-k}$ are the information digits, the coefficients of r(t) must be the check digits. Division of $x_{n-1}t^{n-1} + \ldots + x_{n-k}t^{n-k}$ by g(t) is carried out by the circuit of Figure 4-1.

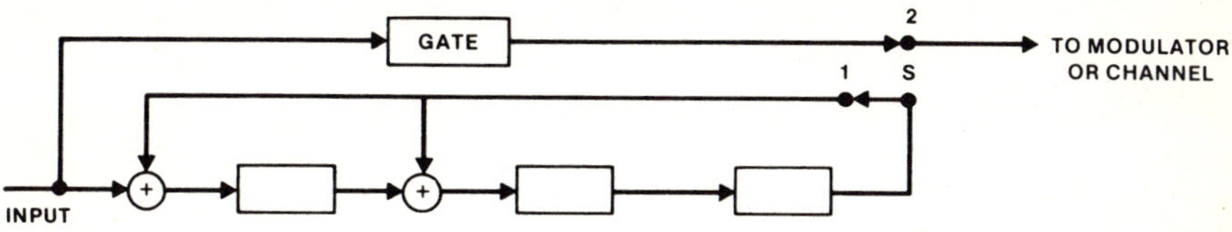

Figure 4-1/(n–k)-stage Encoder for (7,4) Cyclic Code

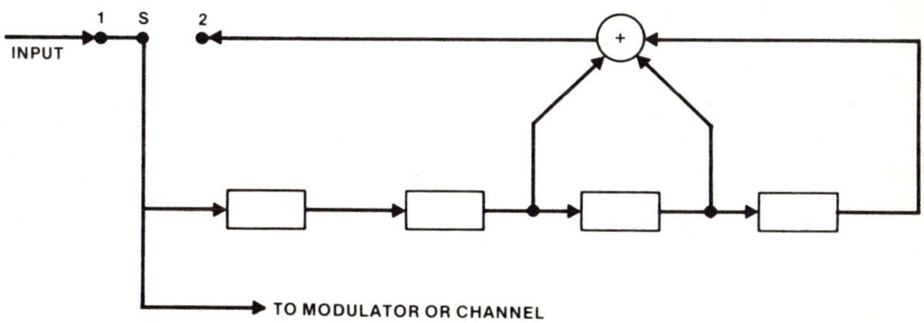

Figure 4-2/k-stage Encoder for (7,4) Cyclic Code

The encoder of Figure 4-2 corresponds to h(t). Initially switch S is in position 1, where it remains until the four information digits are fed into the register and also to the modulator or channel. The switch then moves to position 2 and the shift register is stepped three times to produce the check digits. This method of encoding is based on the following chain of reasoning. If $x(t) = b(t)g(t)$ is a code word, then $x(t)h(t) = b(t)g(t)h(t) = b(t)\ (t^{n-1}) = t^n b(t) - b(t)$, since $g(t)h(t) = t^n-1$. Now, the degree of $x(t)h(t)$, deg(xh), is $\deg(x) + \deg(h) = (n-1) + k = n + k - 1$, and $\deg(gh) = n$. Therefore $\deg(b) = \deg(xk) - n = k - 1$. In view of this, it follows that $t^n b(t)$ has only terms of degree $n, n+1, \ldots, n + k-1$, while b(t) has terms of degree $0, 1, \ldots, k-1$. Thus, $x(t)h(t)$ has no terms of degree k, k+1, . . . , n–1, and we can make use of this face to derive n–k relationships of the form

$$\sum_{i=0}^{k} h_i x_{\ell-i} = 0 \qquad k \leqslant \ell \leqslant n-1$$

which can be rewritten as explicit recurrent relationships for the check digits $x_0, x_1, \ldots x_{n-k-1}$ in terms of the information digits $x_{n-k}, \ldots, x_{n-1}$.

We have

$$x_{\ell-k} = -\sum_{i=0}^{k-1} h_i x_{\ell-i} \qquad k \leqslant \ell \leqslant n-1$$

where the minus sign becomes plus in GF(2) and where we must begin with ℓ=n–1 to make use of the recurrence relation.

Chapter 5
Bose–Chaudhuri–Hocquenghem and Reed–Solomon Codes

5.1 Introduction

In this chapter, we shall make use of the more advanced algebraic concepts and the background in cyclic codes presented in Chapter 4 to develop two classes of cyclic codes. One, the Bose-Chaudhuri*—Hocquenghem** (BCH) codes, is the most powerful known class of binary codes for correcting random errors. More specifically, the BCH codes are the first (and so far, the only) codes which completely generalize the single-symbol*** error-correcting codes to the case of multiple, randomly distributed errors. (Contrast this situation with that of correcting clustered multiple errors; i.e., a burst.) The other class, the Reed-Solomon (R-S) codes, is considered the best set of block codes for dealing with multiple bursts of errors in a code word. Encoding for BCH codes, especially in GF(2), has always been known to be easily implementable in view of their cyclic code properties, and decoding has been greatly simplified, both conceptually and in practice, by the contributions of Berlekamp [15] and Massey [16].

Until very recently, the R-S code hardware implementation has been considered cumbersome because of the non-binary finite-field arithmetic required for manipulating the higher-order symbols of these codes. A number of low-cost implementations are now available. For example, Carhoun, Roome, and Palo [17, 18] have reported on the use of charge-coupled devices. Integrated circuits are also being used.

*Bose and Ray-Chaudhuri [12, 13].

**Hocquenghem [14].

***Note that we say *symbol* rather than *bit* or *binary digit*. Thus, a symbol could be represented by several binary digits. The error correction would be done in the symbol field, not in the binary field.

5.2 Definition, Construction and Properties of BCH Codes

A BCH code, in common with other linear codes, can be defined in terms of its parity check matrix H. Since it is a cyclic code, it can also be defined by its generator polynomial g(x), and hence, its generator matrix G. We shall discuss only the second of these approaches in view of the tabulations of BCH codes in terms of generators. Fortunately, in practice one generally does not need to start from scratch each time a BCH code is desired. An extensive table of code generators is available and will be given later in this chapter. As with all cyclic codes, the matrices G and H uniquely define the generator polynomial g(x) and the check polynomial h(x), respectively. Similarly, given n or n–k, g(x) and h(x) uniquely determine G and H, respectively. Finally the relationships

$$GH = \Phi \tag{5-1a}$$

$$g(x)\,h(x) = x^n - 1 \tag{5-1b}$$

hold for BCH codes just as they do for all block codes (in the case of equation (5-1a) and for all cyclic codes (equation (5-1b)). Here, as before, Φ is an nx (n–k) all zero matrix.

We shall define a BCH code by making use of the fact that BCH codes are cyclic codes with particular conditions on the generator polynomial g(x). We shall use the notation which has come to be generally used in the literature. As in Chapter 4, g(x) is a monic polynomial of degree $r \geqslant 1$, with coefficients over code symbol field GF(q), and n is the smallest integer such that g(x) divides $x^n - 1$. The additional condition on g(x) in forming BCH codes is that g(x) be the polynomial of lowest degree having $\alpha^{m_o}, \alpha^{m_o+1}, \ldots, \alpha^{m_o+d_o-2}$ as roots, where m_o is an arbitrarily chosen positive integer, and $d_o \geqslant 2$ satisfies the condition that the $d_o - 1$ numbers $\alpha^{m_o}, \ldots, \alpha^{m_o+d_o-2}$ are distinct roots of g(x).

Then a polynomial g(x) generates a BCH code if and only if the properties just stated hold. For reasons of greater ease of understanding and practicality of implementation, for the remainder of this discussion of BCH codes we shall deal only with binary codes. Binary BCH codes result if we set $q = 2$. We shall further restrict the choice of code by setting $m_o = 1$ and requiring that α be a primitive element of GF (2^m). It then turns out that the order $2^m - 1$ of α is equal to the code word length n (binary symbols). The parameter d_o is a lower bound to the actual minimum distance d of the code (i.e., $d \geqslant d_o$) and is usually referred to as the designed distance. Note that with α a primitive element of GF(2^m), the definition of d_o stated near the end of the previous paragraph implies that $d_o - 1 \leqslant r$. Another bound can help prevent us from trying to design an impossible BCH code. If t is the actual minimum error-correcting capability of the code, then the relationships $d \geqslant 2t + 1$ and $d \leqslant n$ combine to give

$$2t + 1 \leqslant 2^m - 1$$

or

$$t \leqslant 2^{m-1} - 1. \tag{5-2}$$

Thus, for example, for $m = 4$, $n = 15$, the designed minimum error-correcting capability cannot exceed 7 (which is achieved for the code whose only words are the all-0 and all-1 words).

Example 5-1. Let $m = 2$, $m_o = 1$, $d = d_o = 3$. Then $n = 2^2 - 1 = 3 = d$, $m_o + d_o - 2 = 2$, and α and α^2 are distinct roots of g(x), which must divide $x^3 - 1$ (or $x^3 + 1$, since coefficients are in GF(2)). Furthermore, since α is a primitive element of GF(2^2), it follows that $\alpha^3 = 1$. Thus $(x - \alpha)(x - \alpha^2) = x^2 - (\alpha + \alpha^2)x + 1 = g(x)$. Since the only first-degree polynomial that divides $x^3 + 1$ is $x + 1$, it follows that g(x) must be $(x^3 + 1)/(x + 1)$ or $x^2 + x + 1$. Thus, by matching coefficients in the two expressions for g(x), we see that $\alpha + \alpha^2 = 1$. If we represent the elements 0, 1, and α of GF(2^2) as follows:

Element	Representation
0	(0, 0)
1	(0, 1)
α	(1, 0)

then from the relationship $\alpha + \alpha^2 = 1$, we get $(1, 0) + \alpha^2 = (0, 1)$, or $\alpha^2 = (1, 1)$. The theory of cyclic codes developed in the last chapter tells us that the degree of g(x), which we have found to be 2, is equal to n-k, so that k = n−2 = 1. Furthermore, since generator matrix G has n = 3 columns, the coefficients of g(x) fill the row. Thus the generator matrix is simply G = [1 1 1], since the coefficients of g(x) and 0's (if necessary) make up any row of G. The code then consists of the vectors (0, 0, 0) and (1, 1, 1), which we could have concluded immediately, once we realized that $d_o = 3$. In this example, we have intentionally worked in great and perhaps unnecessary detail for the purpose of giving further practice in finite field manipulations along with some insight. (In particular, the rapid and unique determination of g(x) actually eliminated the need to develop details of $GF(2^2)$, since n = 3 and g(x) turned out to have three terms.)

For the next example, we use what is now virtually a classic example of BCH code generation; it was used in 1960 by Bose and Ray-Chaudhuri [12] in their original paper and subsequently by Gallager [9] and by Peterson and Weldon [11]. Before beginning it, however, we point out that the technique followed in our Example 5-1 of calculating g(x) as a product of linear factors, each having as a root a power of α, rapidly becomes difficult with increasing d_o. One alternative is to choose an α whose minimal polynomial has degree greater than 1. But how can we do this? Perhaps the best way is to use a result stated earlier for Galois fields, in combination with tables of irreducible polynomials over GF(2) which have been developed by various workers. The Galois field result is this: For α a primitive element of $GF(q^m)$ and f(x) the minimal polynomial (of degree n) of α, all elements of $GF(q^m)$ can be represented uniquely as polynomials in α by making use of the fact that $f(\alpha) = 0$. The important word here is "all". The tables of polynomials referred to are most readily available in Appendix C of Peterson and Weldon [11]. Now let us proceed with the next example.

Example 5-2. Let q = 2, m = 4, $m_o = 1$, $d_o = 5$. Then $n = 2^4 - 1 = 15 > d_o$. Since $m_o + d_o - 2 = 4$, we must find minimal polynomials for α, α^2, α^3, and α^4. Since α, α^2, and α^4 all have the same minimal polynomial, we need find minimal polynomials for α and α^3 only. Referring to the referenced tables in Peterson and Weldon [11], we find the following entries for irreducible polynomials of degree m = 4: 1 23F and 3 37D. (We shall not concern ourselves here with the letters shown. The interested reader will find an explanation in the referenced appendix.) In "1 23F", the 1 refers to the exponent of α (i.e., α^1), and 23 is the octal representation of the binary coefficients (highest degree term at the left) of the polynomial. Since 23 octal corresponds to 10 011 binary, this means that $x^4 + x + 1$ is the minimal polynomial of α. Similarly, the minimal polynomial of α^3 is $x^4 + x^3 + x^2 + x + 1$, corresponding to the table entry "3 37D." Thus, as required by the condition on g(x) stated in the definition of a BCH code, g(x) is the product of these two minimal polynomials:

$$\begin{aligned} g(x) &= (x^4 + x + 1)(x^4 + x^3 + x^2 + x + 1) \\ &= x^8 + x^7 + x^6 + x^4 + 1 \end{aligned} \tag{5-3}$$

which, in view of the cyclic nature of BCH codes, gives

$$G = \begin{bmatrix} 1\,1\,1\,0\,1\,0\,0\,0\,1\,0\,0\,0\,0\,0\,0 \\ 0\,1\,1\,1\,0\,1\,0\,0\,0\,1\,0\,0\,0\,0\,0 \\ 0\,0\,1\,1\,1\,0\,1\,0\,0\,0\,1\,0\,0\,0\,0 \\ 0\,0\,0\,1\,1\,1\,0\,1\,0\,0\,0\,1\,0\,0\,0 \\ 0\,0\,0\,0\,1\,1\,1\,0\,1\,0\,0\,0\,1\,0\,0 \\ 0\,0\,0\,0\,0\,1\,1\,1\,0\,1\,0\,0\,0\,1\,0 \\ 0\,0\,0\,0\,0\,0\,1\,1\,1\,0\,1\,0\,0\,0\,1 \end{bmatrix} \tag{5-4}$$

The theory and examples presented above have been intended to develop a basic understanding of BCH code structure and generation. In many cases, even the brief labor of Example 5-2 will not be necessary. For example, Stenbit [19] published a table of generators for all primitive BCH codes up to length 255. This table, reproduced here as Table 5-1, should certainly be consulted first when a BCH code is desired. Coefficients are again in octal, right justified.*

Example 5-3. The code just found in Example 5-2 can be read directly from Table 5-1 as 721 for the (15, 7), 2-error-correcting code.

*i.e., arranged so that the zero — degree coefficient is at the extreme right.

Table 5-1/Generators of Primitive BCH Codes.*

n	k	t	$g(x)$
7	4	1	13
15	11	1	23
	7	2	721
	5	3	2467
31	26	1	45
	21	2	3551
	16	3	107657
	11	5	5423325
	6	7	313365047
63	57	1	103
	51	2	12471
	45	3	1701317
	39	4	166623567
	36	5	1033500423
	30	6	157464165547
	24	7	17323260404441
	18	10	1363026512351725
	16	11	6331141367235453
	10	13	472622305527250155
	7	15	5231045543503271737
127	120	1	211
	113	2	41567
	106	3	11554743
	99	4	3447023271
	92	5	624730022327
	85	6	130704476322273
	78	7	26230002166130115
	71	9	6255010713253127753
	64	10	1206534025570773100045
	57	11	335265252505705053517721
	50	13	54446512523314012421501421
	43	14	17721772213651227521220574343
	36	15	3146074666522075044764574721735
	29	21	403114461367670603667530141176155
	22	23	123376070404722522435445626637647043
	15	27	22057042445604554770523013762217604353
	8	31	7047264052751030651476224271567733130217
255	247	1	435
	239	2	267543
	231	3	156720665
	223	4	75626641375
	215	5	23157564726421
	207	6	16176560567636227
	199	7	7633031270420722341
	191	8	2663470176115333714567
	187	9	52755313540001322236351
	179	10	22624710717340432416300455
255	171	11	15416214212342356077061630637
	163	12	7500415510075602551574724514601
	155	13	3757513005407665015722506464677633
	147	14	1642130173537165525304165305441011711
	139	15	461401732060175561570722730247453567445
	131	18	215713331471510151261250277442142024165471
	123	19	120614052242066003717210326516141226272506267
	115	21	60526665572100247263636404600276352556313472737
	107	22	22205772322066256312417300235347420176574750154441
	99	23	10656667253473174222741416201574332252411076432303431
	91	25	6750265030327444172723631724732511075550762720724344561
	87	26	110136763414743236435231634307172046206722545273311721317
	79	27	66700035637657500020270344207366174621015326711766541342355
	71	29	24024710520644321515554172112331163205444250362557643221706035
	63	30	10754475055163544325315217357707003666111726455267613656702543301
	55	31	7315425203501100133015275306032054325414326755010557044426035473617
	47	42	2533542017062646563033041377406233175123334145446045005066024552543173
	45	43	15202056055234161131101346376423701563670024470762373033202157025051541
	37	45	5136330255067007414177447245437530420735706174323432347644354737403044003
	29	47	3025715536673071465527064012361377115342242324201174114060254757410403565037
	21	55	1256215257060332656001773153607612103227341405653074542521153121614466513473725
	13	59	464173200505256454442657371425006600433067744547656140317467721357026134460500547
	9	63	15726025217472463201031043255355134614162367212044074545112766115547705561677516057

*Reprinted with permission from *IEEE Transactions on Information Theory*, volume IT-10, no. 4, October 1964, p. 391.

5.3 Decoding

With several excellent textbook treatments—most notably Gallager [9], Berlekamp [15], Lin [20], and Peterson and Weldon [11]—already available**, we shall not attempt either to repeat or to break new ground in the matter of describing the decoding of BCH codes. Instead, we shall only sketch out the steps involved. While encoding of BCH codes can be performed exactly as was described in Chapter 4 for any cyclic code, decoding is done in a manner which computes directly the locations and values of the individual symbol errors, in contrast to the storage-consuming table look-up associated with coset leaders and to the time-consuming maximum-likelihood calculation of the transmitted code word.

The decoding proceeds in four main steps:

1. Calculation of syndrome $s = (s_1, s_2, \ldots, s_{n-k})$
2. Formation of the error-locating polynomial based on the components of the syndrome
3. Calculation of the error locations
4. Calculation of the $\lfloor (d-1)/2 \rfloor$ or fewer error values*.

Clearly step (4) is unnecessary in the case of a binary code. Of the remaining steps, step (2) requires by far the most explanation and analysis, although in terms of concept and implementation, it is no more difficult than any of the other steps. We owe much of the ease of understanding and carrying out this step to a set of results published by Berlekamp [15] and Massey [16].

5.4 Performance of BCH Codes

Each BCH code has its designed error-correcting capability specified as a parameter ($d_o = 2t+1$) of its construction. Alternatively, tabulations of codes (e.g., Peterson and Weldon [11], Appendix D, and our Table 5-1) always specify t as one of the code parameters. It is well known, however, that most BCH codes can correct significant numbers of error patterns which exceed the designed error-correcting capability of the code. There are two reasons

**A briefer presentation appears in the paper by Chien [21].

*Here, as usual, $\lfloor x \rfloor$ denotes the largest integer equal to or less than x.

for this. The first is that the designed distance d_o may be less than the actual minimum distance d_{min}. A look at Appendix D of Peterson and Weldon amply bears this out. The second reason is that certain error patterns with weight greater than the guaranteed, rather than designed, error-correcting capability are nonetheless correctable.

On the negative side, it has been shown the ratio $d_o/n \rightarrow 0$ as n becomes large with rate k/n held fixed. Since it can also be shown that $d_{min} \leqslant 2\, d_o$ at all times, it follows that $d_{min}/n \rightarrow 0$ also. Thus, BCH codes show decreasing error-correcting power as block length increases and rate is held fixed.

5.5 Reed-Solomon Codes

The Reed-Solomon [22] codes may be viewed as a subclass of the BCH codes in which m = 1 in GF (q^m), and $q > 2$. In other words, the R-S codes are nonbinary BCH codes having $n = q-1$. A special property of these codes is that their (BCH) decoding algorithm has the symbol field identical to the error-locator field. In terms of minimum distances, the R-S codes do as well as it is possible to do for a given n and k, namely

$$d = n-k + 1.$$

Remember that these numbers all pertain to symbols from a higher-order alphabet ($q > 2$).

If we let $q = p^s$, where p is a prime and s is a positive integer, then we can consider the R-S codes as a class of codes first considered by Gorenstein and Zierler [23]. In particular, if p = 2, we have the Zierler codes discussed in Chapter 10 of this book as a burst-control technique. The case p = 2 has the virtue of being implementable in terms of binary logic elements. Since $n = q-1$ for the R-S codes, we also have $n = p^s - 1$ and $k = n-d + 1 = p^s - d$, all in q-ary symbols. Finally, since $d = 2t + 1$, where t is the (q-ary) error-correcting capability of the code, we have $k = p^s - 2t - 1$. In summary, we can construct an $(n, k) = (p^s-1, p^s-2t-1)$ code capable of correcting any combination of t errors and e erasures satisfying $2t + e \leqslant n - k$, in symbols from GF (p^s). Here, now, is the origin of the multiple-burst-correcting capability of the R-S (and Zierler) codes. Each symbol from GF (2^s) can be represented as a set of binary digits. Thus, 2t q-ary symbols are equivalent to 2ts binary digits. In terms of binary digits, then, we have a code of length $s(2^s - 1)$ digits, of which $s(2^s - 2t - 1)$ correspond to information.

R-S decoders are becoming commercially available, with development spurred by military tactical communications requirements.

Example 5-4. It is not unusual to take s = 4. Then $n = 2^4 - 1 = 15$. If we choose t = 2, then $k = 15 - 2 \times 2 = 11$. In terms of binary digits, this (60, 44) code can correct up to 8 errors, provided they occur in bursts covering no more than two 16-ary digits. (These digits will be one of the 4-tuples 0000, 0001, . . . , 1111.)

Since an R-S code is, in one sense, a special case of the BCH codes, we can construct its generator polynomial in the same way as we do the g(x) for any other BCH code. In this case, however, the roots of the minimal polynomial g(x) are all in the g(x) coefficient field, GF(q). That is, since m = 1, g(x) can be factored completely into *linear* factors. Thus, the BCH code construction rule yields

$$g(x) = (x-\alpha)(x-\alpha^2)\ldots(x-\alpha^{d_o-1}) \qquad (5\text{-}5)$$

for the generator polynomial of a R-S code, where the powers of α are elements of GF(q).

Unlike binary BCH codes, R-S codes have not been tabulated as a special class, so we are unable to provide a table of R-S codes similar to Table 5-1 for BCH codes.

Chapter 6
Convolutional Codes and Encoding

Recall that when we encode for a block code, we usually use some large number (roughly 10 to 100) of information bits per code word or block. In sharp contrast to this, we will see that convolutional encoding generally encodes data bits no more than four at a time and usually just one at a time. Encoding is performed with one or more shift registers (SR's) which compute check symbols as linear combinations of the data bits contained in the SR's. Just as for block codes, there are systematic and nonsystematic convolutional codes, corresponding to the cases in which the information bits are transmitted unaltered or altered, respectively. We shall consider only channels which have binary inputs, although generalization to higher-order alphabets is easy. (See Gallager [9] or Fano [24].)

6.1 Convolutional Encoding

Similar to the case of continuous functions of a continuous variable (for example, a time-dependent voltage and current), convolutional of two digital sequences can be accomplished as follows:

1. Reverse one sequence.
2. Align the digit at one end, say the right, of this reversed sequence with the digit at the other, in this case the left, end of the other sequence.
3. Multiply the digits which are aligned, add the products formed for this alignment of sequences, and regard the sum of products just found as one element of the convolution of the two sequences.

4. Shift the two sequences one position relative to each other.
5. Repeat steps (3) and (4) until the two sequences have been shifted completely past each other.

In the case of binary functions and sequences, the product at each position is either 0 or 1, and summing takes place modulo 2. This will be the case throughout our discussion of convolutional codes.

Example 6-1. Suppose we want to find the convolution of the sequences 1101 and 10011. We customarily indicate this operation by writing (1101)*(10011). We shall keep the sequence 10011 fixed while reversing 1101, thus:

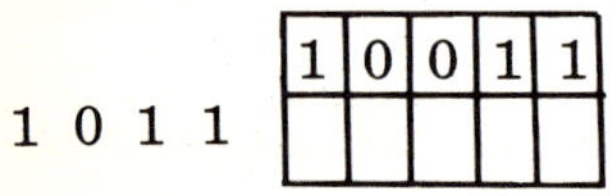

To see how the calculation procedure works, let us look at the first four steps of the convolution. We have assumed all zeroes preceding and following each of the sequences.

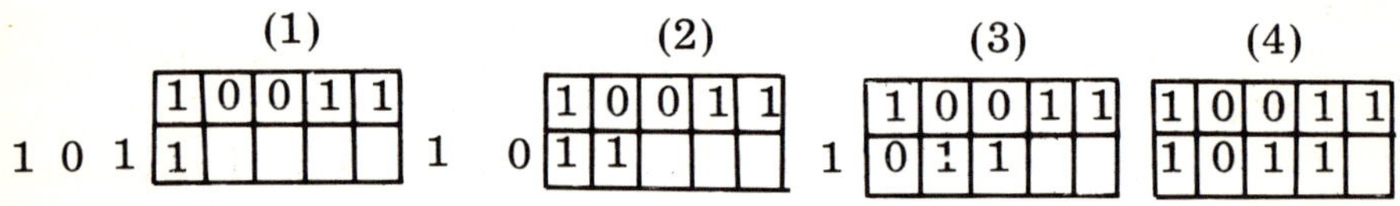

Thus, the results at each of the four steps shown are given by:

Step (1) $1 \cdot 1 = 1$
Step (2) $1 \cdot 1 + 0 \cdot 1 = 1$
Step (3) $1 \cdot 0 + 0 \cdot 1 + 0 \cdot 1 = 0$
Step (4) $1 \cdot 1 + 0 \cdot 0 + 0 \cdot 1 + 1 \cdot 1 = 0$

You should convince yourself that the complete convolution is given by (reading left to right) 11000111.

In convolutional encoding, we generally think of the 1's of the fixed sequence as representing the taps of a shift register while the moving sequence corresponds to the data or information bits as they move through the shift register.

Encoding takes place by advancing the information bits one or a few at a time through one or more shift registers. Let n_0 binits or channel symbols be the total output of the shift registers for every k_0 input bits. Then the code rate is:

$R = k_0/n_0$ bit/symbol

Particularly common cases are $k_0=1$, $n_0=2$, 3, or 4. Obviously, a bit can influence the shift register output only as long as it is in the shift register. Thus, we usually refer to K, the number of stages in the shift register, as the constraint length* of the convolutional code. It is roughly analogous to block length for block codes. The relationship between SR tap connections and mathematical representations of a code will be deferred until Section 6.3.

Figure 6-1 on the next page shows an encoder for a systematic convolutional code having R = 1/3, K=3. This code, chosen for its simplicity, is nonetheless adequate to illustrate all properties of a typical convolutional encoder. For the encoder shown, data bits enter the shift register from the right, one at a time. In addition to being transmitted unchanged (top output line), each bit is added modulo 2 to the preceding bit (middle output line) and to the two preceding bits (bottom output line), giving a total of $n_0=3$ channel symbols out via the commutator for every $k_0=1$ bit into the shift register.

*Some early workers in the theory of convolutional codes used the term constraint length to refer to the maximum number $n_A=n_0K$ of channel symbols influenced by any bit passing through the shift register.

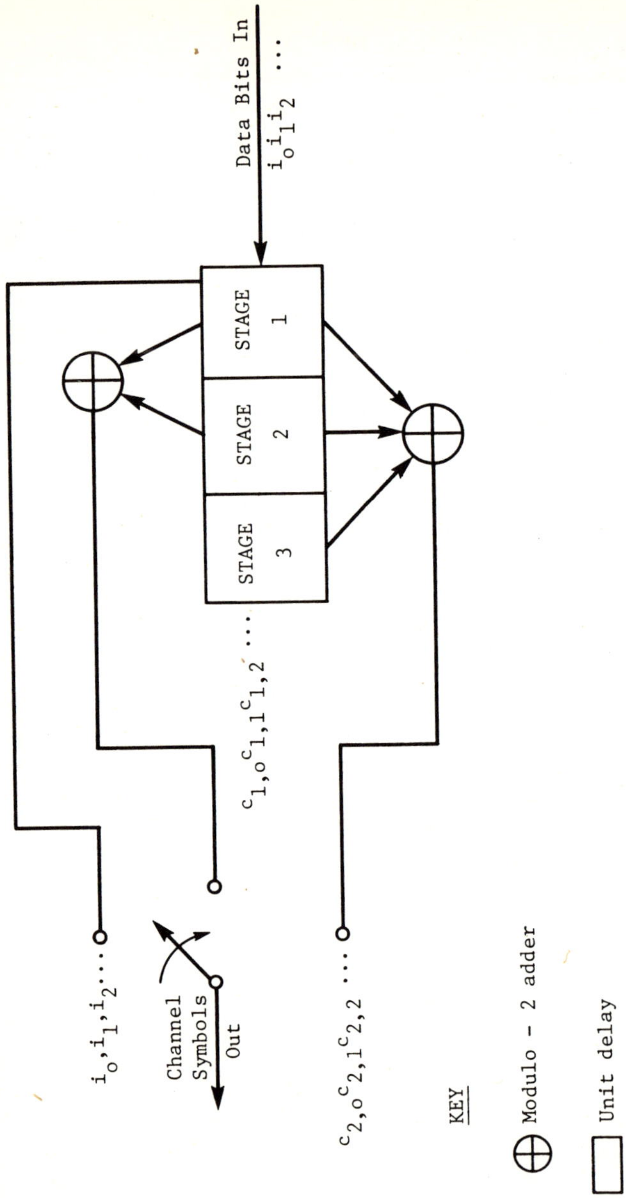

Figure 6-1/Convolutional Encoder.

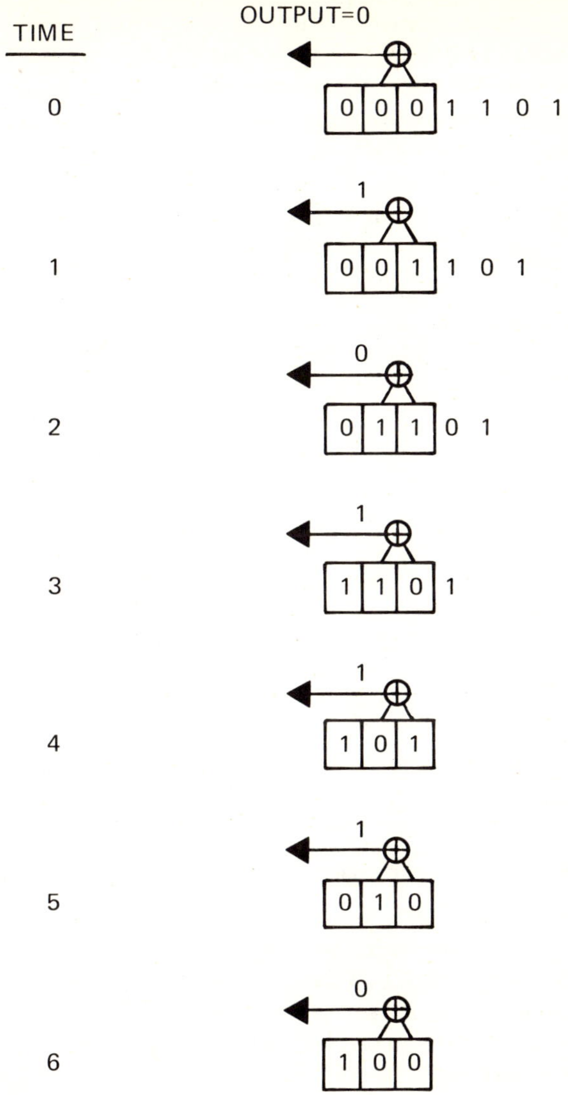

Figure 6-2/Generation of Check Digits by Upper Set of Tap Connections for Figure 6-1 Encoder.

Example 6-2. To see how the encoder SR of Figure 6-1 operates, let us look at "snapshots" of the SR as the successive information bits 1101 enter from the right. For simplicity, we have assumed that the information sequence preceding and following our four-bit sequence consists entirely of zeroes. Figure 6-2 shows the details of computing the first of the two check digits which follow each information bit into the channel. The SR contents along with all information and check digits that make up the encoder output are summarized in the following table.

Time	SR Contents	Output
		i c_1 c_2
0	0 0 0	0 0 0
1	0 0 1	1 1 1
2	0 1 1	1 0 0
3	1 1 0	0 1 0
4	1 0 1	1 1 0
5	0 1 0	0 1 1
6	1 0 0	0 0 1

Notice that the first of the three output digits at each discrete value of time is simply the latest input bit, in keeping with the systematic nature of the code.

6.2 Graphical Representation of Convolutional Codes*

The possible sequences of channel symbols are conveniently displayed by a *tree*. The tree for the code of Section 6.1 is shown in Figure 6-3. Each branch of the tree represents the output corresponding to a particular set of three bits in the shift register; i.e., the two which were shifted left after encoding for the preceding bit time interval, and the new bit just introduced at the right-hand end of the shift register.

*This section and Section 6.4 are based on the excellent tutorial paper by Viterbi [25].

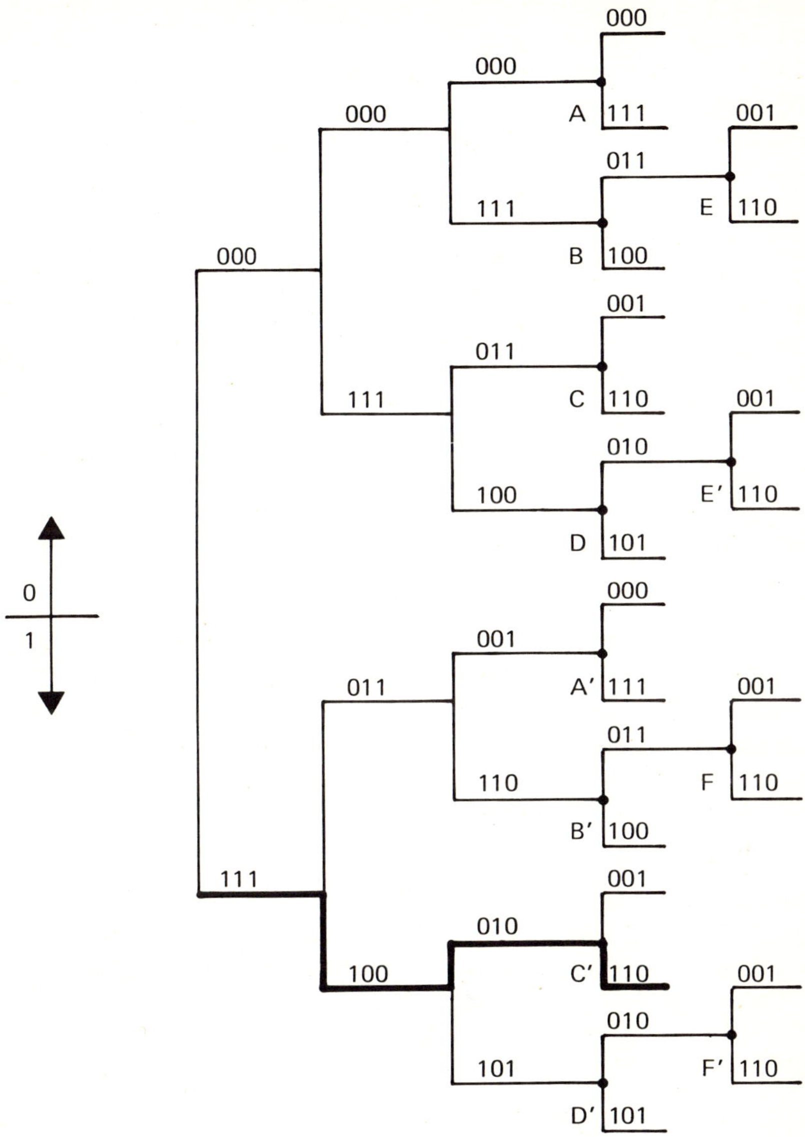

Figure 6-3/Code Tree Corresponding to Encoder of Figure 6-1.

Reading left to right, the channel symbols appear on each branch in the order in which they are transmitted by the clockwise-rotating commutator of Figure 6-1. Each new data bit corresponds to a node of the tree. The number of possible branches emanating from a node of the tree is equal to the size of the input (or data, or information) alphabet; in this case we are dealing with a binary alphabet, so that two branches leave every node. By convention, upper and lower branches from a node correspond to values of 0 and 1, respectively, for the data bits. A particular input sequence to the encoder corresponds to a unique path through the tree. For example, the data sequence 1101001 . . . (oldest digit at left) corresponds to the path shown with the heavy line in Figure 6-3.

Notice several properties of the branches of the tree. First, any succession of the branches shown can be generated by supplying the corresponding set of input bits to the encoder SR of Figure 6-1. Second, of the branches which emanate from any node, all of the digits on one are the binary complement (1 instead of 0, 0 instead of 1) of the digits on the other branch. The reason for this is fairly clear: as long as the SR is such that each new input digit influences all output digits, changing the latest input to the SR changes all $n_0 - 1$ of the modulo-2 sums which determine the check digits.

Now observe that starting with the fourth branch of any sequence, there are identical sets of branches in the upper and lower halves of the tree, implying that certain pairs of nodes could be tied together and hence combined. This is true, for example, at the nodes marked A and A′ in Figure 6-3. The same is true of the portions beyond B and B′, C and C′, and D and D′. In view of this property of the code tree, we may view A and A′ as the same node. Similarly, each of the pairs B and B′, C and C′, and D and D′ reduces to a single node. Looking at the next level of nodes, we observe that E and E′, F and F′, etc., may be tied together in a manner similar to that for A and A′, etc. Note that, with A and A′, . . . , D and D′ tied together in the manner just described, E already coincides with F, and E′ with F′. Thus, at each depth within the tree beyond the depth corresponding to one code constraint length, the number of branches can be halved without reducing the amount of information obtainable from the code tree diagram.

After combining nodes of the code tree in the manner just described, we are left with a structure having a repetitive pattern, whose appearance has led to its being called a *trellis*. We use the terms *node* and *branch* for trellises exactly as we did in the case of the tree. In addition to displaying compactly the possible encoded sequences, the trellis will prove very useful in studying the details of the Viterbi decoding algorithm to be presented in Chapter 8. Since each new bit entering the encoder causes a bit to be "pushed out" at the other end, only the newest K-1 bits can influence the encoder output corresponding to the input bit about to enter the SR. We talk, therefore, of the 2^{K-1} possible *states* of the encoder at any time, along with a set of output symbols corresponding to each choice of input bit. On the trellis of Figure 6-4 (which corresponds to the encoder of Figure 6-1), each encoder state (having oldest bit on the left, newest on the right) is listed alongside the corresponding line of nodes in the trellis, while each set of output symbols appears on the branch connecting the state and its possible successor. As with the tree, we conventionally and arbitrarily choose the upper and lower branches emanating from a node to correspond to the inputs 0 and 1, respectively. You should compare the SR states displayed in Figure 6-4 with the first digits of the SR contents in the table of Example 6-2; similarly, compare the outputs in Figure 6-4 and Example 6-2. The SR input is the last (right-hand) digit shown in the SR Contents column.

The designation of encoder states in conjunction with the trellis leads us to a third and final way of describing the operation of any given convolutional encoder. This is the *state diagram*, a notation widely used in the study of discrete Markov processes and finite-state machines. In fact, a convolutional encoder is a finite-state machine; it has a set of states defined, a set of inputs, and a set of outputs each of which depends on the state and the input. In addition to this, the sequence of states of the encoder is certainly a Markov process in that each state transition depends on the current state but not on any previous state; that is, the way in which the encoder arrived at its present state has no effect on future states.

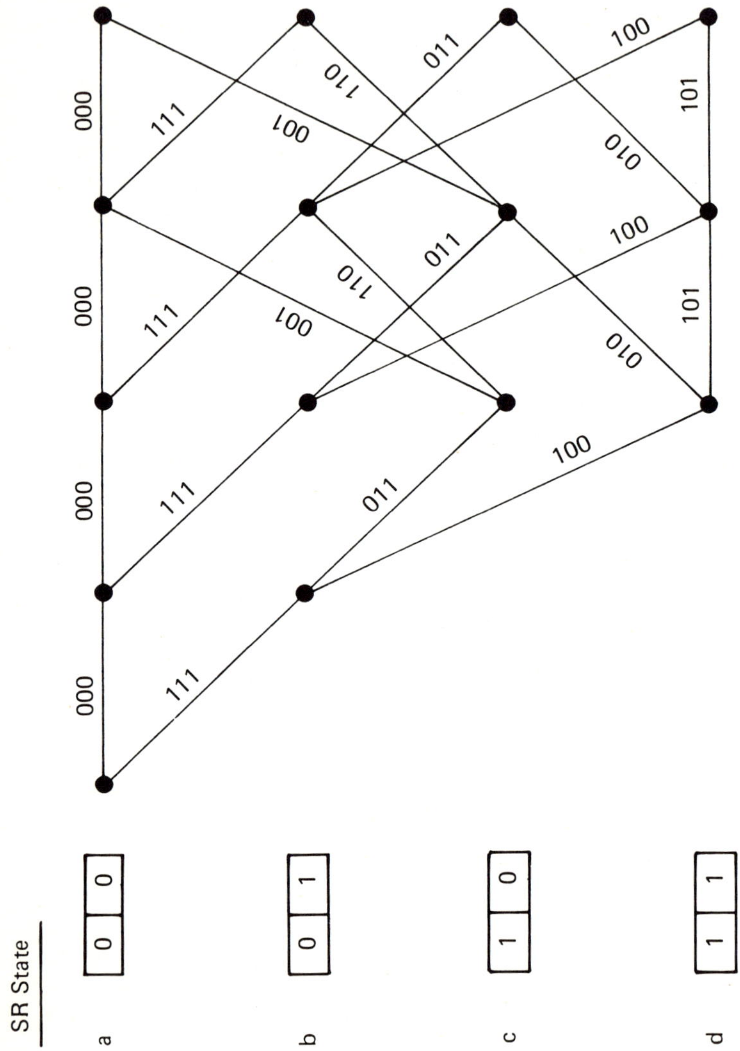

Figure 6-4/Trellis Corresponding to the Encoder of Figure 6-1.

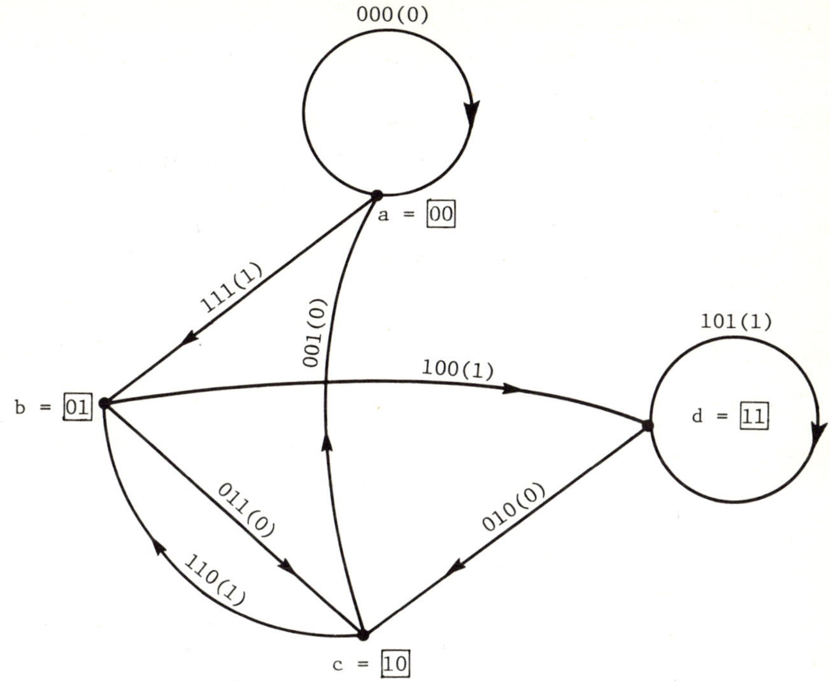

Figure 6-5/State Diagram Corresponding to the Encoder of Figure 6-1.

Refer now to Figure 6-5, which corresponds to the code we have been discussing through Figures 6-3 and 6-4. Each node of the state diagram represents a unique state of the encoder. State transitions are indicated by directed line segments from one node to another. Note that for the 00 and 11 states, the encoder can remain in the same state, given the proper input. In all cases, each line segment is labeled with the encoder output for that state transition and input, with the input given in parentheses following the output. As before, the oldest bit is on the left in the state designation.

6.3 Analytical Representation of Convolutional Codes

In contrast with the pictorial representations of convolutional codes given in Section 6.2, there are two very useful and widely used analytical representations. They are the delay-operator polynomial and the infinite (or semi-infinite) matrix.

In the first representation, both the encoder connections and the sequence(s) to be encoded are represented as polynomials in the delay operator D. For example, the sequence 1101001, with oldest digit at the left, would be written in the delay operator notation* as

$$I(D) = 1 + D + D^3 + D^6 \tag{6-1}$$

so that the exponent of the indeterminate (sometimes incorrectly referred to as a dummy variable) D is the number of time units of delay of that digit relative to the chosen time origin, which is usually taken to coincide with the first bit considered. More generally, the sequence $i_0\ i_1\ i_2\ i_3\ \ldots$ has the transform $i_0 + i_1 D + i_2 D^2 + i_3 D^3 + \ldots$.

In representing shift register tap connections, an output of a stage to the appropriate modulo -2 adder corresponds to a coefficient of 1 in the polynomial, while no output corresponds to a 0. Thus, for upper and lower sets of taps, respectively, the SR of Figure 6-1 has polynomial representations

$$\begin{aligned} G_1\ (D) &= 1 + D \\ G_2\ (D) &= 1 + D + D^2 \end{aligned} \tag{6-2}$$

In this case the lowest degree term corresponds to the stage encountered earliest by the entering bit stream. Following Massey, we shall refer to polynomials which specify the SR tap connections as *generator polynomials*. Each such polynomial is the transform of what Wozencraft and Reiffen [26] referred to as a generator sequence.

*Sometimes called the *transform* of the sequence.

Example 6-4. In contrast to the convolution operation, the use of transforms of the sequences is much more suited to pencil-and-paper computation. For example, the convolution of Figure 6-2 becomes

$$(1+D)\cdot(1+D+D^3+\ldots) = 1+(1+1)D+D^2+D^3+D^4+\ldots = 1+D^2+D^3+D^4+\ldots$$

Compare the final expression in this example with its counterpart in Example 6-2. Note that convolution of sequences corresponds to a multiplication of the respective transforms, just as in Fourier, Laplace, or Z-transform theory.

The other major representation of convolutional codes and encoding uses semi-infinite vectors and matrices, so called because they have a definite beginning but no end. That is, the code vector is of the form:

$$\mathbf{u} = \left[u_1\ u_2\ u_3\ \ldots\right]$$

where the elements of the vector **u** continue indefinitely to the right. Let the transmitted vector **x** be given by:

$$\mathbf{x} = \left[x_{1,1}\,x_{1,2}\,x_{1,3}\,x_{2,1}\,x_{2,2}\,x_{2,3}\,x_{3,1}\ \ldots\right]$$

Example 6-5. Let us work out the form which the matrix G must have to give the transmitted vector $\mathbf{x} = \mathbf{u}\,G$.

Think in terms of the vector **u** entering the SR of Figure 6-1. For u_1 in stage 1 and 0's in the remaining two stages, the expressions for the first three transmitted symbols are

$$x_{1,1} = u_1$$
$$x_{1,2} = u_1$$
$$x_{1,3} = u_1$$

Now shift **u** one stage to the left. This gives

$$x_{2,1} = u_2$$
$$x_{2,2} = u_1 + u_2$$
$$x_{2,3} = u_1 + u_2$$

Finally, for u_1, u_2, and u_3 in the SR, we have

$$x_{3,1} = u_3$$
$$x_{3,2} = u_3 + u_2$$
$$x_{3,3} = u_3 + u_2 + u_1$$

Note that this is the first time that all K=3 stages of the SR have contained information bits; it can be thought of as a "steady state" condition, while the preceeding (K-1)-step build-up is an "initial transient." Thus, in general, the SR output is

$$x_{m,1} = u_m$$
$$x_{m,2} = u_m + u_{m-1}$$
$$x_{m,3} = u_m + u_{m-1} + u_{m-2}$$

The submatrix A_1 of G which gives this must therefore satisfy

$$\begin{bmatrix} u_{m-2} & u_{m-1} & u_m \end{bmatrix} A_1 = \begin{bmatrix} u_m & u_m + u_{m-1} & u_m + u_{m-1} + u_{m-2} \end{bmatrix}$$

A little thought (or grinding out the equation in terms of general elements of A_1) shows that:

$$A_1 = \begin{bmatrix} 0 & 0 & 1 \\ 0 & 1 & 1 \\ 1 & 1 & 1 \end{bmatrix}$$

Now, how do we handle the "initial transient"? As u_1, u_2, and u_3 are shifted into the SR, the initial shift (bringing in u_1) permits only the right-hand stage of the SR to influence the output. Next, the two right-most stages influence. Finally, u_3 enters and all three stages can influence the SR output. The submatrices $T_1, \ldots, T_{K-1} = T_2$, which give this "transient" behavior of the SR are:

$$T_1 = \begin{bmatrix} 1 & 1 & 1 \\ 0 & 0 & 0 \\ 0 & 0 & 0 \end{bmatrix} \quad T_2 = \begin{bmatrix} 0 & 1 & 1 \\ 1 & 1 & 1 \\ 0 & 0 & 0 \end{bmatrix}$$

Thus, we have shown that G is given by

$$G = \begin{bmatrix} [T_1] & [T_2] & [A_1] & 0\,0\,0 & 0\,0\,0 & 0\,0\,0 \\ & & & [A_1] & 0\,0\,0 & 0\,0\,0 \\ & & & & [A_1] & 0\,0\,0 \;\cdots \\ & & & & & [A_1] \end{bmatrix} \tag{6-3}$$

$$G = \begin{bmatrix} 1\,1\,1 & 0\,1\,1 & 0\,0\,1 & 0\,0\,0 & 0\,0\,0 \\ 0\,0\,0 & 1\,1\,1 & 0\,1\,1 & 0\,0\,1 & 0\,0\,0 \\ 0\,0\,0 & 0\,0\,0 & 1\,1\,1 & 0\,1\,1 & 0\,0\,1 \ldots \\ & & & 1\,1\,1 & 0\,1\,1 \\ & & & & 1\,1\,1 \end{bmatrix}$$

where the large ovals indicate all-zeroes entries, and the matrix G extends arbitrarily far down and to the right. In practice, of course, G would be finite but, in a meaningful case, very large. This matrix G is a generator matrix in exactly the same sense as in the block code case. That is, any code (i.e., transmitted) sequence can be represented as a linear combination of the rows of G.

Now look carefully at the rows of G. Notice that they are simply shifted replicas of one another. Since each row by itself is certainly a code sequence, we should be able to find that sequence in the tree for this code. Inspection of Figure 6-3 shows this to be the case. The same argument applies to any linear combination of two or more rows of G. Thus, given the generator matrix, we can generate the tree for the code.

The process can also be reversed since there is a one-to-one correspondence between G and the tree. This gives us a second way of obtaining G from other information about the code. As we follow along one or more successive all-zeroes branches and finally choose our first branch corresponding to a data bit equal to 1, we note that this latest branch is always 111, regardless of where we are in the tree (including, you may notice, the 1's branch at the initial node). Thus, the path to node A′ is

111 011 001

corresponding to the data bit sequence 100, while data bit sequence 0100 gives the path

000 111 011 001,

which is simply the sequence to node A′ shifted three digits to the right. Further shifts of this type occur if we take data sequences 00100, 000100, etc. This suggests that such shifted versions of the same sequence might be used as rows of G, provided that all sequences in the tree can be produced from some smaller number of row vectors. To determine whether this can actually be done, let us use as a basis the following vector **a** and its translations **b** and **c**:

a = 111 011 001 000 . . .

b = 000 111 011 001 000 . . .

c = 000 000 111 011 001 000 . . .

where all additional components are 0's. Now let the path to node A in Figure 6-3 be labeled #1, that to B, #2, etc., with #8 assigned to the path to node D′. Comparing vectors **a**, **b**, and **c**, truncated after $n_o K = 9$ digits, with these paths, we see that **a** = #5, **b** = #3, and **c** = #2. With this bit of encouragement, let us see if linear combinations of **a**, **b**, and **c** give rise to the remaining paths in the tree. We have

a + **b** = 111 100 010 001 000 . . .

a + **c** = 111 011 110 011 001 000 . . .

b + **c** = 000 111 100 010 001 000 . . . .

a + **b** + **c** = 111 100 101 010 001 000 . . .

Again comparing the 9-digit truncated vectors with the tree, we see that we have generated paths 7, 6, 4, and 8, respectively.

To conclude this section, we generalize from $R = 1/n_o$ to $R = k_o/n_o$ with $k_o \geqslant 2$. To do this, we let there be k_o parallel inputs to the encoder and denote the transforms of these input sequences by $I^{(1)}(D), I^{(2)}(D), \ldots, I^{(k_o)}(D)$. For a nonsystematic code, each transmitted sequence will be a linear combination of all k_o input sequences and will have transform

$$T^{(j)}(D) = G^{(j,1)}(D)\, I^{(1)}(D) + G^{(j,2)}(D)\, I^{(2)}(D) + \ldots + G^{(j,k_o)}(D)\, I^{(k_o)}(D)$$

for $j = 1, 2, \ldots, n_o$. We notice tht there can be up to $k_o n_o$ generator polynomials $G^{(j,\ell)}(D)$. Each polynomial specifies the tap connections from one shift register to one output (transmitted) sequence line. An encoder for a systematic convolutional code of rate k_o/n_o is shown in block diagram form in Figure 6-6. Each SR is of length K and has n_o sets of taps, one set for each transmitted sequence. For a systematic code, there are only $k_o(n_o - k_o)$ nontrivial generator polynomials, since $T^{(j)}(D) = I^{(j)}(D)$ for $j = 1, 2, \ldots, k_o$.

The matrix representation of encoding becomes somewhat more cumbersome in detail. The input message vector will be written

$$u = [u_1^{(1)}\, u_1^{(2)} \ldots u_1^{(k_o)}\, u_2^{(1)}\, u_2^{(2)} \ldots u_2^{(k_o)} \ldots]$$

where the subscript refers to time, as before, and the superscript identifies the input sequence. Similarly, the output vector will be

$$x = [x_1^{(1)}\, x_1^{(2)} \ldots x_1^{(n_o)}\, x_2^{(1)}\, x_2^{(2)} \ldots x_2^{(n_o)} \ldots]$$

The structure of the generator matrix G is also modified, of course. We can write

$$G = \begin{bmatrix} G_0 & G_1 & G_2 \ldots & & G_N & \ldots & & \\ & G_0 & G_1 & G_2 \ldots & & G_N & \ldots & \\ & & G_0 & G_1 & G_2 & \ldots & G_N & \ldots \\ & & & \ddots & & & & \ddots \end{bmatrix}$$

Here each sub-matrix G_i contains k_o rows and n_o columns. All other entries in G are zero. An example using a generator matrix for $k_o > 1$ will be given in Section 6.6.

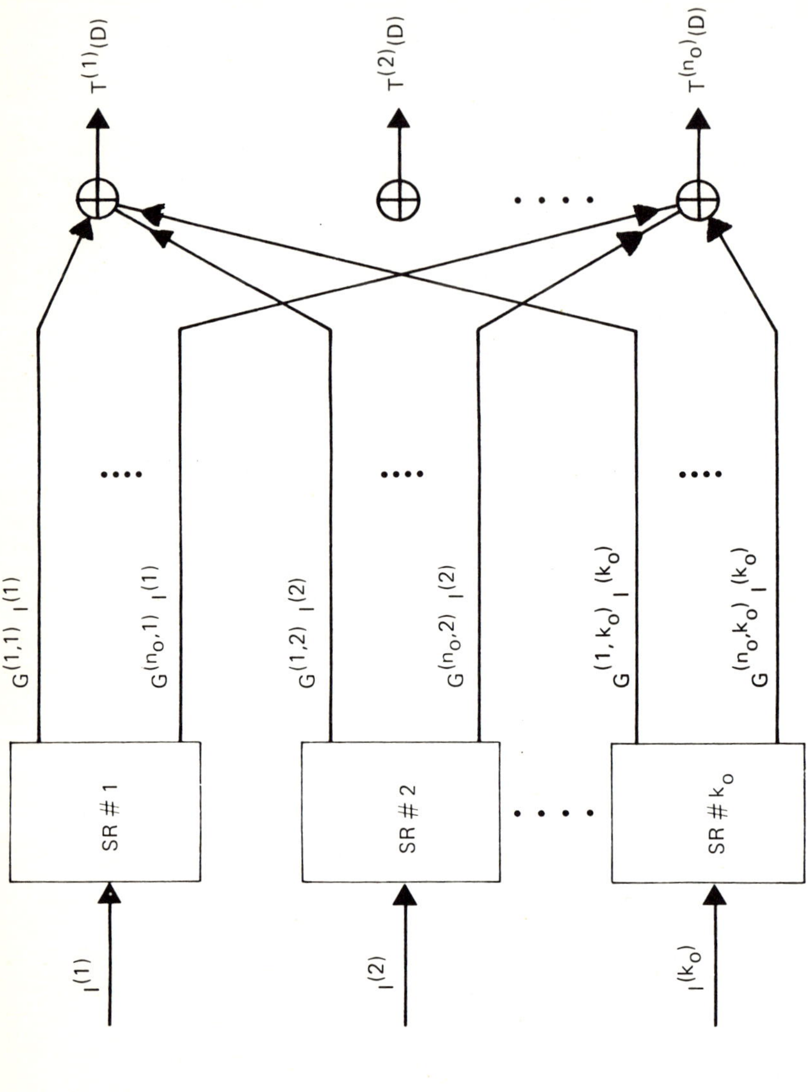

Figure 6-6/Encoder Block Diagram for $k_o > 1$

6.4 Distance Properties

Recall that for block codes, we defined the concept of distance between two code words to give us a way of quantitatively describing the extent to which the code words and block-length sequences were different. We made a distinction between this measure, distance, and the manner in which distance was actually computed, calling the latter *metric*. For block codes, the most popular metric by far was found to be Hamming distance — the number of positions in which two words (or block-length sequences) differ. It was shown to be desirable that a code have the largest possible minimum distance between code words.

Convolutional codes also have a distance concept defined for them. In fact, there are two types of distance in use, each of which is important and useful. Corresponding to distance between words of block length n, we have distance between sequences of various lengths which differ in their initial information bit i_o. (Hamming distance will again be used as the metric.) The first type of distance defined in this way is the distance between encoded sequences of length $n_0 K$, corresponding to the code constraint length K. The smallest value of this distance, denoted d_{min}, has always been an important code parameter. In fact, for many years, it was the only distance concept used for convolutional codes.

In 1968, however, Massey [27] coined the term "free distance," d_{free}, to denote another type of distance which was found to be an important parameter for two of the decoding techniques in use for convolutional codes. *Free distance* is defined to be the minimum distance between arbitrarily long (i.e., possibly infinite) encoded sequences, one corresponding to an initial information bit $i_o = 0$ and one to $i_o = 1$. The definitions of d_{free} and d_{min} in terms of code sequences corresponding to $i_o = 0$ and $i_o = 1$ are of interest because one of these values of i_o represents correct decoding, while the other represents incorrect decoding. Because of linearity, we can, without loss of generality, choose $i_o = 0$ as the correct value. Going one step further, we can define the *correct subset* S_c and *incorrect subset* S_I as the sets of all encoded sequences corresponding to $i_o = 0$ and $i_o = 1$, respectively. Also because of linearity, we observe that the encoded sequence corresponding to the difference of a sequence in S_c and a sequence in S_I is itself in S_I since it corresponds to an information sequence beginning with a 1. Thus, in determining d_{min} and d_{free}, we need only consider sequences in S_I. From this it follows that d_{min} and d_{free} are the minimum number of 1's in encoded sequences of lengths $n_o K$ and infinity, respectively, which are members of S_I.

Since free distance is defined in terms of an infinitely long encoded sequence, it turns out to be particularly important with regard to convolutional code performance with a decoding algorithm which can make use of searches over more than one constraint length. This means sequential and Viterbi decoding. While we obviously must always have $d_{min} \leqslant d_{free}$, it is also true that for many codes, $d_{free} = d_{min}$.

Example 6-6. To illustrate the notions of minimum distance and free distance, refer again to the systematic code defined by the tree in Figure 6-3. To determine d_{min}, it is necessary only to find the weights for the four code sequences, corresponding to information sequences of length K=3, which terminate at nodes A′, B′, C′, and D′. Let w(A′), etc., denote the weights of these code sequences. It is easy to see that w(A′)=6, w(B′)=7, w(C′)=5, and w(D′)=6. Thus, d_{min} =5. Now, can we find d_{free} without too much difficulty? In this case, yes. Observe that the weight of a code sequence stops growing once that sequence corresponds to an all-zeroes information sequence. This is already the case at A′ if we continue to take the upper branch each time. If we let w(A′, ∞), etc., denote the minimum weight of any infinitely long code sequence starting at the specified node (e.g., A′), then we find that w_{min} (A′, ∞) = 0, while w_{min} (B′, ∞), W_{min} (c′,∞), and w_{min} (D′, ∞) are all at least equal to 1. Adding each of these weights to the weight of the code sequence from the base of the tree out to the corresponding node, we see that the minimum-weight infinite-length sequence through A′ has w=6, while for all other paths $w \geqslant 6$. Thus, $d_{free} = 6$.

Searching for a code which has the largest minimum distance is at best tedious and at worst practically impossible by hand; and even with the aid of a computer it can become quite time-consuming due to the exponential growth (with K) in the number of sequences to be examined. Fortunately, a number of clever ways have been found to reduce this effort, particularly by reducing the number of codes which need to be examined in the effort to determine the optimum (i.e., maximum d_{min} or d_{free}) code for a given constraint length K. A number of computer-based search techniques have been developed. Results of applying these techniques are displayed in the tables of Section 6.6. Especially useful, of course, are those cases in which the code generators are given along with values of the distance parameter(s).

6.5 Distance Bounds for Convolutional Codes

Both upper and lower bounds can be computed on the minimum distance of a convolutional code having given rate $R = k_o/n_o$ and constraint length $= n_o K$. These bounds are similar in nature and derivation to those for block codes, with block length corresponding to constraint length. Unfortunately, in general, neither the upper nor the lower bound is very tight, so that their usefulness is generally restricted to giving a rough idea of how good a code is in terms of how closely its minimum distance approaches the values of minimum distance given by the bounds. We shall present the bounds without proof, and only for the case of binary codes.

For the lower bound on d, we have a Gilbert-like bound characterized as follows. For rate R and constraint length $n_o K$, let d be the largest integer which satisfies

$$H\left(\frac{d}{n_o K}\right) \leqslant 1 - R. \tag{6-4}$$

Then there is at least one binary convolutional code with minimum distance d for which expression (6-4) holds. Here, H(x) is the familiar entropy function for the case of a binary alphabet:

$$H(x) = -x \log_2 x - (1 - x) \log_2 (1 - x)$$

One upper bound on minimum distance corresponds to the Plotkin bound for block codes. It can be stated as follows. For a binary code with $R = 1/n_o$, the minimum distance d_{min} satisfies

$$d_{min} \leqslant \lfloor (1/2)(n_o K + n_o) \rfloor \tag{6-5}$$

where $\lfloor I \rfloor$ denotes the largest integer equal to or less than I; that is, the integer portion of I.

A simple upper bound on d_{free} has been found by Heller [28]. It is given by

$$d_{free} \leqslant \min_{j \geqslant 1} \left\lfloor \frac{n_o}{2} \quad \frac{2^j}{2^j - 1} \quad (K + j - 1) \right\rfloor \qquad (6\text{-}6)$$

where, as before, $\lfloor \ \rfloor$ denotes the integer portion of the enclosed expression and n_o and K have already been defined. Let us consider the calculation of this bound on d_{free}. For any given case, n_o and K are fixed, being parameters of the code. The fraction $2^j/(2^j - 1)$ quickly approaches the value 1 from above with increasing j. The expression $(K + j - 1)$ obviously grows linearly with j. Thus, we should expect that the minimum value of the expression in brackets should be reached for a small value of j. This can be verified analytically by regarding d_{free} and j in equation (6-6) as continuous variables and applying the usual first-derivative test.

As stated earlier, these bounds are usually quite coarse, although occasionally we come across a code which actually achieves one of them.

Example 6-7. Let us apply the bounds of equations (6-4), (6-5) and (6-6) to the code of Figure 6-3 and Example 6-6. We have $n_o = 3$, $K = 3$, $R = 1/3$, with $d_{min} = 5$ and $d_{free} = 6$.

a. The Gilbert bound becomes

$$H\,(d/9) \leqslant 2/3$$

Direct calculation or table look-up (e.g., Fano [29], Appendix B) shows that

$$H\,(0.1735) = 0.6656$$

$$H\,(0.1740) = 0.6668$$

so that $d/9 \leqslant 0.1740$, $d \leqslant 1.566$. Thus, the largest integer d which satisfies the equation (6-4) is d=1, giving $d_{min} \geqslant 1$, obviously a poor lower bound in this case.

b. After substitution, the Plotkin bound expression becomes

$$d_{min} \leqslant \lfloor (1/2)\,(9 + 3) \rfloor = 6,$$

a good upper bound.

c. The Heller bound on d_{free} is tabulated below for j=1, . . . , 5. From these values we find $d_{free} \leqslant 8$, again a rather good bound.

j	$\lfloor \cdot \rfloor$	
1	$\lfloor 9 \rfloor$	= 9
2	$\lfloor 8 \rfloor$	= 8
3	$\lfloor 60/7 \rfloor$	= 8
4	$\lfloor 48/5 \rfloor$	= 9
5	$\lfloor 336/31 \rfloor$	= 10

6.6 Known Good Convolutional Codes

In this section we present tables of optimum or near-optimum codes as they have appeared in the literature during the past few years. In some cases, we have modified the author's original notation to bring it into conformity with our own. You will notice the terms catastrophic and non-catastrophic code used in conjunction with the codes by Larsen in Tables 6-1 through 6-3. This terminology will be explained in Chapter 7. Lack of familiarity with the concept will not present any difficulty for the present discussion.

Larsen [30] has tabulated non-catastrophic codes having rates R = 1/2, 1/3 and 1/4, and $3 \leqslant K \leqslant 14$, and catastrophic R = 1/2 codes for K = 5, 12, and 14. These codes are given in Tables 6-1, 6-2, and 6-3. Some of the codes listed had been published earlier by Odenwalder [31] while the majority of them were new results by Larsen. The bound referred to is equal to or 1 greater than the Heller bound discussed in Section 6.5*. In cases where this bound is not actually achieved, optimality was established by an exhaustive search of all codes. The generator is given as the sequence 1, $g_1^{(i)}$, $g_2^{(i)}$, etc., where

*See Larsen [30] for a detailed explanation of the bounds.

$$G^{(i)}(D) = 1 + g_1{}^{(i)} D + g_2{}^{(i)} D^2 + \cdots + g_{K-1}{}^{(i)} D^{K-1}$$

is the transform of the code generator. Note that all of the codes listed are nonsystematic.

Table 6-1/Rate 1/2 Codes with Maximum Free Distance*

*Reproduced, with permission, from Reference [30].

A. Noncatastrophic Codes

ν	N	generators(octal)		d_{free}	bound
3	6	5	7[1]	5	5
4	8	15	17[1]	6	6
5	10	23	35[1]	7	8
6	12	53	75[1]	8	8
7	14	133	171[1]	10	10
8	16	247	371[1]	10	11
9	18	561	753[1]	12	12
10	20	1167	1545	12	13
11	22	2335	3661	14	14
12	24	4335	5723	15	16
13	26	10533	17661	16	16
14	28	21675	27123	16	17

B. Catastrophic Codes

ν	N	generators(octal)		d_{free}	bound
5	10	27	35	8	8
12	24	5237	6731	16	16
14	28	21645	37133	17	17

[1] This code was found by Odenwalder [31] and is listed here for completeness.

Table 6-2/Rate 1/3 Noncatastrophic Codes with Maximum Free Distance*

	N	generators (octal)			d_{free}	bound
3	9	5	7	7[1]	8	8
4	12	13	15	17[1]	10	10
5	15	25	33	37[1]	12	12
6	18	47	53	75[1]	13	13
7	21	133	145	175[2]	15	15
8	24	225	331	367[1]	16	16
9	27	557	663	711	18	18
10	30	1117	1365	1633	20	20
11	33	2353	2671	3175	22	22
12	36	4767	5723	6265	24	24
13	39	10533	10675	17661	24	24
14	42	21645	35661	37133	26	26

[1] This code was found by Odenwalder [31] and is listed here for completeness.
[2] This code was also found by Odenwalder [31], but was overlooked. The corresponding code in [31] has free distance only 14.

Table 6-3/Rate 1/4 Noncatastrophic Codes with Maximum Free Distance*

ν	N	generators(octal)				d_{free}	bound
3	12	5	7	7	7	10	10
4	16	13	15	15	17	13	13
5	20	25	27	33	37	16	16
6	24	53	67	71	75	18	18
7	28	135	135	147	163	20	20
8	32	235	275	313	357	22	22
9	36	463	535	733	745	24	24
10	40	1117	1365	1633	1653	27	27
11	44	2387	2353	2671	3175	29	29
12	48	4767	5723	6265	7455	32	32
13	52	11145	12477	15573	16727	33	33
14	56	21113	23175	35527	35537	36	36

*Reproduced, with permission, from Reference [30].

Example 6-8. The rate 1/2 non-catastrophic code having K = 4 has $n_A = K \times 1/R = 8$ and has generators given in octal notation by 15 and 17, corresponding respectively to $G^{(1)}(D) = 1 + D + D^3$, $G^{(2)}(D) = 1 + D + D^2 + D^3$. This code has $d_{free} = 6$, which achieves the bound given by Equation (6-6) for these code parameters. (The reader should verify this last statement.)

Earlier, Bahl and Jelinek [32] published two tables of rate 1/2 convolutional codes whose free distance has turned out to be far superior to that of any other codes, published since then, except Larsen's and Odenwalder's noted above. The data from these two tables are reproduced here as Tables 6-4 and 6-5. The first of these tables gives all codes found for $3 \leqslant K \leqslant 9$, while the second presents only one code for each K. This latter table resulted from taking, in those cases when more than one code was found having the maximum d_{free}, that code with the largest d_{min} whose generator had the smallest weight W. The purpose of this last criterion was the minimization of the number of adders in the encoding circuitry.

A complementary code of rate ½ (as in Table 6-5) is defined as follows. The high-order and low-order coefficients $g_{K-1}^{(i)}$ and $g_0^{(i)}$ are all 1, and the remaining coefficients of one generator polynomial are the binary complements of those in the other generator polynomial. For example, the first code of Table 6-5 has generator polynomials $1+D^2$ and $1+D+D^2$ corresponding to 101 and 111.

Tables 6-6 through 6-8 present results obtained by Paaske [33] in a computer-based search for optimal (in the sense of having maximum d_{free}) short convolutional codes of rates 2/3 and 3/4. Paaske utilized several criteria based on theoretical results obtained in his paper to discard unpromising codes quickly, thus reducing the search effort. Note that some of the upper bounds on free distance in Table 6-6 were, in fact, not achieved.

Table 6-4/Generators of Codes with $d_f = v + 2$*

v	Generator
3	101
4	1011
5	10011
6	100011
	100101
7	1000101
	1001101
	1010011
8	10001001
	10011011
	10011101
	10101101
9	100010011
	100011011
	100100011
	100101001
	100110101
	101000011
	101001011

Table 6-5/R=1/2 Complementary Codes*

v	Generator (Octal)	d_{free}	d_{min}	Weight
3	5	5	3	2
4	13	6	3	3
5	31	7	4	3
6	61	8	4	3
7	121	9	5	3
8	211	10	5	4
9	503	11	6	4
10	1065	12	6	5
11	2415	13	7	5
12	5121	14	7	5
13	12043	15	7	5
14	24421	16	8	5
15	51303	17	7	7
16	120643	18	8	7
17	346411	18	9	8
18	425551	20	8	9
19	1411041	20	9	6
20	2734605	20	10	11
21	5011303	22	9	8
22	11047441	22	10	9
23	22517023	24	10	11
24	51202215	24	10	9

*Reproduced, with permission, from Reference [32].

Table 6-6/Upper Bounds for Short Rates 2/3 and 3/4 Convolutional Codes*

constraint length ν	free distance R=2/3 upper bound	R=2/3 achieved	R=3/4 upper bound	R=3/4 achieved
2	4	3		
3	4	4	4	4
4	6	5	4	(4)
5	6	6	6	5
6	8	7	6	6
7	8	8	8	(6)
8	8	(8)	8	7
9	10	9	8	8
10	10	10	9	

Table 6-7/Generator Matrices of the (3,2) Convolutional Codes in Table 6-6.*

ν	$\underline{G}_0$	$\underline{G}_1$	$\underline{G}_2$	$\underline{G}_3$	$\underline{G}_4$	$\underline{G}_5$
2	101 011	111 100				
3	101 011	011 001	000 101			
4	101 011	100 101	110 011			
5	101 011	111 001	011 101	000 101		
6	101 011	111 111	010 101	101 011		
7	101 011	110 001	011 101	011 111	000 110	
9	101 011	001 010	101 011	011 100	110 001	000 101
10	101 011	100 111	010 100	011 010	101 100	110 011

*Reproduced, with permission, from Reference [33].

Table 6-8/Generator Matrices of the (4,3) Convolutional Codes in Table 6-6.*

ν	$\underline{G}_0$	$\underline{G}_1$	$\underline{G}_2$	$\underline{G}_3$
3	1111 0101 0011	0000 0110 0100	0000 0000 0011	
5	1001 0101 0011	1111 0101 0100	0000 1001 0011	
6	1001 0101 0011	1001 1001 1110	0101 1010 0110	
8	1001 0101 0011	1110 0000 0010	1100 1101 0110	0000 1001 1010
9	1001 0101 0011	0011 0111 1011	0110 0001 1000	0110 1100 1001

*Reproduced, with permission, from Reference [33].

Table 6-9†/ODP Systematic Convolutional Codes with Rate 1/2 which are also OMD Codes

M	$G^{(2)}$		d_M	#paths	d_∞	#paths
1	6	B	3	2	3	1
2	7	B	3	1	4	2
3	64	B	4	3	4	1
4	72	B	4	1	5	2
5	73	B	5	5	6	3
6	730	B	5	2	6	3
	734		5	3	6	1
7	714	B	6	11	6	2
8	715	B	6	5	7	2
	671		6	6	7	1
9	6710	B	6	1	7	1
	7154		6	3	8	4
10	6710	B	7	12	7	1
	7152		7	13	8	3
11	6711	B	7	5	8	2
	7153		7	6	9	3
12	67114	B	8	29	9	1
13	67114	B	8	12	9	1
14	67115		8	6	10	4

Note: B denotes that this generator was previously found by Bussgang [53].

†Reproduced, with permission, from Reference [34].

Table 6-10/ODP Systematic Convolutional Codes with Rate 1/2*

M	$G^{(2)}$	d_M	#paths	d_∞	#paths
15	714474	8	1	10	1
16	714476	9	18	10	1
	671166	9	22	12	13
17	671145	9	7	11	1
	671166	9	13	12	13
18	6711454	9	3	12	4
19	7144616	10	31	12	3
20	7144616	10	13	12	3
	7144761	10	18	12	1
21	67114544	10	4	12	1
22	71446162	10	1	13	2
	71446166	10	6	14	6
23	67114543	11	27	14	6
	67115143	11	32	14	2
24	714461654	11	11	15	5
	671151434	11	16	15	4
25	714461654	11	5	15	5
	671145536	11	9	15	3
26	671145431	11	1	15	1
	671151433	11	4	16	8
27	7144616264	12	21	14^L	1
	7144760524	12	26	16	7
28	6711454306	12	8	16	4
	6711514332	12	13	16	3
29	7144616573	12	2	17^L	3
	7144760535	12	6	18	22
30	71446162654	13	43	16^L	2
	67114543064	13	44	16^L	1
31	71446162654	13	15	16L	2
	67114543066	13	24	18	11
32	71446162655	13	4	17^L	2
	71447605247	13	13	18^L	2
33	714461626554	13	1	18^L	5
	671145430654	13	4	18^L	1
34	714461626554	14	34	18^L	5
	714461625306	14	42	18^L	1
35	714461625313	14	14	18^L	3
	714461626555	14	19	19^L	2

Note: L denotes that this number is actually d_{71} which is a lower bound on d_∞.

*Reproduced, with permission, from Reference [34].

More recently, Johannesson [34] has discovered optimum codes of short to medium length, both systematic and nonsystematic, all at rate 1/2. He has defined several types of optimality. A code is called an optimum minimum distance (OMD) code when its minimum distance d_{min} is equal to or greater than that of any code of the same constraint length. Similarly, an optimum free distance (OFD) code has its free distance d_{free} equal to or greater than that of any code of the same constraint length. To define the third type of optimality, we must first define the concept of distance profile. The distance profile of a convolutional code is the set of minimum weights of paths resulting from an information sequence having $i_o = 1$, taken over path lengths (measured in branches) of 1, 2, . . . , K. Then a code is said to be an optimum distance profile (ODP) code if its distance profile is equal or superior to the distance profile of any code of the same constraint length.

A quick-look-in (QLI) code is a nonsystematic code with the property that the information digits can be obtained simply by adding the two encoded sequences together modulo 2. Thus, without actually decoding, it is possible to get an idea of the transmitted information bits. This capability may be highly desirable in a situation in which one needs at least a rough idea of the data being sent, at the earliest possible time. Obviously, there is no way of knowing whether errors have been committed when using the quick-look-in technique, but if the E_B/N_o is known for the channel, one knows the average bit error rate and is usually prepared to live with it.

Some explanation of the notation used in Tables 6-9 through 6-13 must be given. Johannesson's ν is our K-1, and his d_m and d_∞ are our d_{min} and d_{free}, respectively. His generators $G^{(1)}$ and $G^{(2)}$ are given in octal notation with the highest-order bit corresponding to the lowest-degree term in the generator polynomial. Furthermore, the high-order bit positions of the first (left-most) octal digit are always filled in, which is just the reverse of the notation commonly used. The notation "# paths" refers to the number of paths in the tree which have the distance shown.

Table 6-11/ODP QLI Codes with Rate 1/2*

M	$G^{(1)}$	$G^{(2)}$	d_M	#paths	d_∞	#paths
1	6	4	3	2	3	1
2	7	5	3	1	5	1
3	74	54	4	3	6	1
4	72	52	4	1	6	1
5	71	51	5	5	7	1
	75	55	5	6	8	2
6	704	504	5	2	7	1
	714	514	5	3	8	1
7	742	542	6	11	9	1
8	742	542	6	5	9	1
9	7404	5404	6	1	9	1
	7434	5434	6	2	10	2
10	7406	5406	7	12	10	1
	7422	5422	7	13	11	2
11	7421	5421	7	5	11	1
	7435	5435	7	6	12	5
12	74044	54044	8	29	11	1
13	74042	54042	8	12	11	1
	74046	54046	8	17	13	2
14	74042	54042	8	6	11	1
	74047	54047	8	7	14	2
15	740414	540414	8	1	13	1
	740470	540470	8	3	14	2
16	740416	540416	9	18	14	1
	740462	540462	9	22	15	3
17	740415	540415	9	7	15	3
	740463	540463	9	9	16	2
18	7404244	5404244	9	3	15	1
	7404634	5404634	9	4	16^L	1
19	7404242	5404242	10	31	15	1
20	7404241	5404241	10	13	14^L	1
	7404155	5404155	10	18	18^L	2
21	74042404	54042404	10	4	15	1
	74041550	54041550	10	8	18^L	2
22	74041566	54041566	10	1	18	1
	74042436	54042436	10	8	19^L	2
23	74042417	54042417	11	27	18^L	1
	74041567	54041567	11	32	19^L	1

Note: L denotes that this number is actually d_{71} which is a lower bound on d_∞.

*Reproduced, with permission, from Reference [34].

Table 6-12/Nonsystematic QLI Codes with Maximum Free Distance for QLI Codes*

M	$G^{(1)}$	$G^{(2)}$		d_M	#paths	d_∞	#paths
1	6	4	1,2,3	3	2	3	1
2	7	5	1,2,3	3	1	5	1
3	74	54	1,2,3	4	3	6	1
4	66	46	1, 3	4	2	7	2
5	75	55	1,2,3	5	6	8	2
6	654	454	3	5	3	9	4
7	742	542	2,3	6	11	9	1
8	751	551	3	6	7	10	1
9	7664	5664		5	1	11	3
10	7506	5506	3	7	14	12	3
11	7503	5503		6	2	13	8
12	76414	56414		7	7	14	10
13	66716	46716		6	1	14	3

Notes: 1. This code is OFD.

2. This code is ODP.

3. This code is OMD.

Table 6-13/Nonsystematic Codes which are simultaneously ODP, OMD, and OFD*

M	$G^{(1)}$	$G^{(2)}$	d_M	#paths	d_∞	#paths
1	6	4	3	2	3	1
2	7	5	3	1	5	1
3	74	54	4	3	6	1
4	62	56	4	2	7	2
5	75	55	5	6	8	2
6	634	564	5	3	10	12
7	626	572	6	11	10	1
8	751	557	6	6	12	10
9	7664	5714	6	2	12	1
10	7512	5562	7	13	14	19
11	-	-	7	-	15	-
12	-	-	8	-	16	-
13	60676	45662*	8	17	16	5

* The search for the code with the smallest number of $d_\infty=16$ paths was not exhaustive and hence a slightly better code might exist.

*Reproduced, with permission, from Reference [34].

A look at the two generators for any nonsystematic QLI code reveals that they are identical except for the single bit which is second from the left; this position, which corresponds to D in the generator polynomial, is present in $G^{(1)}$ but not in $G^{(2)}$. Thus, $G^{(1)} - G^{(2)} = D$, always, so the QLI sequence is

$$(G^{(1)}(D) + G^{(2)}(D))\, I(D) + E^{(1)}(D) + E^{(2)}(D) =$$

$$D \cdot I(D) + E^{(1)}(D) + E^{(2)}(D)$$

which gives the information sequence one time unit after the two received sequences enter the decoder's encoder, corrupted by the mod-2 sum of the two noise sequences $E^{(1)}(D)$ and $E^{(2)}(D)$.

Example 6-9. Consider the code specified by the third line of Table 6-13. This code has K=4 with the following encoder tap connections:

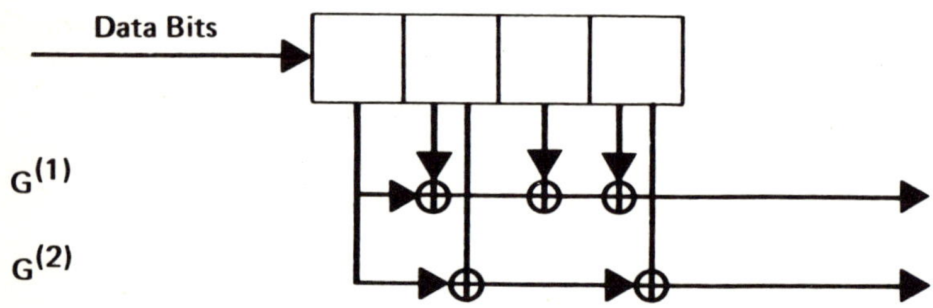

Johannesson [34] has also compared minimum and free distances for his various classes of optimum codes with these parameters for six classes of codes found earlier by others (as indicated), and with the Gilbert lower bound. Figures 6-7a and 6-7b together present all of these comparisons.

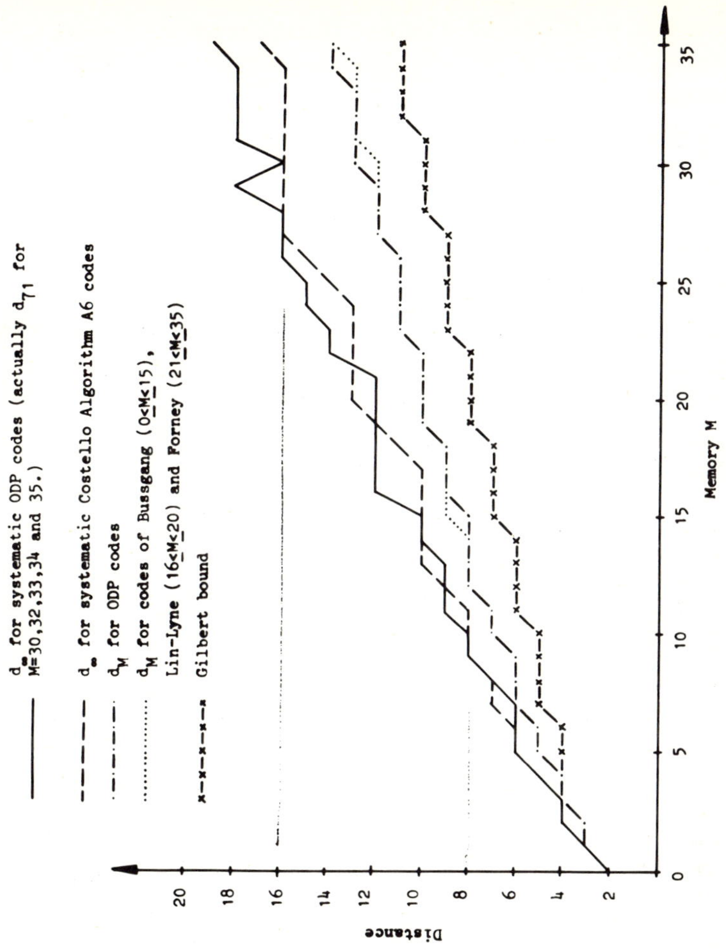

Figure 6-7a/Minimum Distance d_M and Free Distance d_∞ for some Rate 1/2 Convolutional Codes*

*Reproduced, with permission, from Reference [34].

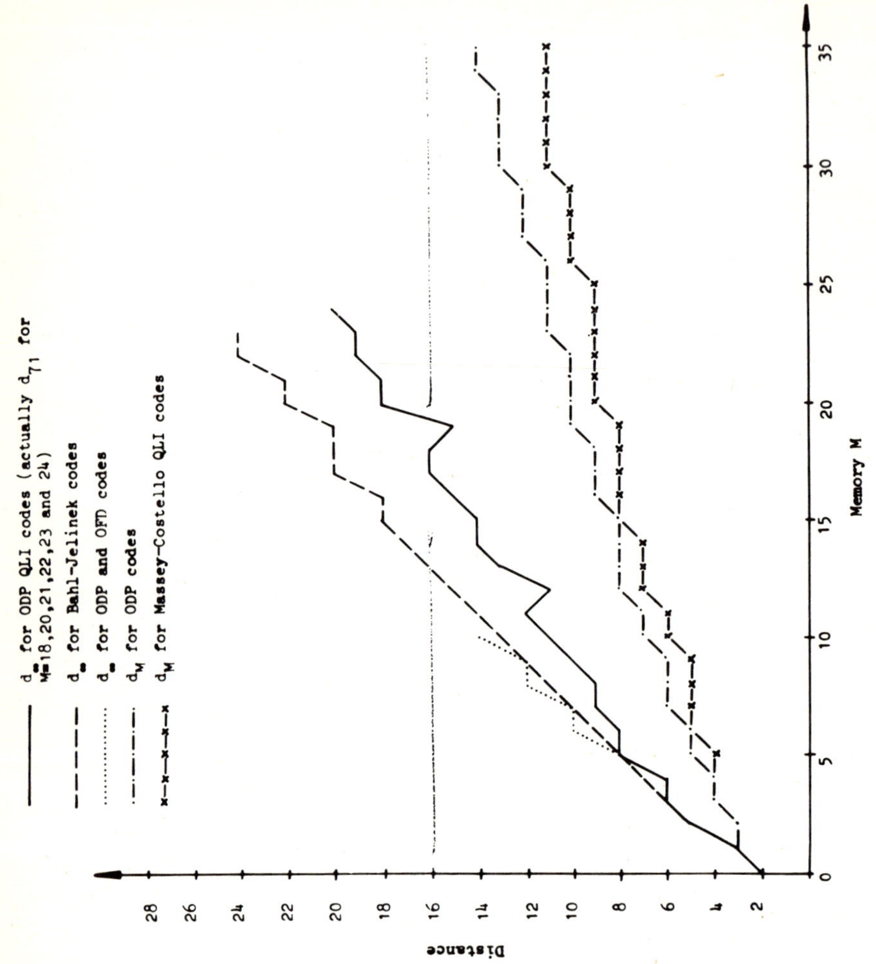

Figure 6-7b/Minimum Distance d_M and Free Distance for some Rate 1/2 Convolutional Codes*

*Reproduced, with permission, from Reference [34].

Example 6-10. As a final example in this chapter, let us derive the generator matrix and encoder for the rate 2/3 code having K=2 in Table 6-7. Here

$$G_0 = \begin{bmatrix} 1 & 0 & 1 \\ 0 & 1 & 1 \end{bmatrix} \qquad G_1 = \begin{bmatrix} 1 & 1 & 1 \\ 1 & 0 & 0 \end{bmatrix}$$

so that

$$G = \begin{bmatrix} 1\ 0\ 1 & 1\ 1\ 1 & & \\ 0\ 1\ 1 & 1\ 0\ 0 & & \\ & 1\ 0\ 1 & 1\ 1\ 1 & \\ & 0\ 1\ 1 & 1\ 0\ 0 & \\ & & & \ddots \end{bmatrix}$$

Each block of n_o = 3 columns specifies encoder output at some instant of time. Alternate rows (for k_o = 2) specify the stages of one shift register which are to be **added** modulo 2 into the output line corresponding to that column. The shift register tap connections can be deduced by noting that, for any column in a block of k_o columns, odd and even numbered rows correspond to SR #1 and SR #2, respectively. Thus, we have

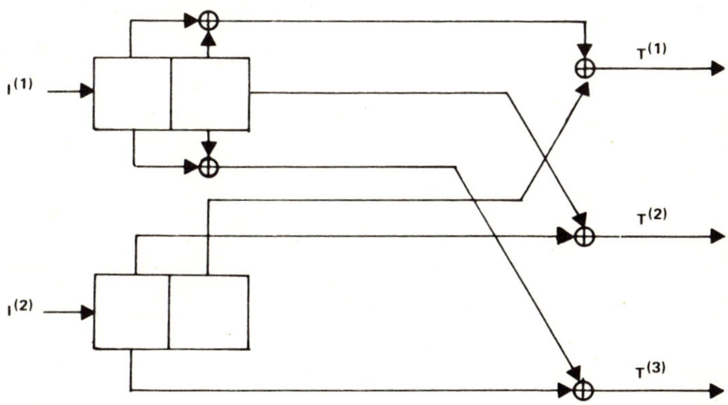

Chapter 7

Threshold Decoding

7.1 Introduction

A significant portion of the currently known theory of threshold decoding of convolutional codes is due to J.L. Massey [35]. In common with sequential and Viterbi decoding, techniques which also use convolutional codes, threshold decoding has the distinction of having been implemented on a production basis. For threshold decoding, this implementation will be discussed near the end of this chapter. Of the three techniques just mentioned for decoding convolutional codes, threshold decoding is conceptually and practically the closest to block decoding. The conceptual similarity stems from the fact that threshold decoding of convolutional codes begins with the calculation of a set of syndrome digits, defined for convolutional codes in a manner very similar to their definition for block codes. This causes threshold decoding to lack the search aspects characteristic of Viterbi decoding and sequential decoding. The role of the syndrome sequence also makes implementation somewhat similar to that for decoding block codes, with the exception of the threshold element and the special type of parity checks involved.

The early popularity of threshold decoding as an error-control technique was due in part to this simplicity and in part to the fact that Massey's published results included several sizable families of suitable convolutional codes of various rates and structures. While these original codes and their decoding algorithm were designed to handle random errors, refinements such as diffuse threshold decoding (see Chapter 10 for details) were soon developed to cope with bursts as well.

It should be mentioned in passing that certain classes of reasonably good block codes have also been found to be threshold, or majority-logic, decodable. In fact, the earliest published work on majority-logic decoding was Reed's [36] algorithm for decoding Muller's block codes.

Threshold decoding requires the calculation of a syndrome at the receiver in a manner similar to that used for block codes. Recall that in the block code case the received vector, which consists of information digits and check digits all possibly corrupted by noise, is operated on by the parity-check matrix to produce a syndrome vector s. With **x**, **y**, and **e** representing transmitted, received, and error vectors respectively, we found that $s = \mathbf{y}H = (\mathbf{x} + \mathbf{e})\,H = \mathbf{e}H$, since $xH = 0$. Each multiplication of a vector by a column of H produces one parity-check equation; i.e., one equation relating specific information digits and one or more specific check digits by means of a modulo-2 sum. For the received vector, each multiplication by a column of H produces one digit of s. If $\mathbf{e} = \mathbf{O}$ or has an even number of errors in the positions checked by a column of H, then the corresponding component of s is 0. Note that what the syndrome calculation does in effect is to recompute check digits on the basis of the received information digits and add each of these recomputed checks to the corresponding received check. If the corresponding computed and received check digit are the same, the result, a component of s, is 0.

In the case of convolutional codes the syndrome definition is similar, except that the syndrome is a sequence because the information and check digits occur as sequences. This is illustrated in the portions of Figure 7-1 labeled ENCODER and SYNDROME CALCULATION.

For the explanation which follows, we shall assume a rate-1/2 code and modify slightly the notation used in conjunction with Figure 6-1. At the transmitter, let $i_0, i_1, i_2, \ldots$ represent information digits, and let $c_0, c_1, c_2, \ldots$ represent corresponding check digits. Let i'_j and c'_j be the received digits (possibly in error) corresponding to i_j and c_j, respectively. Finally, let e_{Ij} and e_{cj} be the error digits at the j-th position in the information and check sequences, respectively, giving

$$\begin{aligned} i'_j &= i_j + e_{Ij} \\ & \qquad\qquad\qquad j = 0, 1, 2, \ldots \qquad (7\text{-}1) \\ c'_j &= c_j + e_{cj} \end{aligned}$$

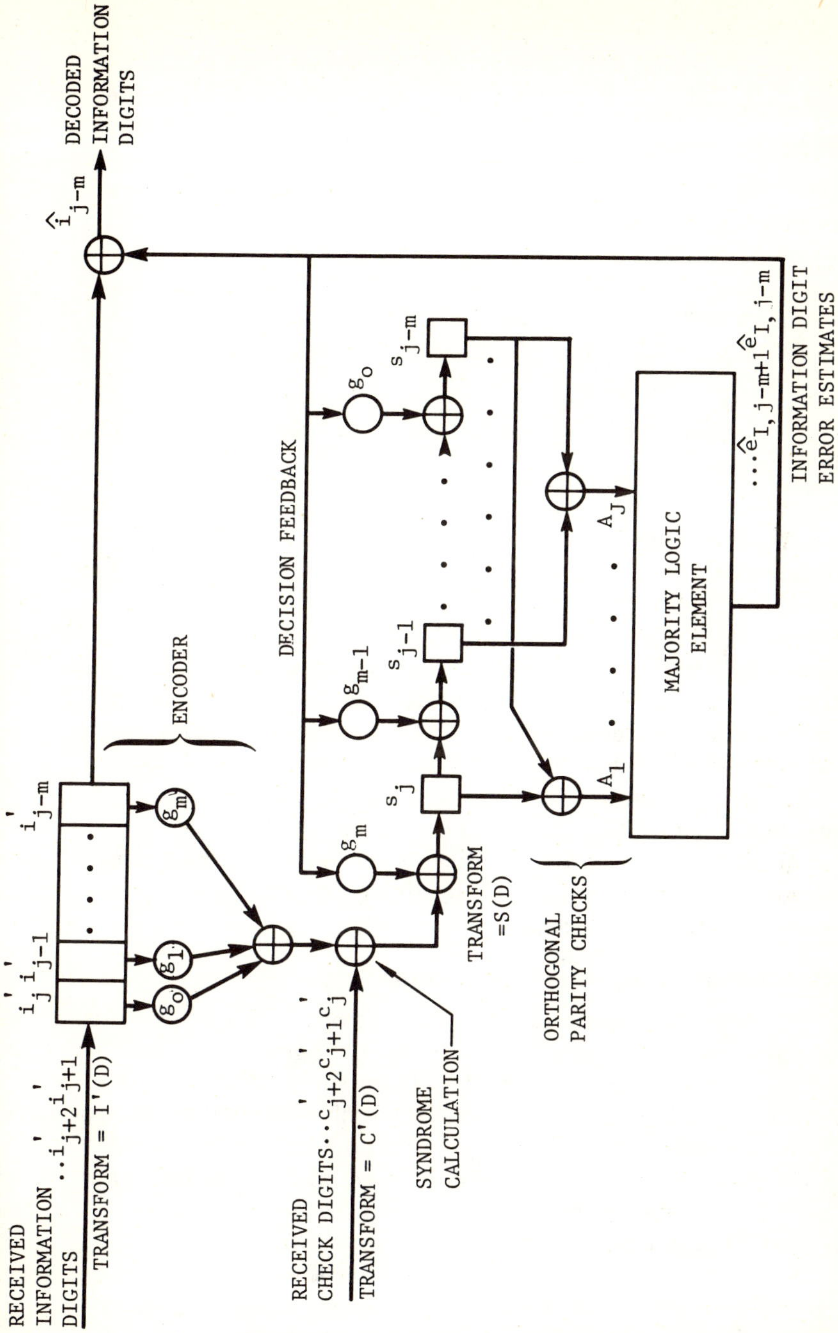

Figure 7-1/Majority-Logic Threshold Decoder for Rate-1/2, Binary Systematic Code

To understand how the system of Figure 7-1 works, let us start with j = 0 and assume that all shift register stages have initially been set to 0. Let a double prime denote a check digit calculated at the decoder.

Then

$$
\begin{aligned}
c''_0 &= g_0\, i'_0 & s_0 &= c''_0 + c'_0 \\
c''_1 &= g_1\, i'_0 + g_0\, i'_1 & s_1 &= c''_1 + c'_1 \\
c''_2 &= g_2\, i'_0 + g_1\, i'_1 + g_0\, i'_2 & s_2 &= c''_2 + c'_2\,.
\end{aligned}
\tag{7-2}
$$

If the encoder SR is three stages long (i.e., m = 2), then subsequent calculations are

$$
\begin{aligned}
c''_3 &= g_2\, i'_1 + g_1\, i_2 + g_0\, i'_3 & s_3 &= c''_3 + c'_3 \\
c''_4 &= g_2\, i'_2 + g_1\, i_3 + g_0\, i'_4 & s_4 &= c''_4 + c'_4
\end{aligned}
\tag{7-3}
$$

In threshold decoding, with the exception of one special case, the syndrome digits are not usually used directly to perform decoding. Rather, certain linear combinations of the syndrome digits are formed and these are used in conjunction with a majority logic element to provide an estimate $\hat{e}_{Ij}$ of the information error digit e_{Ij}. Before discussing the threshold decoding process itself, we must understand the meaning, utility, and construction of these special linear combinations of the syndrome digits. This will be undertaken in the next section.

7.2 Orthogonal Parity Check Equations

The key concept in threshold decoding of convolutional codes is that of parity check equations which are orthogonal on a digit. This concept of orthogonality differs from the well-known one from mathematics and signal theory in which two vectors or two functions are orthogonal to each other if and only if their inner or dot product, appropriately defined, is equal to zero. Rather, orthogonality of parity check equations is defined as follows: Given a set of equations which relate various information and check digits through checksums, we say that these equations are *orthogonal on digit* d_j if d_j is checked by every equation and if no other digit is checked by more than one equation. Note that in order to achieve orthogonality it may be necessary to combine two or more of the original syndrome digit equations. An additional goal while constructing orthogonal sets of equations is to maximize the total number of digits checked.

Example 7-1. Denote information digits by i, check digits by c, and syndrome digits by s. Then the set of equations

$$
\begin{aligned}
s_1 &= i_1 + i_2 + c_1 + c_3 \\
s_2 &= i_1 + i_3 + c_2 + c_5 \\
s_3 &= i_1 + c_4
\end{aligned}
\qquad (7\text{-}4)
$$

is orthogonal on i_1.

If the three equations in Example 7-1 are the complete set of orthogonal equations for a code, then we call such a code *self-orthogonal* because orthogonality has been achieved in terms of single syndrome digits without the need for combining them.

Before proceeding any further, let us generalize our notation somewhat in order to gain both compactness and additional insight. Consequently, let

$$
\begin{aligned}
I(D) &= i_0 + i_1 D + i_2 D^2 + \ldots \\
I'(D) &= i_0' + i_1' D + i_2' D^2 + \ldots \\
E_I(D) &= e_{I_0} + e_{I_1} D + e_{I_2} D^2 \ldots
\end{aligned}
\qquad (7\text{-}5)
$$

be the transforms of the transmitted information sequence, received information sequence, and received information error sequence, respectively, so that

$$I'(D) = I(D) + E_I(D)$$

Similarily, let $C(D)$, $C'(D)$, and $E_c(D)$ be the transforms of the transmitted and received check sequences and the received check error sequence, respectively, so that

$$C'(D) = C(D) + E_c(D) \qquad (7\text{-}7)$$

Now, since information and check sequences are related by

$$C(D) = G(D)I(D), \tag{7-8}$$

the syndrome calculation at the decoder gives us (referring to Figure 7-1 and using Equations (7-6) and (7-7)):

$$\begin{aligned} S(D) &= G(D)\, I'(D) + C'(D) \\ &= G(D)\, [I(D) + E_I(D)] + C(D) + E_c(D) \\ &= G(D)\, E_I(D) + E_c(D) \end{aligned}$$

We note here that, since syndrome digits are actually linear combinations of digits of the error sequences, the notion of orthogonality applies to the error digits in exactly the same way as it does to the information and check digits.

Example 7-2. This is a systematic code from Massey's [35] set of "trial-and-error" codes. It has $R = 1/2$ and $n_A = 12$*, with 4 orthogonal check equations. The generator polynomial for the check digits is $G(D) = 1 + D^3 + D^4 + D^5$. The complete decoder is shown in Figure 7-2. Let us look only at the encoder and syndrome positions for the moment. Figure 7-2 shows the calculation of s_5.

The syndrome digits are given (with all addition modulo 2) by

$$\begin{aligned} s_0 &= e_{I0} + e_{c0} \\ s_1 &= e_{I1} + e_{c1} \\ s_2 &= e_{I2} + e_{c2} \\ s_3 &= e_{I0} + e_{I3} + e_{c3} \\ s_4 &= e_{I0} + e_{I1} + e_{I4} + e_{c4} \\ s_5 &= e_{I0} + e_{I1} + e_{I2} + e_{I5} + e_{c5} \end{aligned} \tag{7-9}$$

*Note that Massey [35] used $n_A = (m+1)\, n_0$ where we use Kn_0.

These six equations are obviously not orthogonal on e_{I0}. To achieve orthogonality on e_{I0} we must examine various sums of equations as Massey did, with the additional goal of maximizing the number of orthogonal equations. Clearly s_1, s_2, and $s_1 + s_2$ are of no help since they do not involve e_{I0}, while s_0 and s_3 are acceptable as they are. This leaves s_4 and s_5 for consideration. To use them both, we need to eliminate e_{I1} from one of them without involving e_{I2} more than once. We would also like to avoid eliminating e_{I2} entirely. There are several ways of accomplishing this as trial and error will show, but the solution chosen by Massey is the simplest: use s_4 and $s_1 + s_5$. The resulting set of equations is orthogonal on e_{I0} and checks all digits except e_{c2} of the maximum of 12 possible. We shall denote each member of a set of orthogonal parity checks by A_j. Then we have in this case

$$A_1 = s_0 \qquad A_3 = s_4$$
$$A_2 = s_3 \qquad A_4 = s_1 + s_5 \tag{7-10}$$

7.3 The Threshold Decoding Algorithm

Remember that each received digit is actually given in equation (7-1) as

$$i'_j = i_j + e_{Ij}$$
$$c'_j = c_j + e_{cj} \tag{7-1}$$

and that each expression for an s_j holds with e_{ij} replacing i'_j and e_{cj} replacing c'_j. Our aim then is to estimate correctly the single noise digit e_{I0}. Call this estimate $\hat{e}_{I0}$, and let $\hat{i}_0$ be the estimate of i_0. Then $\hat{i}_0 = i'_0 + \hat{e}_{I0} = (i_0 + e_{I0}) + \hat{e}_{I0}$. Thus, as expected, i_0 is correctly decoded (i.e., $\hat{i}_0 = i_0$) if e_{I0} is correctly estimated. Following Massey [35], we let J represent the total number of parity check equations orthogonal on i_0. Then the majority decoding rule is: Set $\hat{e}_{I0} = 0$ if one-half or more of the orthogonal check equations are equal to zero; otherwise set $\hat{e}_{I0} = 1$. This rule results in correct decoding as long as the error-correcting capability of the code has not been exceeded. It was shown in Reference 35 that for majority decoding, $\lfloor J/2 \rfloor$ or fewer errors among the digits actually checked by the orthogonal equations always permit correct decoding of i_0.

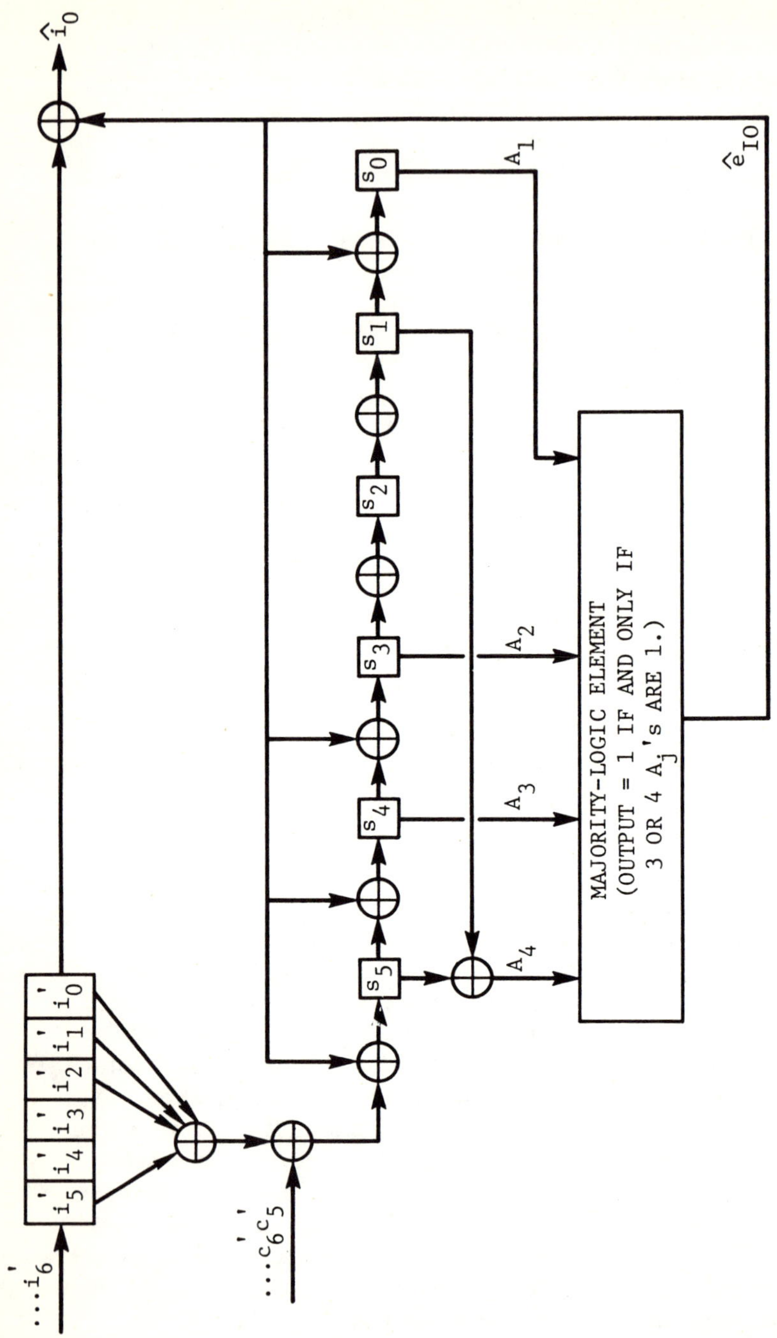

Figure 7-2/Decoder for Example 7-2

How does this capability relate to d_{min} for a code? It turns out that if $d_{min}-1$ check equations orthogonal on e_{I0} (or i_0) can be formed, then i_0 will be correctly decoded for any error pattern of weight $\lfloor (d_{min}-1)/2 \rfloor$ or less. Nearly all of the trial-and-error codes found by Massey [35] meet this condition.

The majority-logic threshold decoder for the BSC has the block diagram shown in Figure 7-1. Note the portion marked DECISION FEEDBACK. This concept, which has not been mentioned up until this point, involves picking off the estimates $\hat{e}_{Ij}$ of the information digit errors and feeding them back through a parity network based on the parity network used in the encoder, and then adding the output digits of this feedback parity network into corresponding stages of the syndrome register. This feedback is carried out for the purpose of removing from the digits in the syndrome register the effects of the error in the information digit just decoded. If the error estimate is correct, then the effect of the feedback is to provide a syndrome which "acts" as if there were no prior errors in the information sequence, identical to the initial conditions when i_0 was being decoded. If, however, the error estimate is wrong, then obviously not only is a decoding error committed but incorrect information is fed back to the syndrome. This incorrect feedback usually has the effect of causing decoding errors where none may have been committed in its absence. This so-called *error-propagation* effect is probably the most serious flaw in algorithms using convolutional codes. We shall defer any further discussion of error propagation until the next section, now stating only that there are ways of avoiding it or minimizing its effects.

To understand how decision feedback works (or doesn't work, in the case of an incorrect decision), let us consider once again the rate-1/2 code of Example 7-2. We repeat the essential code parameters here.

$$G(D) = 1 + D^3 + D^4 + D^5$$

$$A_1 = s_0,\ A_2 = s_3,\ A_3 = s_4,\ A_4 = s_1 + s_5$$

Thus, we have

$$
\begin{aligned}
A_1 &= e_{I0} + e_{c0} \\
A_2 &= e_{I0} + e_{I3} + e_{c3} \\
A_3 &= e_{I0} + e_{I1} + e_{I4} + e_{c4} \\
A_4 &= e_{I0} + e_{I2} + e_{I5} + e_{c1} + e_{c5}
\end{aligned}
\qquad (7\text{-}11)
$$

Consider first the expression

$$s_0 = e_{I0} + e_{c0}$$

If $e_{I0} = 0$, there is nothing for which to compensate. If, however, $e_{I0} = 1$, then its effect should be removed from the syndrome digits. This can be done more easily if the (correct) estimate $\hat{e}_{I0} = 1$ is added to s_0 to give $\tilde{s}_0 = s_0 + \hat{e}_{I0}$. Here we use the tilde ($\sim$) to indicate syndrome digits modified by decision feedback. More generally, whether $e_{I0} = 0$ or 1, addition to s_0 of the *correct* estimate $\hat{e}_{I0} = e_{I0}$, yields

$$\tilde{s}_0 = e_{I0} + \hat{e}_{I0} + e_{c0} = e_{c0} \qquad (7\text{-}12a)$$

Similarly, this same correct feedback also yields

$$
\begin{aligned}
\tilde{s}_3 &= e_{I3} + e_{c3} \\
\tilde{s}_4 &= e_{I1} + e_{I4} + e_{c4} \\
\tilde{s}_5 &= e_{I1} + e_{I2} + e_{I5} + e_{c5}
\end{aligned}
\qquad (7\text{-}12b)
$$

showing that the effects of e_{I0} have been completely removed. The next step in the decoding is to estimate e_{I1}. Before this is done, the encoder and syndrome SR contents are both shifted one stage to the right, "bumping" i'_0 and $\tilde{s}_0$. The new contents of the syndrome SR (with Stage 1 at the right) are:

$$
\begin{array}{llllllllllllll}
\text{Stage 1:} & e_{I1} & & & & & & + e_{c1} & & & & & & \\
\text{Stage 2:} & & e_{I2} & & & & & & + e_{c2} & & & & & \\
\text{Stage 3:} & & & e_{I3} & & & & & & + e_{c3} & & & & \\
\text{Stage 4:} & e_{I1} & & & + e_{I4} & & & & & & + e_{c4} & & & \\
\text{Stage 5:} & e_{I1} & + e_{I2} & & & e_{I5} & & & & & & + e_{c5} & & \\
\text{Stage 6:} & e_{I1} & + e_{I2} & + e_{I3} & & & + e_{I6} & & & & & & + e_{c6} &
\end{array}
\qquad (7\text{-}13)
$$

This is identical to Equations (7-9) except that all subscripts have been increased by 1. Note that Stage 6 concurrently has received the newest syndrome digit. Thus, we are ready to determine e_{I1} in exactly the same way e_{I0} was determined.

What happens if $e_{I0} \neq e_{I0}$? Look at the expressions for s_0, s_3, s_4, and s_5. In each case, the effect is to add 1 (modulo 2) to the correct expression, causing (in this case) these four digits to be in error as long as they remain in the syndrome register, unless changed by another error. In general, the effect of this incorrect feedback is to cause subsequent decoding decisions to be based on incorrect information in the syndrome register. This can be avoided, however.

The most obvious way is to break the feedback connection in Figure 7-2. This has the disadvantage of failing to feed back correct information, which shows up as increased probability of decoding error. There is, however, never any error propagation. This type of decoding has been termed *direct decoding* by Robinson [37] who has analyzed it.

A second way is to design the code to prevent all but a minimal (2 to 3 constraint lengths) propagation of decoding errors. The worst situation of this sort is catastrophic error propagation, in which the decoder continues to make errors even when its syndrome inputs are all 0's, signaling no transmission errors. This problem and its solution are discussed in Section 7.4.

A third way, suggested by Massey [35], is to count errors. When the decoder appears to be correcting errors beyond its design capability by producing a great many 1's as error estimates, it must actually be propagating one or more decoding errors.

The receiver can then signal the transmitter to restart at some time in the past, or it can clear itself out and start anew without any retransmission.

7.4 Error Propagation

As shown in Section 7.3, the use of decision feedback to remove the effects of received errors in information digits can lead to a serious problem if the decoding decision is incorrect, since the wrong information is being fed back. At the very least, this incorrect information results in error propagation; that is, making additional errors which would not have been made with correct feedback or with no feedback at all. In spite of this error propagation, subsequent receipt of error-free channel digits usually causes the syndrome register to return to the all-zero state because all syndrome inputs are zero. Sometimes, however, incorrect decision feedback causes a majority of ones to occur repeatedly in the syndrome even with zeros as input. In this case the decoder continues to decide that there are errors in the received information digits. This is catastrophic propagation of decoding errors in which bits can be decoded in error indefinitely.

It has been shown by Massey and Sain [38] that certain properties of code generators result inevitably in catastrophic error propagation, while other properties assure the lack of error propagation. The test is a simple one: Catastrophic error propagation is possible if and only if the code generators, written in the usual delay-operator notation, contain a common factor of degree one or greater. An important class of codes which do not suffer from catastrophic error propagation is the set of all systematic codes, since one of the generators is simply 1.

Example 7-3. The code with generators $1 + D$ and $1 + D^2$ permits catastrophic error propagation, since $1 + D^2 = (1 + D)^2$ (modulo 2). On the other hand, the code with generators $1 + D$ and $1 + D + D^2$ does not allow catastrophic propagation.

7.5 Performance Assessment

Threshold decoders are simple to build, operate at a constant output rate, and are inexpensive in off-the-shelf models. Aside from error propagation, which has been shown in the preceding section to be a solvable problem, the chief disadvantage of the threshold decoding technique for convolutional codes is that bit error probability is asymptotic to a value greater than zero as constraint length increases, though this is a flaw not shared by Viterbi and sequential decoding. Nonetheless, the performance of threshold decoding is still considered quite adequate for many situations. Although Viterbi and sequential decoding of convolutional codes offer superior performance at greater cost, compared to threshold decoding, the latter is still considered preferable for some situations such as bursts of errors. (See Chapter 10.)

Chapter 8

The Viterbi Decoding Algorithm

8.1 Introduction

The Viterbi [39] decoding algorithm is a powerful, fast, and easily implemented technique for decoding convolutional codes. Furthermore, its analysis and simulation are rather easily carried out. We shall see that the amount of decoding computation needed is independent of the noise in the received sequence of channel symbols.

We shall continue to use the R=1/3, K=3 systematic convolutional code and encoder introduced in Chapter 6. That encoder is reproduced for convenience in Figure 8-1 on the next page. It will also be very useful to have at hand the corresponding trellis. This is shown again in Figure 8-2. In both figures, the oldest symbols are at the left, as they were in Chapter 6. The reason for showing the trellis once more is that the Viterbi algorithm is based on finding the most likely path, in a sense to be defined shortly, through the trellis. Remember that the trellis exploits the fact that there is no dependence between encoded symbols which lie more than one constraint length from each other.

For instance, if 1101 . . . is a bit sequence entering the encoder of Figure 8-1, then the first three bits of the input sequence produce the following encoder output: 111 100 010. (See Figure 8-2). Now shift in the fourth bit, placing 101 in the encoder. The first encoder output (100) with this latest bit in the encoder is independent of whether the very first input bit was a 0 or a 1. Stated another way, the last node reached in the trellis (arrow, Figure 8-2) could have been reached by any of the following input sequences: 1101, 1001, 0101 and 0001.

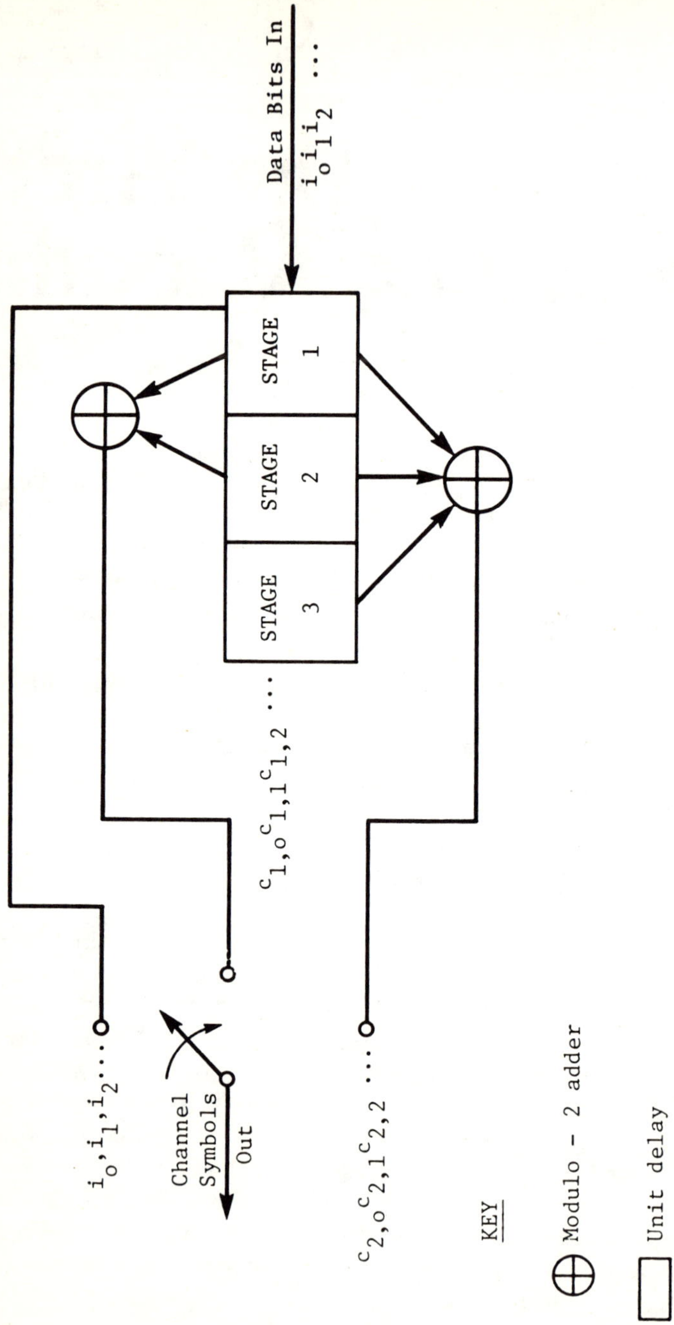

Figure 8-1/Convolutional Encoder.

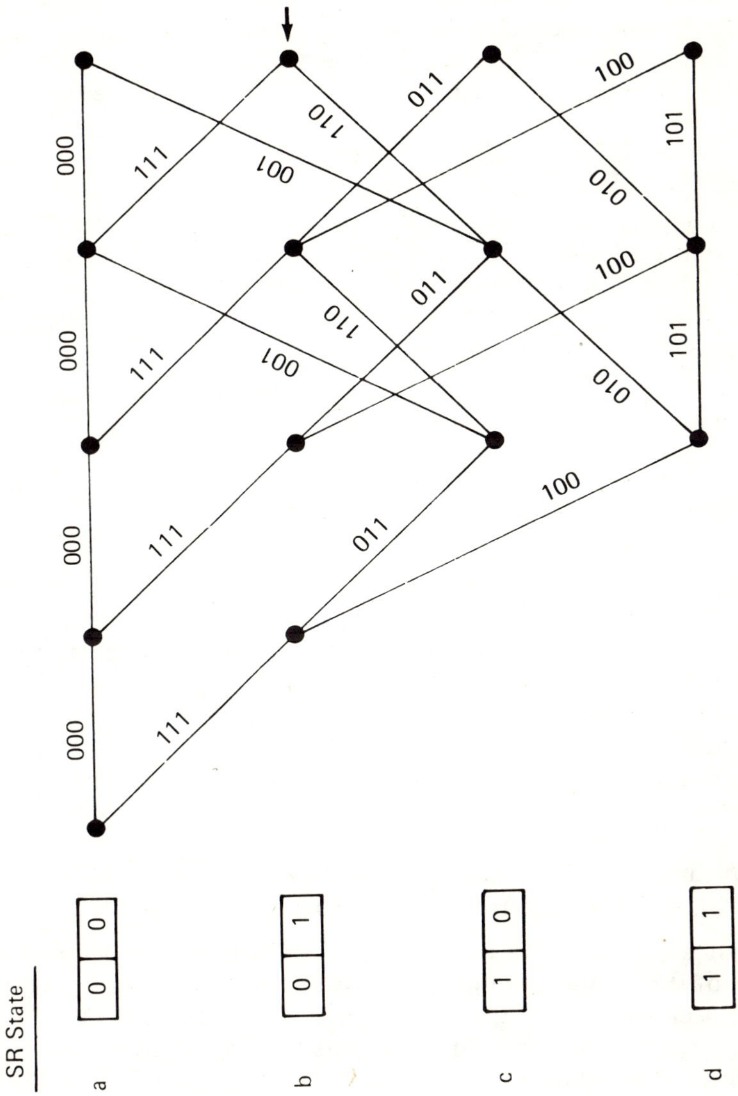

Figure 8-2/Trellis for Encoder of Figure 8-1.

As with block codes, we are interested in finding that transmitted sequence which is the best match in some sense to the received sequence. Initially, we shall work only with a binary-output channel. Later in the chapter, however, we shall present simulation results for soft-decision channels; in this case, the channels have a binary input but more than two quantized outputs, with each quantization level having a measure of confidence associated with it.

8.2 Decoder Operation

Viterbi decoding, in common with other techniques, involves choosing that trial information sequence whose encoded version is in some sense closest to the received sequence. For the time being, we shall use Hamming distance as our measure of closeness or similarity of two binary sequences.

Now let us suppose that the all-0's sequence was transmitted and that the following sequence was received (oldest symbol at the left):

010 000 100 001

Let us try to decode, that is, correctly estimate the transmitted sequence using the trellis of Figure 8-2 and Hamming distance, keeping in mind that we are using a systematic code. The trellis has been redrawn in Figure 8-3, this time to display the distance between corresponding branches of the trial and received sequences, with the latter shown below the trellis. A circled number at a node is the cumulative distance between the received sequence and one of the paths from the base of the trellis out to that node. When there are two numbers, the first number corresponds to the upper path into that node. For example, the first branch received, 010, is distance 1 from 000 and distance 2 from 111.

The distances between the second branch of the received sequence and each of the corresponding four possible trial sequence branches are easily seen to be 0, 3, 2, and 1 for the branches 000, 111, 011, and 100, respectively. Thus, the four possible transmitted sequences of length six channel digits are at distances 1, 4, 4, and 3 from the first six received digits.

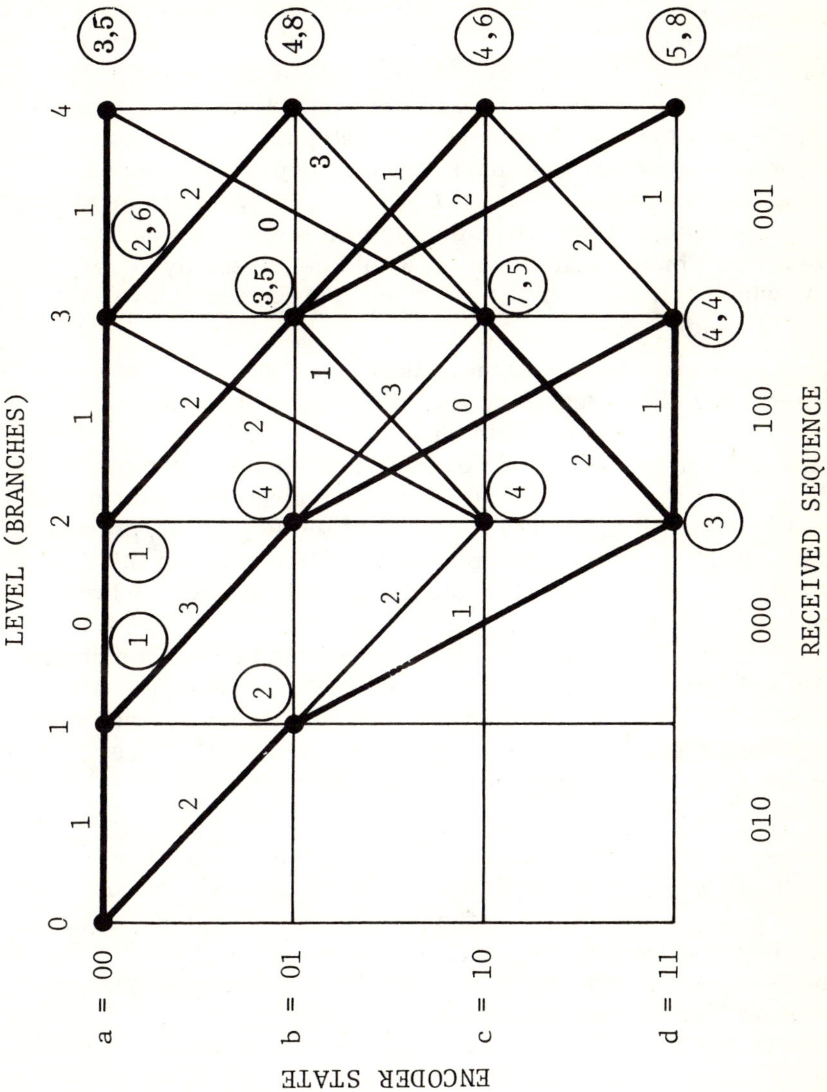

Figure 8-3/Code Trellis Showing Branch and Path Hamming Distances

Thus far, there has been only one possible way to reach each node on the path. We have tested all possible transmitted sequences having 2 (in general, K-1) branches. At the next (3rd or K-th) level node, we see for the first time a node being reached by more than one path. In general, this results in there being two distinct distances to that node, one for each of the two unique paths leading to it from the base of the trellis. Here, for the first time, we must make a decision as to which path to choose to retain for subsequent extensions. If this choice were not made at the K-th or later levels, the number of paths would grow exponentially, with proportional growth in both computation and storage requirements. This growth, however, would be limited by *decoding delay*, which is the length of the sequence processed before a decoding decision is made.

With the above discussion as motivation, we come to the key step in Viterbi decoding. Beginning with the K-th branch and continuing for as long as there are data on which to operate, the decoder retains for each node only one of the two branches leaving that node. The branch retained in the one which gives the better overall path distance with respect to the received sequence. This process of discarding one of the two branches at each level from the K-th onward holds constant at 2^{K-1} the number of paths which are extended to the next level. Furthermore, Viterbi [37] has shown that this process is optimum in the sense of producing a maximum likelihood decision as to the correct path. For our example, a look at Figure 8-3 shows that the paths indicated with heavy lines will be retained in going from level 3 to level 4. Viterbi [25] has, appropriately enough, called these paths *survivors.*

The situation at node (d,3) shows two survivors at this point, corresponding to the two distance–4 paths, 000 111 100 and 111 100 101. Which one should we keep? It turns out that it doesn't matter! In either case, the path distances from node (d,3) to the next level will be the same. Therefore, we could either flip a coin or we could arbitrarily, though regularly, choose a particular branch (say the upper) into such a node.

Let us examine what the decoder has accomplished so far. At level 3 there are four survivor sequences with distances as shown below:

Sequence	Distance from received sequence
000 000 000	2
000 000 111	3
111 100 010	5
000 111 100	4

It is interesting to note that the sequence having the best distance turns out (in this case) to be the one actually transmitted. Furthermore, the three best distances belong to the three paths which begin with the correct transmitted initial branch.

Now let us continue the decoding process. The terminal branch of each survivor at level 4 is shown in Figure 8-3 as a heavy line. Note that survivors at states c and d at level 3 did not survive to level 4. Rather, each of the level-3 survivors at nodes a and b produced two survivors to level 4. At this stage, the details are

Survivor	Distance
000 000 000 000	3
000 000 000 111	4
000 000 111 011	4
000 000 111 100	5

Note that now all four survivors happen to be correct not only in the first but also the second transmitted branch. In fact, the survivors at nodes a and b are the correct path over the first constraint length.

The brief tables in the two preceding paragraphs show that there are two kinds of quantities that must be "remembered" by the decoder: the surviving path and its distance from the received sequence for each node at each level in the trellis.

The next question is: how do we terminate the decoding process and make decisions (i.e., best estimates) as to the transmitted data bits? One way is to produce a decision at each level of the trellis, starting with the K-th level. In this case, the obvious output is the oldest bit in the trellis path having the smallest distance from the received sequence. Once the decision has been made, the decoder can delete from its memory the 2^{K-1} branches at the position of the decoded bit in the trellis. Note that while we have used a systematic code here, the case of a non-systematic code poses no additional burden for the decoder since it has labeled each branch from a node according to whether it was generated by a 0 or a 1 data bit. Another way of making decoding decisions is to withhold any decision until the entire received sequence has been processed. To do this, of course, depends on the availability of sufficient storage. The encoder at the transmitter is then cleared by inserting K-1 successive 0's, which forces the decoder to the node on the all-0's path as this tail sequence is processed. This operation assumes that the decoder knows the total number of bits to be transmitted, which is often the case in any situation of practical interest. The trellis for our example would appear as in Figure 8-4 if this were done. Notice that the effect of each successive 0 is to halve the number of paths to be considered.

8.3 Decoder Parameters

The discussion of the preceding section should have made it clear that the decoder progresses at a fixed rate through the trellis. For real-time operations, a speed advantage of about 2K relative to the channel data rate is necessary since the decoder must process 2K branches at each stage, discarding half of them. Depending on the decoding delay, there must be storage for some multiple of $K \times 2^{K-1}$ pairs of branch and distance values (K branches per constraint length, 2^{K-1} trial paths retained).

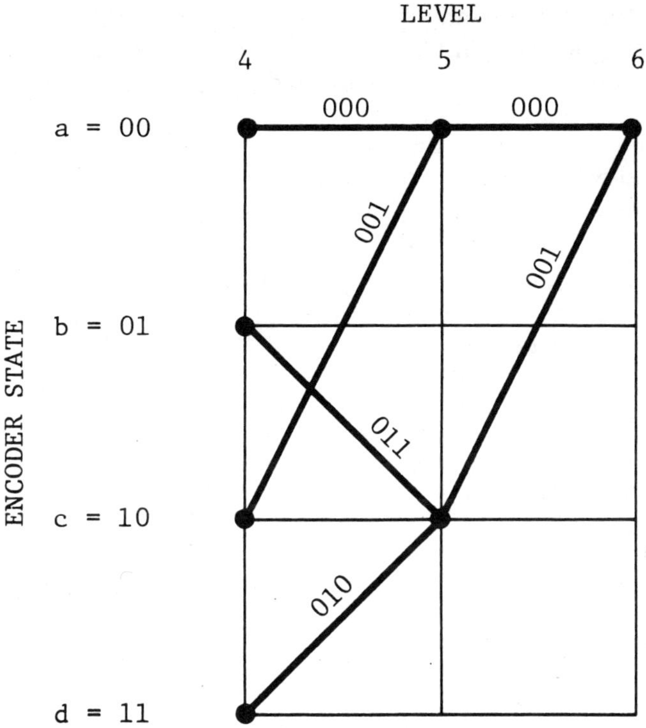

Figure 8-4/Truncation of Trellis Forced by All-0's Input

8.4 Simulation and Implementation Results

Viterbi decoding has been extensively simulated by a number of organizations and individuals, both as a research effort and in conjunctions which offer Viterbi decoder hardware for sale.

The results which follow were obtained by one organization engaged in the building of error-control hardware. A rate-1/2, non-systematic, binary convolutional code used on a Gaussian channel was simulated using both hard (1-bit quantization) and soft (3–, 4–, and 5–bit quantization) decisions on channel digits. Constraint lengths K of 5, 6, and 7 were used, along with decoding delays of

3, 4, 5, and in a few instances, as many as 10, constraint lengths. Results were presented in terms of data bit error probability (P_B) as a function of the ratio of data bit energy to noise power density (E_B/N_o). Comparisons are made at $P_B = 10^{-5}$, which is frequently used as a baseline P_B. The results are presented in Tables 8-1, 8-2, and 8-3. Comparison of Tables 8-1 and 8-2 shows that:

a. Some improvement in E_B/N_o is achieved by increasing constraint length with both hard and soft decisions.

b. Improvement with increasing decoding delay is moderate in going from 3 to 4 constraint lengths, with only marginal improvement beyond 4.

Table 8-1†. E_B/N_o (dB) for Hard-Decision Viterbi Decoding ($P_B = 10^{-5}$)

Decoding Delay, L (Constraint Lengths)	Code Constraint Length		
	5	6	7
3	7.4	7.2	6.7
4	7.25	6.8	6.5
5	7.2*	6.7*	6.4
10	—	—	6.3

* L ⩾ 5

Table 8-2†. E_B/N_o (dB) for Soft-Decision (3 bits) Viterbi Decoding ($P_B = 10^{-5}$)

Decoding Delay, L (Constraint Lengths)	Code Constraint Length		
	5	6	7
3	5.7	5.2	5.1
4	5.3	5.0	4.7
5	5.2*	4.9*	4.5
27	—	—	4.4

* L ⩾ 5

†Data in Tables 8-1 through 8-3 published with permission from the Magnavox Company, Advanced Products Operation, Philadelphia, Pa.

Table 8-3[†]. Coding Gain vs Bits of Quantization (Constraint Length = 6, $P_B = 10^{-5}$)

Number of Bits of Quantization	E_B/N_o (dB)	Coding Gain (dB)
3	4.9	4.7
4	4.8	4.8
5	4.7	4.9

c. Significant improvement takes place with 3-bit quantization compared with hard decisions at any constraint length and decoding delay.

Finally, Table 8-3 shows that there is only marginal improvement in E_B/N_o with quantization beyond 3 bits. It is useful, also, to observe the coding gain, which is the improvement in E_B/N_o with coding compared with ideal (coherent) PSK and no coding at $P_B = 10^{-5}$. We can infer that the latter requires $E_B/N_o = 9.6$ dB to give $P_B = 10^{-5}$. Knowing this, we could, if we desired, compute the coding gain associated with each of the data points in Tables 8-1 and 8-2.

8.5 Assessment and Conclusions

We have seen in Section 8.3 that the decoder must keep track of 2^{K-1} paths through the trellis in order to identify each path on a branch-by-branch basis and to keep a complete record of all path metrics. Thus, storage and computation speed requirements both grow exponentially with constraint length. For these reasons, the applicability of the Viterbi algorithm is restricted to relatively small values of constraint length (usually $K \leqslant 7$). On the other hand, the exponential decrease in bit error probability as a function of constraint length and the constant required decoder speed (independent of channel noise) make it the preferred choice within this range of constraint lengths among convolutional code techniques for use on memoryless channels. We point out that Viterbi decoding does not perform well against bursts of errors, producing output error bursts, due to error propagation, of several times the input burst length.

Chapter 9

Sequential Decoding

9.1 Introduction

In this chapter we will discuss sequential decoding, a very powerful decoding technique for convolutional codes. Sequential decoding exhibits exponential decrease in probability of bit error P_B as a function of code constraint length n_A and is easy to implement for high-speed (megabits/sec) operation with a manageable amount of hardware and/or software using present technology. Both memory and computation effort grow at rates which are less than exponential.

Sequential decoding for the BSC was invented and first studied by J.M. Wozencraft [40]. Major refinements and extensions have been made by Reiffen [41], Fano [24], and Jelinek [42] and Zigongirov [43]. Reiffen extended Wozencraft's theoretical results to the discrete memoryless channel (DMC) and improved upon the efficiency of the decoding algorithm. Fano generalized Wozencraft's and Reiffen's encoding scheme and refined and formalized the tree-searching technique used in decoding. Finally, Jelinek and Zigangirov, working independently of each other, developed what they have called a "stack algorithm," in which increased memory requirements are accepted in return for increased speed (relative to the Fano algorithm).

We shall discuss these three sequential decoding techniques in the order in which they evolved, beginning with a brief discussion of the Wozencraft-Reiffen (W-R) decoding technique. Conceptually, all three techniques are simple, although the details may be somewhat involved. All of the techniques entail searching for a path through a message tree. This path, even though seldom correct over its entire length, has very high probability of being correct at the end corresponding to the information digits about to be decoded. The Fano and Jelinek-Zigangirov algorithms will be discussed as improvements on the W-R technique.

Sequential decoding differs fundamentally from decoding schemes developed for block codes and from other algorithms developed for convolutional codes. The basic task in sequential decoding involves searching the code tree to determine a trial information sequence whose encoded version most closely matches in some sense the corrupted received sequence. Just as in the case of Viterbi decoding (Chapter 8), the notion of closely matching sequences involves the concept of a *decoding metric.* The simplest of these (and the one used by Wozencraft [40]) is Hamming distance, which has already been used extensively in this book for block and convolutional codes. Other functions of the trial and received sequences which could be used as decoding metrics include the mutual information of a particular trial sequence and the received sequence* and the sum of the squares of the differences between matched filter outputs for pairs of corresponding trial and received digits for a channel with a binary input space and a finely quantized output space**. We shall use the term "distance" to refer to the value which the decoding metric takes on for a particular pair of received and trial sequences.

9.2 A Fundamental Limit on Sequential Decoding

Before beginning our discussion of sequential decoding techniques, we must become aware of a fundamental limitation of sequential decoding in general. This limitation has a serious impact on the decoder speed required (especially in real time) to handle particularly noisy received sequences. As we shall see, such a received sequence usually results in a search of the message tree before the sequence is accepted by the decoder. While this search is taking place, received digits continue to enter the decoder. (In a non-real-time situation, valuable computer time is consumed.) It has been possible to characterize this limitation quantitatively in terms of a parameter R_{comp}, the computational cutoff rate. It turns out that as the channel rate R approaches R_{comp} from below, the computational load increases tremendously. In fact, in theory at least, the average decoding computational effort becomes infinite when

*See, for example, Reiffen [41] and Fano [24].

**As in the simulation reported by Reiffen and Wiggert [44].

$R = R_{comp}$. While this does not happen in practice (since the theoretical result is only a bound), the dramatic increase in computation, even as R exceeds about 0.9 R_{comp}, has certainly been observed.

The parameter R_{comp} is determined in part by the channel noise. For the DMC with I input symbols, J output symbols and symbol input probabilities p_i, R_{comp} is given by

$$R_{comp} = \max_{\{p_i\}} \left\{ -\log \sum_{j=1}^{J} \left[\sum_{i=1}^{I} p_i \sqrt{p\,(j|i)} \right]^2 \right. \tag{9-1}$$

where the p (j | i) are channel transition probabilities and the maximization takes place over all possible sets of input probabilities. For the BSC, equation (9-1) reduces to

$$R_{comp} = 1 - \log \left[1 + 2\sqrt{p\,(1-p)} \right] \tag{9-2}$$

while for the binary-input, continuous-output channel of Section 2.2, we get

$$R_{comp} = \log \left[2/(1 + \exp(-E_r/N_o)) \right] \tag{9-3}$$

where E_r is the energy per channel digit, given by $E_r = E_B R$ for energy per data bit E_B and rate R. If logarithms to the base 2 are used, equation (9-3) becomes

$$R_{comp} = 1 - \log_2 (1 + \exp(-E_r/N_o)) \quad \text{bits/symbol} \tag{9-4}$$

Thus, we see that R_{comp} depends on the average properties of the channel (through N_o) and on the transmitted energy. Note that the received energy E_r actually depends also on properties of the transmission medium in ways ($1/r^2$ attenuation, absorption, and/or dispersion, for example) that are beyond the scope of this book.

The quantitative discussion of the dependence of decoding computation effort on the ratio R/R_{comp} will be deferred until after our detailed discussion of sequential decoding algorithms.

Sequence Length (branches) \ Family	1	2 . . .	J
m + 1	$T_{m+1}^{(1)}$	$T_{m+1}^{(2)}$	$T_{M+1}^{(J)}$
.	.	.	.
.	.	.	.
.	.	.	.
3	$T_3^{(1)}$	$T_3^{(2)}$	$T_3^{(J)}$
2	$T_2^{(1)}$	$T_2^{(2)}$	$T_2^{(J)}$
1	$T_1^{(1)}$	$T_1^{(2)}$	$T_1^{(J)}$
Note: In general, $T_i^{(j)} < T_{i+1}^{(j)}$, $T_i^{(j)} < T_i^{(j+1)}$.			

Figure 9-1/Relationships Among Thresholds for Sequential Decoding

9.3 Wozencraft-Reiffen Sequential Decoding

Because it is the simplest in concept, the Wozencraft-Reiffen (W-R) algorithm will be discussed first. An understanding of W-R makes it easier to follow the more general but more efficient Fano algorithm and the "stack" algorithm.

As in encoding, a proposed transmitted (or trial) sequence is generated k_o information digits or n_o channel digits at a time, starting at the base of the message tree. As each new set of n_o digits is added to the existing sequence, the total distance between trial and received sequences is computed. This distance is compared with a threshold which is, in general, a function of the length of the trial sequence and of the number of times the decoder has returned to the base of the tree during its search. This threshold is, in fact, just one value in a family of thresholds for the present level of strictness in rejecting trial sequences. There are K values in each family — one for each possible length, in branches, of the trial sequence — and there are several families. These thresholds can be visualized as shown in Figure 9-1.

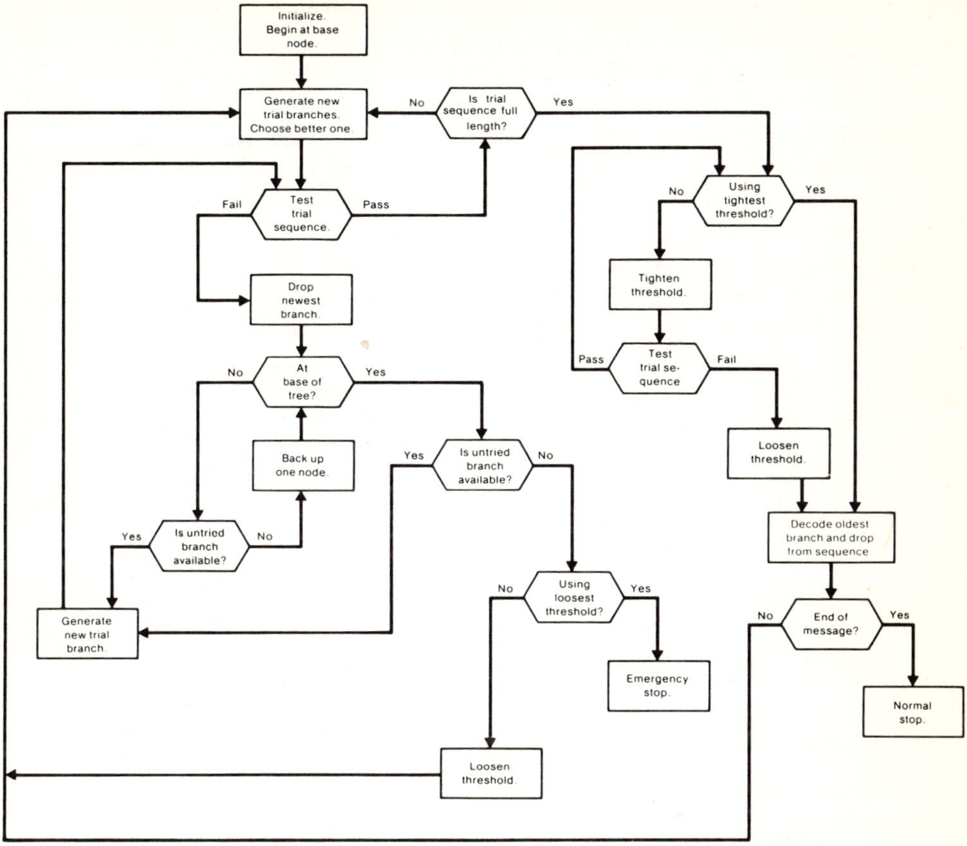

Figure 9-2/Flow Diagram of Wozencraft-Reiffen Sequential Decoding Algorithm

The W-R sequential decoding algorithm will now be described in detail with reference to Figure 9-2. Note first the "transient" or search loop and the "steady state" loop. The search loop is entered under either of two conditions: (1) at the initiation of decoding and (2) any time the decoder fails to decode a new information digit on the first try. When the decoder is successful in decoding on the first attempt, operation continues in the "steady state" loop. We define the decoding of a digit to mean the acceptance by the decoder of a full-length trial sequence which begins with that digit.

The decoder begins operation by generating all q^{k_o} branches emanating from the base of the tree and choosing the best of these in terms of its distance from the first received branch. In our description and in most applications up to now, $q = 2$ and $k_o = 1$, giving two branches leaving each node. From now on, our discussion will assume the case $q = 2$, $k_o = 1$. At the next level node, both branches are generated and tested using the next threshold from the same family. The branch giving the better value of the distance function is chosen. As long as the trial sequence satisfies the threshold at that length, the decoder continues to add branches until the sequences are being compared over a full constraint length. At this point, each time the threshold is satisfied, k_o information digits are decoded, and the decoder drops the oldest (decoded) branch and attempts to add a new branch. Wozencraft [40] and Reiffen [41] call this operation "extending". In one variant of the algorithm, an attempt is made to tighten the threshold each time a digit is decoded.

Any time the trial sequence fails to satisfy the threshold, the decoder enters the transient state. It goes back to the node prior to the one from which it was working and checks to determine whether the other branch there has already been used at the current threshold. If it has not, the branch is chosen and the new trial sequence is checked against the threshold. If this sequence satisfies the threshold, the decoder again moves out in the tree. If this sequence fails, the decoder backs up another node and repeats the test for trial of the other branch there, etc. If the decoder backs to a node for which the other branch has already been used and subsequently rejected at the current threshold strictness, it must go back still another node. If the decoder is finally forced all the way back to the base of the tree, it then loosens the threshold (i.e., designates the next family of thresholds) and begins working its way out as if it were just starting up.

9.4 The Fano Sequential Decoding Algorithm

The Fano [24] algorithm differs from that of Wozencraft and Reiffen in several aspects:

(1) The manner in which the path likelihood is defined.
(2) The manner in which the threshold is handled, both in setting it as the decoder search procedure works its way

steadily into the message tree and in loosening or tightening the threshold as the decoder moves backward or forward in the tree depending on the behavior of the path likelihood.

(3) The fact that the W-R algorithm requires a decoding decision once the oldest digit has been processed through one encoder constraint length, whereas Fano's procedure permits decoding delays as far beyond the first constraint length as desired (within the limits of time and of decoder storage capabilities).

In common with W-R, Fano's algorithm will work with a wide variety of decoding metric functions, as described in Section 9.1. Perhaps the most commonly used metric for all sequential decoding techniques is the logarithm of the likelihood ratio:

$$\log \frac{P(z \mid y)}{P(z)} \tag{9-5}$$

for channel output z and input (trial sequence) y, where z and y are usually taken to be branches of the code tree. It is this last form which Fano has modified to include a bias term, giving the *branch metric* or likelihood function for the i-th branch:

$$\lambda_i = \log \frac{P(z_i \mid y_i)}{P(z_i)} - B \tag{9-6}$$

The branch likelihood functions are combined to give a path likelihood function

$$L_n = \sum_{i=1}^{n} \lambda_i \tag{9-7}$$

whose value and behavior for n = 1, 2, . . . determine the movement of the decoder through the code tree.

The threshold levels T_i with which values of L_n are compared are taken to be uniformly spaced with increments of T_o. Unlike the W-R algorithm, in which T_i is a predetermined function of the trial sequence length which reflects the number of times the threshold has been loosened or tightened, Fano's procedure uses whichever value of T_i is most suitable in a sense soon to be made precise.

We assume binary data at the input to the encoder and therefore binary representation of the transmitted and trial sequences throughout the encoding and decoding processes. At the input to the decoder, however, we may allow 2^n quantized levels (i.e., "soft" decisions with n-bit quantization) as a way of preserving and utilizing additional information about the received channel noise. (Note that n = 1 gives the case of "hard" decisions, i.e., either 0 or 1 as the received channel digit.) Regardless of the number of levels of quantization, it should be noted that the use of a binary code means that each node in the code tree can have exactly two branches coming from it leading to the node corresponding to the next information bit. The effect of the quantization will appear in terms of additional values for branch and path likelihoods.

In Fano sequential decoding, it is helpful to make use of the concept of a search tree, which corresponds to (but is not the same as) the code tree. The search tree displays quantitatively, in terms of the values of the various branch and path metrics which result, the movement of the decoder through the code tree along various trial sequences. Thus the search tree is not a redrawing of the code tree. For the metric of equation (9-6), upward motion in the search tree (that is, increases in L_n) corresponds, in general, to correct hypotheses, regardless of whether a 1 or 0 was sent. For example, a correctly hypothesized bit with low-level channel noise will produce a branch whose terminal node in the search tree is higher than it would have been in the event of greater received noise.

Before discussing the actual operation of the Fano sequential decoding algorithm, we must introduce one more set of concepts. We need to make a distinction between the concept of being at or moving forward or backward to a node, on the one hand, and the concept of looking ahead or back to a node, on the other hand. In each of these cases, the path metric value for the node in question is computed, and a comparison is made between this value and one of the threshold values. The distinction between the two concepts becomes apparent when we consider the node which is serving as a reference point for the current portion of the search for the correct path. Being at (or moving to) a node signifies that a decision has been made to accept for the present the branch and trial sequence terminating at that node. In looking ahead (or back) to a node, there is only a tentative look at the node, with acceptance only a possibility.

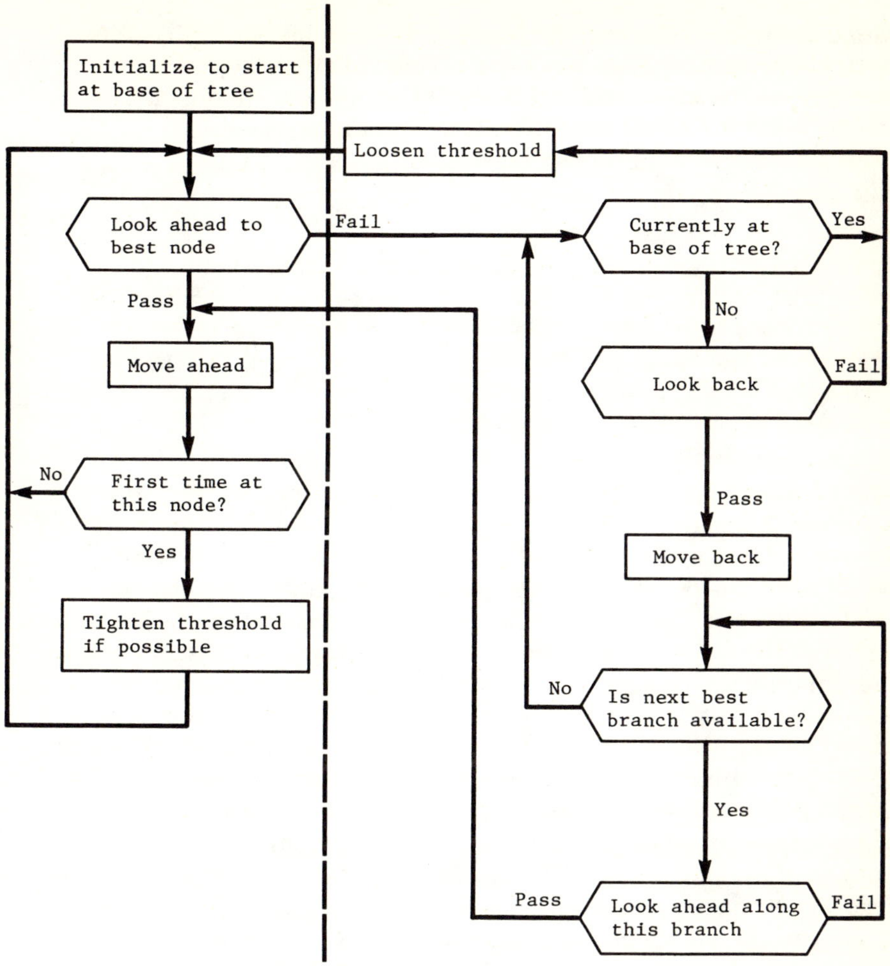

Figure 9-3/Flow Diagram of Fano Sequential Decoding Algorithm

The Fano sequential decoding algorithm is shown in simplified form in Figure 9-3. The terminology used there has been made as general as possible so that the steps can be applied without rewording to any desired decoding metric. In particular, either Hamming distance or a likelihood ratio can be used for the decoding metric. These two metrics result, respectively, in decreasing and increasing trends in the value of the path metric for the correct path. Note the word "trends". On a short-term (3-4 nodes) basis, the path in the search tree may actually head in a direction opposite to that expected for the correct path, usually as a result of increased channel noise. It is the long-term behavior of the path metric and search tree path that is of most importance.

The portion of Figure 9-3 to the left of the dashed line constitutes the forward loop, in which the decoder advances steadily through the search tree. Decoding decisions, when wanted, can be obtained for any digits that are at least one constraint length behind the branch which was just accepted by the box labeled "move ahead" in the forward loop. The portion of Figure 9-3 to the right of the dashed line constitutes the search loop. We shall say that a decoding computation has taken place whenever the decoding metric is computed for a branch. In terms of the flow diagram, this occurs whenever a "look ahead" box is executed.

The forward loop continues to be executed as long as the sequence resulting from adding the newest branch is accepted, which is the "pass" path from the "look ahead to best node" box. A "fail" decision at this point, however, puts the decoder in the search mode. The first thing the decoder must do is to determine if it is already at the base of the tree. If it is, then since the best branch did not pass, the decoder cannot advance until the threshold is loosened. This step is repeated if necessary. If the decoder is not at the base of the tree, then it obviously must retreat (look back) to the preceding node in the path. If the value of the path metric there does not satisfy the threshold, the threshold is loosened and the decoder returns to the forward loop to attempt to extend the path with this looser threshold, starting at the node from which it just looked back. That is, the decoder does not actually move back if the path metric fails at this point. If, however, the value of the path metric does satisfy the threshold, the decoder then moves back to this node and begins to try other branches if one or more are available. When a branch is found which enables the path metric to pass, the decoder returns to the forward loop. If no satisfactory branch is found at this node, the decoder, after checking as to whether it is at the base of the tree, backs up another node.

Example 9-1. The best way of gaining an understanding of the operation of the algorithm is to work through an example, which we shall now do. In order to maintain a focus on the algorithm itself without digressing to compute branch and path metrics, we take the search tree of Figure 9-4 as our starting point. This tree shows only the path values and thresholds. Note that it is irrelevant

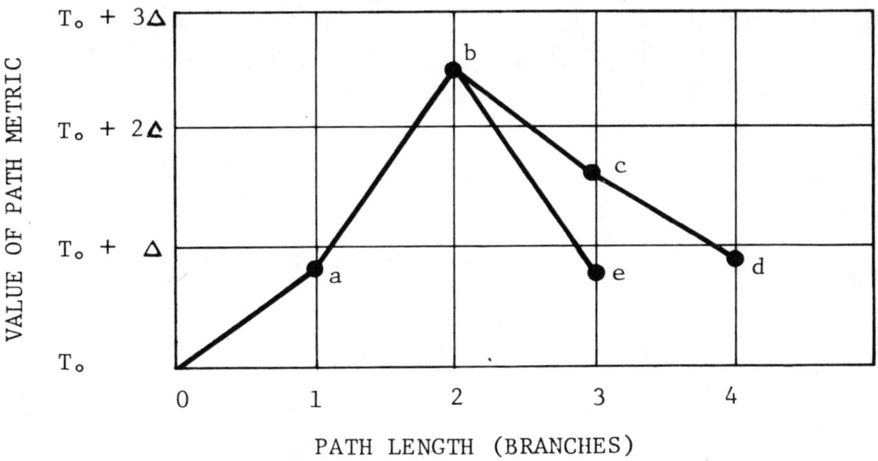

Figure 9-4/ Paths in Search Tree

for the present discussion to know whether a branch at a node corresponds to a 0 or a 1 information digit; therefore no attempt has been made here to identify branches in this way. We have assumed for our metric a function (such as logarithm of a likelihood ratio) which tends to increase with sequence length; that is, while there may be short-term decreases in the metric value, the overall trend is upward.

In Figure 9-4, the abscissa shows path length, starting at the base of the tree; the ordinate specifies the value of the path metric and shows the various possible threshold values. The column headings of Table 9-1 should be self-explanatory. You should correlate each step of Figure 9-4 and Table 9-1 with movement through the steps in the flow diagram of Figure 9-3.

The main points of difference between the W-R and Fano algorithms can be summarized as follows:

(1) The W-R produces a decoding decision any time the trial sequence has reached a length of one constraint length and has satisfied the threshold; the Fano algorithm may produce a decision at this point but generally is programmed to defer a decision until three to five constraint lengths have been processed successfully. This strategy, while reducing the probability of a decoding error, requires increased storage for received digits and branch metrics plus increased bookkeeping.

Table 9-1/Moves and Rationales for Example 9-1

Path Length and Node	Loop: Forward (F) or Search (S)	Looking at Node	Current Threshold	Pass (P) or Fail (F)	Move	Threshold Increment
0	F	a	T_o	P	Forward	0
1 (a)	F	b	T_o	P	Forward	$+2\Delta$
2 (b)	F	c	$T_o + 2\Delta$	F	None	0
2 (b)	S	a	$T_o + 2\Delta$	F	None	$-\Delta$
2 (b)	F	c	$T_o + \Delta$	P	Forward	0
3 (c)	F	d	$T_o + \Delta$	F	None	0
3 (c)	S	b	$T_o + \Delta$	P	Back	0
2 (b)	S	e	$T_o + \Delta$	F	None	0
2 (b)	S	a	$T_o + \Delta$	F	None	$-\Delta$
2 (b)	F	c	T_o	P	Forward	0
3 (c)	F	d	T_o	P	Forward	0
4 (d)			T_o			

(2) The Fano algorithm attempts to tighten the threshold after each successful extension of the trial sequence (i.e., regardless of sequence length), whereas W-R does this only after a decoding decision.

(3) The Fano metric includes a bias term whose effect is to render the various thresholds constant, making visualization easier during analysis and potentially decreasing storage requirements during implementation (although at the expense of additional computation).

(4) The W-R algorithm assumes that threshold values will be calculated from an appropriate mathematical formula and (usually) stored. As a result, there is a set of "loosest" threshold values; if one of these is violated, the decoder must stop, unless provision has been made to compute additional values. In contrast to this, the Fano algorithm must store only one baseline threshold value and one fixed increment value from which all necessary threshold values are computed.

9.5 "Stack" Decoding

The following discussion of the so-called stack decoding algorithm is presented to display the potential benefits of this simple but powerful technique. The stack algorithm is described here, even though there presently exists no commercially available implementation of it, because the author believes that the student or practicing engineer should be aware of the potential of this technique both for the limits it may impose and for consideration in an advanced development or research situation.

To motivate the discussion, we will first present the advantages offered by the stack algorithm, followed by a description of its operation relative to that of the Fano algorithm. (The material to be presented here follows Jelinek [42]. The chief advantage of the stack algorithm is a greatly reduced average number of computations per decoded digit, relative to this same quantity for the Fano algorithm. This advantage of the stack algorithm has been explored by Jelinek via simulation on a general-purpose computer and is shown graphically in Figure 6 of his paper [42]. Results given there show that the stack and Fano algorithms are nearly equivalent at $R=0.8\ R_{comp}$, with the stack algorithm showing an advantage of about 2:1 at $R=0.9\ R_{comp}$ and better than 7:1 at $R=R_{comp}$. The stack algorithm has an additional benefit. Neither the Wozencraft-Reiffen nor the Fano decoder can do anything but the single computation per branch required during quiet intervals of the channel noise, and thus cannot "work ahead" to build an advantage to be drawn upon during noisier periods. In contrast to this, if the highest path in the stack is as long as the received sequence, the stack decoder can compute the path likelihood for the next highest path to full length and store it for potential future use. This last statement correctly suggests that computer memory is the commodity being traded for the impressive speed advantages of the stack decoder. As a side benefit for those interested in following the derivations of results, the stack algorithm is analytically far more tractable than either the Wozencraft-Reiffen or the Fano algorithm. (Compare for example, the effort leading to the expressions for number of computations in an incorrect subset and for the upper bound on the probability of error in the original works of Reiffen [41], Fano [24], Zigongirov [43], and Jelinek [42].)

While the stack algorithm is valid for an arbitrary number r branches leaving each node of the code tree, we shall for simplicity develop and explain it in terms of a binary tree; i.e., r = 2. The stack algorithm can be described in terms of the following steps:

(1) Compute branch likelihood λ for the 0- and 1- branches.
(2) Compute path likelihoods $L_o(n_1)$ and $L_1(n_1)$ for the n_1-branch paths terminating in the 0-branch and 1-branch, respectively.
(3) Arrange $L_o(n_1)$, $L_1(n_1)$ and any other available path likelihood values in descending order. Eliminate the lowest path value in this set. (Note that this ordering and elimination are done without regard to the corresponding path lengths.)
(4) For the node corresponding to the largest likelihood value in the stack, compute branch likelihoods and path likelihoods corresponding to each of the two branches leaving that node; then eliminate from the stack memory the likelihood value for the path out to that node and insert in the stack, in proper position according to descending order, the two path likelihoods just found.
(5) Repeat Step 4 until the largest path likelihood value in the stack corresponds to a path whose length is equal to the (predetermined) decoding delay. Decode the initial branch

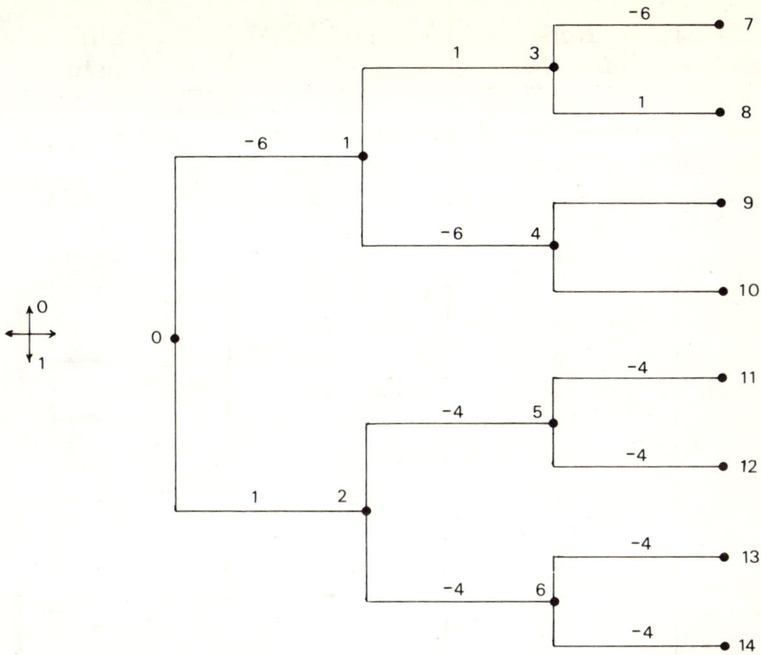

Figure 9-5/Branch Likelihoods for the Tree Considered in Example 9-2

of that path. (If the decoding delay is equal to the message length, the entire sequence corresponding to the largest stack entry can be presented as output to the user.)

On the other hand, if the message length exceeds the decoding delay, only the initial branch need be released. In this case, all stack entries corresponding to paths of the incorrect subset (i.e., those paths beginning with the other branch from the base node of the tree) must be purged from the stack before continuing. At the same time, the decoded branch likelihood can be subtracted from the path likelihoods remaining in the stack, although this is not necessary.

Example 9-2. To illustrate the stack algorithm, we shall elaborate upon the details of the example used by Jelinek [42]. The tree to be considered is shown in Figure 9-5. Nodes are numbered for identification and easy reference, and the likelihood value found for each branch is written just above the branch. For this example we need not know the correct (transmitted) sequence.

Step	Node Number	L	Path Length
1	0	0	0
2	2	1*	1
	1	-6	1
3	5	-3*	2
	6	-3	2
	1	-6	1
4	6	-3*	2
	1	-6	1
	11	-7	3
	12	-7	3
5	1	-6*	1
	11	-7	3
	12	-7	3
	13	-7	3
	14	-7	3
6	3	-5*	2
	11	-7	3
	12	-7	3
	13	-7	3
	14	-7	3
	4	-12	2
7	8	-4**	3
	11	-7	3
	12	-7	3
	13	-7	3
	14	-7	3
	7	-11	3
	4	-12	2

*Largest L in stack, but not for full-length sequence.
**First time largest L achieved for full-length sequence.

Figure 9-6/Example of Stack Algorithm Operation

The contents of the stack are shown in Figure 9-6. At each node, the path likelihood L and path length (in branches) are given. The algorithm terminates when a node with path length = 3 appears at the top of the stack. The lines at the right of the figure indicate the disposition of the node which was at the top of the stack at the start of that step. At Step 7, the top stack entry corresponds for the first time to a path which is three branches long. Through stored information giving linkages between nodes, the decoder determines that path 8 corresponds to an initial information bit value of 0. It decodes this first bit (or the entire path through nodes 1, 3, and 8, depending on circumstances.

Following this decoding decision, the likelihood of the decoded branch can be subtracted from the values of L for nodes in the correct subset (in this case nodes 8, 7, and 4). Nodes in the incorrect subset (in this case 11, 12, 13, and 14) can be purged from the stack. We would then have

Node Number	L	Path Length
8	2	2
7	−5	2
4	−6	1

Jelinek has compared his version of the stack algorithm with the Fano algorithm on the basis of the required average decoding speed advantage $\overline{A}$ (defined as the number of decoding steps performed in the time one branch is received). A code having $R = ½$ was used on the BSC at various crossover probabilities p up to $R_{comp} = R$, which corresponds to $p = 0.045$. The algorithms are virtually identical at $R/R_{comp} = 0.8$ with $\overline{A} = 1$. At $R/R_{comp} = 0.9$, $\overline{A}$ is about 2 for the Fano algorithm and still about 1 for the stack algorithm. At $R = R_{comp}$, these values are, respectively, 14 and 2, showing the significant speed advantage of the stack algorithm at high information rates for the BSC.

9.6 Decoder Parameters

We have described the operation of three variations of sequential decoding. It is clear that there will usually be a great variability, as a function of time, in the number of decoder computations necessary to extend the trial sequence by one branch. This translates into a similar variability in the number of computations required to decode one digit. The effect of this variability on decoder hardware in the case of real-time operation or on cost of computer time for off-line operation is profound. Long searches, which result when a particularly noisy received sequence is encountered, cause the continuing stream of in-coming digits to accumulate in the meantime. In order to preclude the loss of these digits, there must be an input buffer to store them. To minimize the number of digits which enter the buffer during a search, the decoder must have a speed advantage (or speed factor, as it is often called) on the order of ten times the information rate.

As pointed out in Section 9.2, the decoder computation effort depends strongly on the ratio R/R_{comp}. In particular, we have the following result, due to Gallager [9]: For sequential decoding applied to a DMC, the average number of forward moves (in the search tree) per decoded subblock of $k_o = n_o R$ information digits is bounded by

$$4\Big/\left[1 - e^{n_o (R - R_{comp})}\right]^2, \quad R < R_{comp} \tag{9-8}$$

Clearly, this expression becomes infinite as $R \rightarrow R_{comp}$.

Typical values of code constraint length n_A for sequential decoding range from about 20 up to several hundred channel digits. High information rates ($\geqslant$ ½ bit/symbol) and channel rates (on the order of tens of megabits per second) have been achieved in commercially available hardware offered by several vendors.

9.7 Summary and Conclusions

We have shown both the power and the limitations of sequential decoding. The power of this technique arises from the fact that it can provide bit error rates which decrease exponentially with code constraint length at information rates below channel capacity, in combination with a computation load whose moments of all orders are bounded by a constant independent of constraint length as long as $R < R_{comp}$.* Further more, storage requirements grow linearly with code length. The limitation is the variability in computation time to advance one node or branch. This variability,

*See, for example, Gallager [9], p. 279.

forces the decoder to include buffer storage amounting to some small number of constraint lengths and to possess a speed advantage, relative to the channel data rate, to enable it to keep up during noisy periods or at least to be able to catch up quickly once the channel has again become quiet. Because of this behavior on noisy channels, sequential decoding has been found unsuitable as a burst-correcting technique.

Chapter 10
Coding to Combat Impulse Noise

10.1 Introduction

This chapter discusses techniques of coping with bursts of errors, as opposed to the random errors for which most schemes are designed. We shall consider some codes such as the Reed-Solomon previously discussed, along with other techniques. As you may be aware, in considering real-life communication channels, one frequently encounters channels whose behavior is strongly influenced by impulsive noise having large amplitude and relatively short duration. At high transmission rates, even a short noise pulse can affect a large number of bits. The effect of such noise is the production of a burst of errors in the received channel symbols. We will be concerned here with ways of coping with error bursts in the case of binary transmission. We shall consider techniques both with and without a feedback channel, with emphasis on the latter. In that case the burden of error control falls squarely on forward error correction by means of either block or convolutional codes. The material of this chapter applies and, in the case of threshold decoding, extends results obtained in earlier chapters.

We begin with a definition. A noise *burst* of length b is usually defined relative to a *guard space* of length g. The guard space contains all 0's as error digits. The burst is a sequence of b binary digits such that:

(1) the first and last of its digits are 1's (errors);
(2) a guard space must precede and follow the noise burst; and
(3) the sequence of b burst digits does not include a sequence of g or more consecutive 0's.

We see from this definition that not all of the burst need be 1's.

Example 10-1. The noise sequence 00001100111000 could be regarded as containing a burst of length 7 (fifth through eleventh digits) relative to a guard space of length 3, or it could be considered as containing bursts of lengths 2 and 3 relative to a guard space of length 2.

Example 10-2. The sequence 0001001000 can be viewed either as containing two random errors or a burst of length 4 relative to a guard space of length 3.

10.2 Coding with Feedback

The simplest scheme for handling bursts consists of error detection and retransmission using block codes. In this scheme, a relatively unsophisticated, easily implemented (e.g., cyclic) code may be used. A block diagram of a reasonably sophisticated system is shown in Figure 10-1. The noiseless feedback channel is attainable in practice because of the very low data rate of the feedback signal, which permits large values of E_B/N_0. Before describing the operation of this system, we point out that an elementary version of it might be one in which the transmitter waits after sending out a code word until it receives a signal that the word was either correctly received in which case it sends the next word, or was incorrectly received in which case it re-transmits the word just sent.

At the receiver, the syndrome s is computed. If $s \neq 0$, one or more errors has occurred and a request for retransmission is sent; if $s = 0$, the code word is sent on to the user under the assumption that no errors have occurred. In the situation shown in Figure 10-1, storage beyond that necessary for error correction is required at both the receiver and the transmitter. As with error correction, the receiver must store the word following the one being decoded. In addition, if the decoding results in the detection of one or more errors, the decoder initiates a repeat request, by which time the second word following the word just decoded is on its way. If either or both of these last two words turn out to be error-free, they can be passed on to the user immediately, once their turn comes to be decoded. The situation at the decoder forces the same three words to be stored at the transmitter, in addition to subsequent words if the data source cannot be turned off at will. Logic must be provided at the receiver to initiate a repeat request when necessary and to enable the buffer to release information bits from a correct codeword to the user. Logic at the transmitter

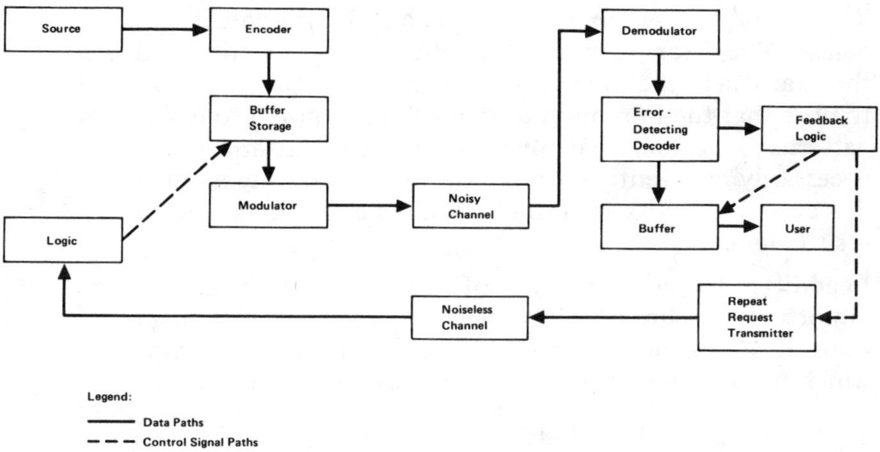

Figure 10-1 / Error Control Using Error Detection and Retransmission.

responds to a repeat request by signaling the buffer there to re-transmit the proper word. This logic would also turn off the source during periods of re-transmission if that happens to be possible.

We have described the operation of a block code system using feedback. We now discuss briefly the performance capability of such a system. Two performance measures are important: the probability of an undetected error and the throughput rate.

An undetected error occurs when s = 0 because the received error sequence was actually a code word. Since an (n, k) binary code contains 2^k code words each of which could be received as any of 2^n possible sequences, the probability of receiving such a sequence is very nearly $2^k/2^n$ or $2^{-(n-k)}$. Thus, for example, for the modest values n = 31, k = 16, this probability would be 2^{-15} or about 3×10^{-5}, a value which would be more than adequate for many purposes.

The following theorem relates code redundancy to the ability of the code to detect a single burst of a specified length.

Theorem 10.1. For detecting any burst of length b or less with a linear code of length n, b parity check symbols are necessary and sufficient.

Thus, in particular, an (n, n–b) cyclic code will detect up to b consecutive errors occurring anywhere within a code word. For the example in the preceding paragraph, b = 15. It is also useful to note that the minimum distance 2t+1 required to correct all patterns of t errors is adequate to *detect* all patterns of 2t (not necessarily consecutive) errors. Conversely, if only a t-error-detection capability is desired, then a minimum distance of t + 1 is sufficient.

In addition to the probability of undetected error, an equally important measure of effectiveness for schemes involving retransmission is the *throughput rate*, which is the time rate at which information is accepted at the decoder. Thus, if

N_t = total number of attempts at transmitting code words

N_a = total number of code words accepted at decoder

N_r = total number of repeat requests

R_{tr} = transmission rate in bits/second

R_{th} = throughput rate in bits/second

then

$$N_t = N_a + N_r$$

and

$$R_{th} = \frac{N_a}{N_t} R_{tr}.$$

The scheme described in this section works very well when the forward channel has relatively long intervals of many block lengths of error-free behavior. On the other hand, a prolonged noisy period could result in drastically reduced throughput at best and loss of data at the worst if the input to the encoder cannot all be stored or temporarily halted.

A very thorough investigation which considers throughput rate as more important than block error rate has been reported by Benice and Frey [45]. They evaluated BCH codes of lengths 7, 15, . . . , 1023 and by means of computer simulation. Similar results are reported in the excellent paper by Burton and Sullivan [52].

A most impressive use of BCH codes in an error detection role was first simulated by Fontaine [46] and then implemented by Reiffen, Yudkin, and Schmidt [47]. The repeat request logic used is a refinement of the scheme presented in Figure 10-1. A (255, 231) error detecting binary BCH code was used on a telephone channel. The predicted time to first undetected error was close to 300 years!

10.3 Interleaving

With interleaving, as shown in Figure 10-2, the data stream (the i's) is separated into a number of parallel streams, each of which is encoded separately. The encoded sequences (the x's) are then commutated for serial transmission over the channel. At the receiver the stream is again split, each resulting stream is decoded, and the decoder outputs recombined to give the originally encoded data. This technqiue can be applied equally well to block and convolutional coding schemes. Its success is based on the fact that for m sufficiently large, bursts of channel errors are spread out over the m separately encoded streams, thus resulting in the need for much less potent error-correction on any given stream. That is, each of the m streams appears to have passed through a standard memoryless channel.

As shown in Figure 10-2, implementation can be carried out in terms of m encoders. Similarly, m decoders are necessary. If a cyclic code is being used, each encoder and decoder consists of shift registers, mod-2 adders, and some decision logic for the decoders. An alternate method is to interleave the stages and taps of the encoder shift registers into a single shift register m times as long. For cyclic block codes, this converts an (n, k) code with generator polynomial g(x) in each of the original m encoders into an (mn, mk) code having generator $g(x^m)$. A similar relationship holds for convolutional codes, in which m–1 stages are inserted after each stage in one of the original m encoders. It can be shown that if the original (n, k) cyclic code had the ability to correct bursts up to b symbols in length, the the (mn, mk) interleaved code can correct bursts up to mb symbols long.

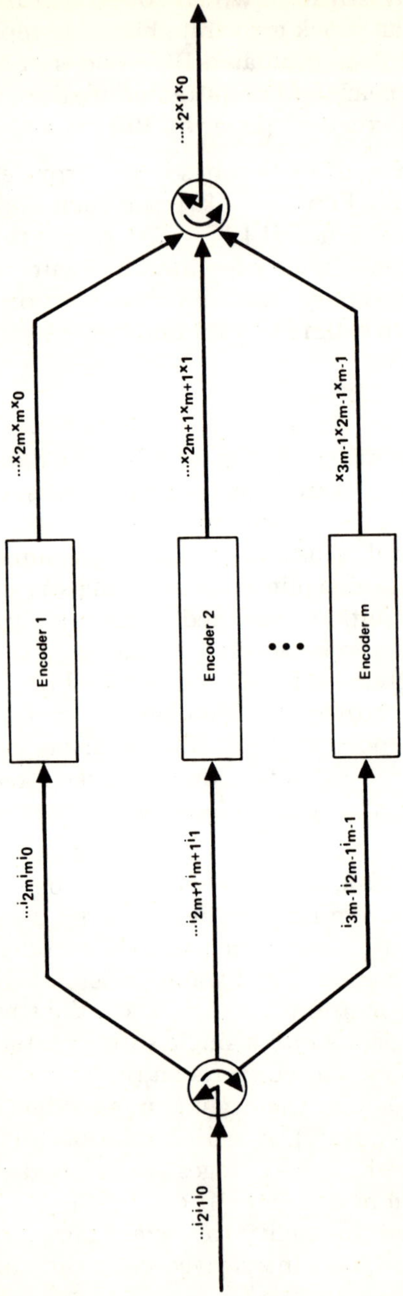

Figure 10-2/ Interleaved Encoding

We point out the useful property that as far as a cyclic code is concerned, a burst of any length b_1 can just as well occupy the first b_2 ($< b_1$) positions and the last $b_1 - b_2$ positions of the code word; i.e., it can be an "end-around" burst.

10.4 Burst-Correcting Block Codes

In contrast to interleaving are techniques which rely on codes especially constructed to deal with bursts of channel noise. The following theorem is useful in evaluating the capabilities and efficiencies of these codes.

Theorem 10.2. *In order to correct any possible error burst of length b or less, a linear code must have at least 2b parity-check symbols. In order to correct any burst of length b or less and simultaneously detect any burst of length $d \geqslant b$ or less, a linear code must have at least b + d parity-check symbols.**

The two best known classes of burst-correcting block codes are the Fire [48] and Reed-Solomon [22] codes. The latter have been described in Chapter 5, and the former will be discussed below.** The unpleasant truth is that for both block and convolutional burst-correcting codes, code design is still largely an art, leaning heavily on trial-and-error techniques. Encoding for the Fire and R-S codes is done just as it is for any other cyclic code, with arithmetic in $GF(2^m)$ for the R-S code.

A general burst-correcting decoder is shown in Figure 10-3. As usual, the g's are the coefficients in generator polynomial g(x) and are therefore implemented as open circuits or wires for g(x) over GF(2). This decoder contains only delay elements, mod-2 adders, gates, and combinational logic.

As with all cyclic codes, a Fire code is most easily defined in terms of its generator polynomial, which is of the form $g(x) = p(x)(x^i + 1)$, over GF(2). Here p(x) is an irreducible polynomial of degree m with roots of order e, and p(x) and $x^i + 1$ are relatively prime. Then code length n is the least common multiple of i and e. The number of parity checks is i+m, so that the number of information symbols is k=n–i–m. A Fire code can correct a single burst of length b or less and simultaneously detect a burst of length $d \geqslant b$ or less if $i \geqslant b+d-1$ and $m \geqslant b$. Alternatively, it

*This theorem holds for non-binary as well as binary codes.

**Peterson and Weldon [11] present a much more thorough discussion of burst-correcting codes, including a list of good codes.

can detect any combination of two bursts in which the length of the shorter burst is no greater than m, and the sum of the lengths is no more than i+1; or it can certainly detect any single burst of length i+m. The factor x^{i+1} gives rise to sets of parity checks spaced i digits apart in each set, so that no burst of length less than i will affect both checks of a set.

First, let us compare the ability of a Fire code to detect or correct bursts with the performance bounds of Theorems 10.1 and 10.2. According to Theorem 10.1, i + m parity checks are necessary and sufficient to detect a burst of length i + m, which is exactly what is claimed for the Fire codes. Applying the bounds of Theorem 10.2 to the simultaneous burst correcting and detecting capability, we see that the number of parity check symbols must satisfy $i + m \geqslant b + d$, which is certainly true for the nontrivial case $b > 1$, since $i \geqslant b + d - 1$ and $m \geqslant b$.

Finally, note that since the number of parity checks is i + m, this fact combined with the relationships $m \geqslant b$, $i \geqslant b + d - 1$, and $d \geqslant b$ implies that $i + m \geqslant 2b + d - 1 \geqslant 3b - 1$, which is well in excess of the minimum number required to detect or correct a burst of length b.

Example 10-3. Let

$$g(x) = (x^7 + x^2 + 1)(x^{16} + 1)$$

With $x^{16} + 1 = (x + 1)^{16}$, you can verify that x + 1 does not divide $x^7 + x^2 + 1$ evenly. Then m=7, i=16, and it turns out that e=127, which is prime. Then n=ie=2032, n–k = 7+16 = 23 parity checks, and k = 2032–23 = 2009 information digits. We must choose $b \leqslant m = 7$. Choosing b=7, we find $10 \geqslant 7 + d - 1$. That is, the code corrects any burst of length 7 or less and simultaneously detects a burst of length 10 or less; if used for pure detection, it can detect a single burst of length 23 or less. In this example, then, we have a code in which a code word of more than 2000 symbols is required to correct bursts no more than 7 symbols long. On the positive side is the fact that the rate in transmitted symbols per bit of information is high, nearly 0.99; and the implementation is extremely simple, requiring only n–k=23 stages in the encoder shift register.

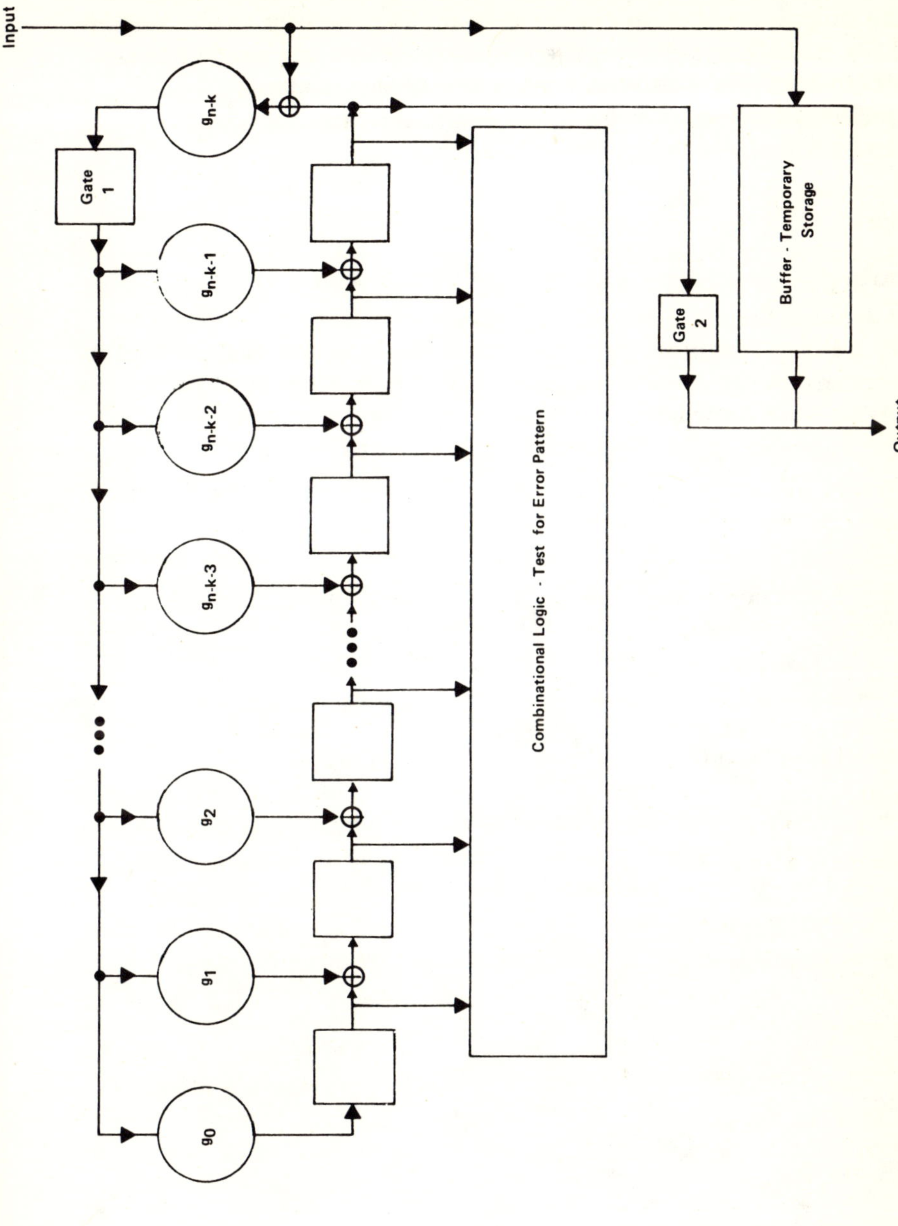

Figure 10-3 /General Burst-Correcting Decoder for a Block Code

The Fire codes are not as efficient as some more recent additions to the set of known burst-correcting codes. For example, Burton [49] has defined codes of length n=be which correct any burst of length $b_1 \leqslant b$, as long as such a burst starts at the 1st, (b + 1) th, (2b + 1) th, . . . , or (eb + 1) th position of the code word. These codes have

$$g(x) = p(x)\,(x^b + 1)$$

with p(x) and $x^b + 1$ relatively prime and p(x) of degree b and exponent e.

This raises the question, when can a Fire code be used profitably? The answer is: if one wants protection against short to fairly long bursts with a high-rate, easily implemented code, then use a Fire code or one by Burton or any of several others.* For example, such a code is ideally suited to detecting errors occurring in data stored in a digital computer.

If a higher-order code alphabet is used, more powerful burst-correcting codes are possible. Thus, if we group r binary digits together, each symbol thus formed is an element of an alphabet of $R=2^r$ symbols. With this point of view, we see that a burst of length (t–1) r+1 binary digits or less can affect at most t successive symbols of the R-ary alphabet. This is the basis for the use of Reed-Solomon (R-S) codes, discussed in Chapter 5, in burst-correction. By Theorem 10.2 an R-S code which corrects t errors in an R-ary code word needs at most 2t R-ary check symbols (i.e., 2tr binary check digits) out of the $n=2^r-1$ R-ary symbols in a code word. Note that this makes it possible to correct more than one binary burst contained within the R-ary burst of length t.

Example 10-4. If r=7 and t=4, the R-S code has symbols consisting of blocks of 7 binary digits each. The code can correct all bursts of length (t-1) r+1 = 22 binary digits or less using 2tr = 56 check binary digits out of a word length of $r(2^r-1) = 889$ binary digits. This compares very favorably, from the standpoint of code efficiency and burst-correcting power, with the Fire code discussed previously. Decoding is slightly more complicated, requiring a special-purpose computer to carry out finite-field algebra. Subsequent advances in theory and recent advances in technology have resulted in substantial reductions in decoding time and complexity.

*See, for example Table 11.1 in Peterson and Weldon [11].

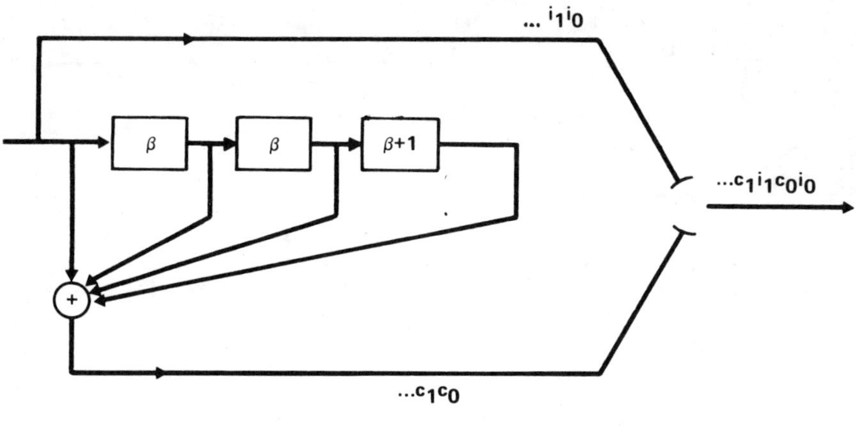

Figure 10-4 /Encoder for Diffuse Threshold Decoding

It is of passing interest to observe that a Fire code to correct a burst of length 22 or less would require only 65 binary parity-check symbols but would have a code length of possibly 1.6×10^8 binary digits.

10.5 Burst Correction with Convolutional Codes

Finally, we mention briefly two techniques (there are others) which can be applied to correct bursts when using convolutional codes. Both techniques relate to threshold decoding, and hardware may be commercially available for implementing both. They are characterized by the ability to cope with very large bursts with little increase in equipment complexity as they require only additional delay units in direct proportion to the increase in burst length b.

The first is diffuse threshold decoding, developed in the early 1960's and later published by Kohlenberg and Forney [50]. The encoder and decoder are shown in Figures 10-4 and 10-5, respectively. The code illustrated corrects bursts of $b = 2\beta$ binary digits relative to a guard space of $g = 6\beta+2$. Note that the technique is not quite the same as the interleaving defined earlier, since not all taps of the shift register are separated by exactly β stages.

The second technique is due to Gallager and is shown implemented in Figures 10-6 and 10-7. For the code shown, most bursts up to $b = 2\beta$ relative to $g = 2(\beta+k_1+k_2)-1$ are corrected. Note that $b \approx g$

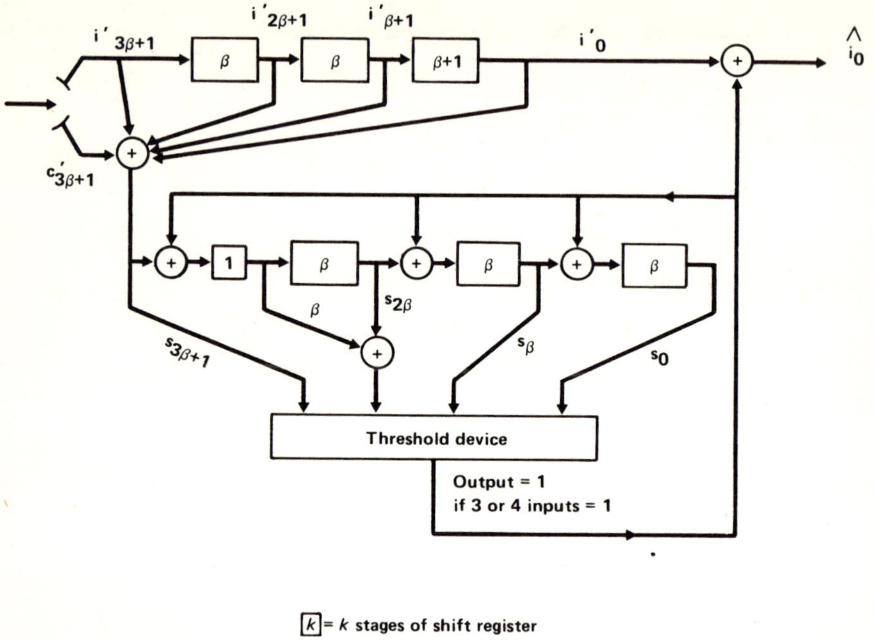

Figure 10-5/ Diffuse Threshold Decoder

for $\beta >> k_1$ or k_2 (typically, $\beta \sim 1000$, while k_1 and k_2 are less than 10). As noted, this power is achieved at the expense of not being able to correct all bursts relative to the specified guard space. Implementation is again extremely simple. Basically, the decoder operates as follows. A burst of errors in the encoder section will cause a corresponding burst of 1's to enter the syndrome register. The latter burst will be in the last $5+k_1+k_2$ stages of this register, and will therefore cause an output from the burst detector, at just the time that the leading edge of the channel error burst reaches the right-hand end of the $(\beta+k_1+6)$–stage portion of the encoder. With very high probability, this output is the correct estimate of the error in information digit $\hat{i}$ about to be emitted from the decoder.

10.6 Summary

The techniques discussed in the preceding sections for burst noise channels are summarized in Table 10-1. This set of techniques is not exhaustive, but it is certainly representative of those currently available.

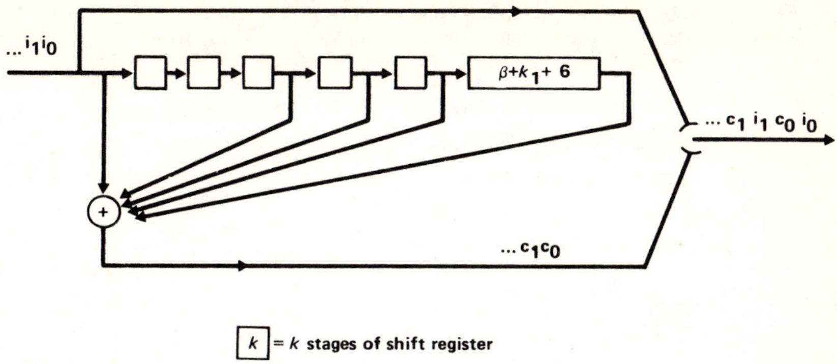

Figure 10-6/ Gallager Burst Encoder

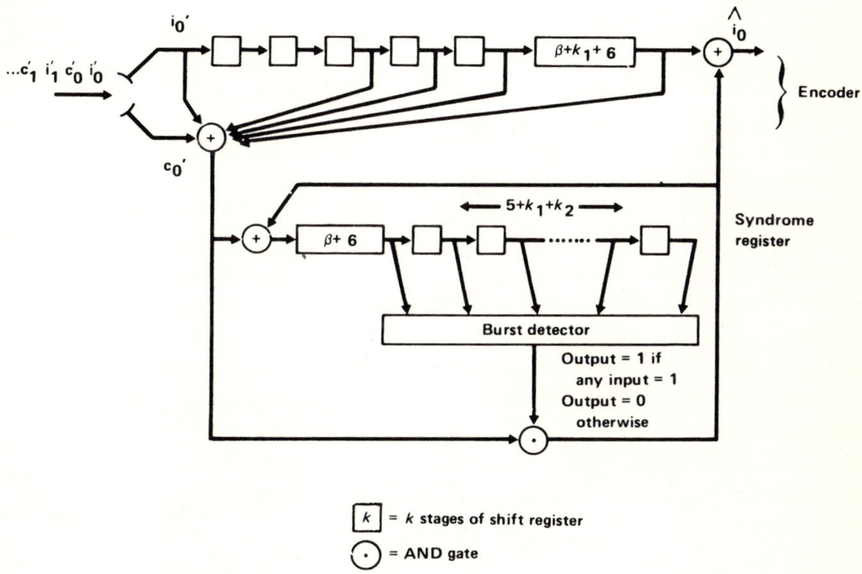

Figure 10-7/ Gallager Burst Decoder

Technique	Advantages	Disadvantages
1. Error detection and retransmission	Easy to implement. Less redundancy required than to correct same number of errors. Independent of burst length.	Requires reliable feedback link, possibly buffer storage & logic at receiver and transmitter. Low throughput with noisy forward channel.
2. Simple interleaving	"Dilutes" effects of noise burst by distributing over separately coded data streams. Easy to implement; many good random-error-correcting codes are known.	Dependence of errors in burst not fully exploited in decoding.
3. Fire codes	Very high code efficiency. Very simple implementation.	Long codes required for modest burst-correcting capability.
4. Reed-Solomon codes	Code efficiency typically greater than 90%. Code construction easy. Hardware becoming commerically available.	No serious disadvantages.
5. Threshold decoding techniques	Capable of handling large bursts (~2000). Hardware commercially available.	Code design for bursts is still an art. Equipment may exist for only limited range of code rates.

Table 10-1/ Comparison of Burst-Correcting Techniques

Chapter 11
Applications and Trade-Off Analyses

11.1 Introduction

In this chapter, we will present examples of the application of error-control techniques to situations which have occurred in practice. Summaries of the trade-offs will be presented. An important fact to bear in mind is that a technology-based factor such as speed, cost, weight, or power, which was decisive in reaching a certain conclusion at the time, may with new technology be either irrelevant or may lead to a conclusion different from the one reached based on the older technology.

System parameters which must be considered include:

a. Data rate in bits per second; i.e., the rate at which data are generated and/or must be transferred by the system.

b. Available or required ratio of signal energy per bit to noise power density (E_B/N_o).

c. Communication channel or storage medium characteristics — Gaussian, impulse, or other type of noise; depth, duration, and frequency of occurrence of fades, if any; interference, either accidental or intentional (jamming).

d. Availability of processing (encoding and decoding) and implementation (software versus hardware, general- versus special-purpose computer).

e. Processing speed compared to data rate; possible need for buffering to allow for variations in rate at which processing can take place; e.g., input buffer with sequential decoding.

f. Tolerances of the message (data, digital voice, video) to errors; i.e., required output bit or block error rate.

g. Required throughput rate.

h. Existence and characteristics of a feedback link.

i. In case of jamming, expected type, duty cycle, frequency coverage, and jamming-to-signal ratio.

11.2 Example #1: A Floating Data-Collection Platform

The first application concerns the choice of a coding technique to meet specified performance requirements for a data-collection system consisting of 1,000 to 10,000 floating (both fresh and salt water) data collection platforms which periodically transmit a burst of data from each platform through a geosynchronous satellite to a common receiving and processing station on earth. This transmission is at a rate of 100 bits/sec for 10 to 20 seconds. Thus, if error control coding is to be used, the encoder must be inexpensive indeed, so that 1,000 to 10,000 such encoders will not cost the user a small fortune.

The data were to be transmitted using an antenna whose pattern is shown in Figure 11-1. The gain from this pattern is at most 3 to 4 dB relative to that of a perfectly spherical (isotropic) antenna pattern; i.e., 3 to 4 dBi. This type of coverage was specified by the user. While giving essentially complete hemispherical coverage, the pattern has two serious disadvantages, both of which lead to nearly the same result as far as received signal strength at the satellite is concerned. Note in Figure 11-1 that there is a rapid drop in gain both along the pattern's axis of symmetry and near the plane normal to this axis. Thus, any time either of these low-gain portions of the pattern is oriented toward the satellite during transmission as the result of motion caused by the floating platform, low signal strength, or fading occurs. Even if platform motion does not occur, the phenomenon of multiple propagation paths (multipath) also can produce low signal strength at the satellite as a result of destructive interference between the direct and reflected signals.

At the time, there were no known experimental results on fading channels for the UHF band (400-460 MHz) to be used. Therefore, data were used which had been obtained with an earlier satellite system involving various data-gathering buoys operating in a high VHF band at around 150 MHz. These data, which were quite extensive and consistent, showed 5 to 6 dB average and 10 dB maximum fades in one case, and maximum fades of 12 dB lasting anywhere from 5 to 20 seconds in another case. There was strong evidence to suggest that the broad, deep fades were caused primarily by multipath.

The challenge to error-control can now be seen: at 100 bits per second, even a 5-second fade will affect 500 bits. Thus, a rate-1/2 code would have to be able to correct 1,000-digit bursts. More fundamental in the present situation is the fact that 5 seconds represents 25 to 50% of a single transmission. In fact, it was concluded that for fades of two seconds or more, a platform's transmission would have to be repeated or lost.

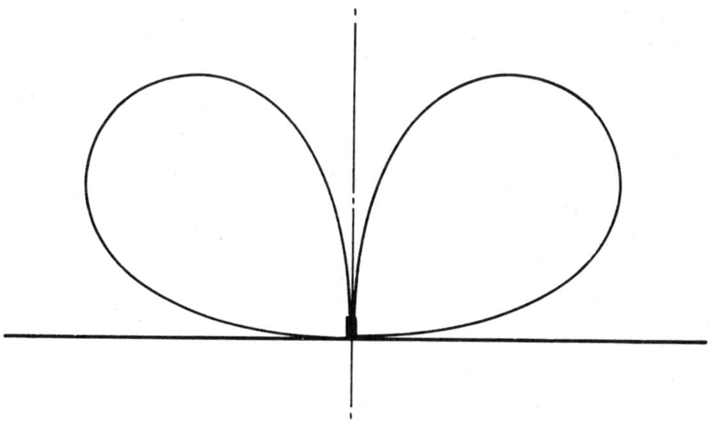

Figure 11-1/Antenna Pattern for Floating Data-Collection Platform

During intervals between fades, the channel between each floating platform and the satellite is the one assumed to exist at most times between any earth station and a satellite; i.e., the Gaussian channel. The average bit error probability P_B for this channel was estimated based on one of the sets of experiments from which were extrapolated the fading channel statistics just discussed. For tests in which threre were bit errors, P_B ranged from 3×10^{-5} to 10^{-2}; these results included effects of any fading which may have occurred.

We have described the physical aspects of the situation and have presented data for what was expected to be a channel with behavior very similar to the one actually being studied. With this as the setting, the following question was posed: how well can one do in coping with bursts of errors caused by deep fades while providing protection against randomly occurring errors, all within the additional constraints of lowest possible cost, physically small size, and low power consumption? The following error-control (four correction and one detection) schemes were considered in this light:

- Interleaved BCH codes
- Nonbinary (Zierler) codes
- Sequential decoding
- Diffuse threshold decoding
- Error detection with re-transmission

Interleaved BCH codes were considered by reviewing some simulations performed on data from an HF link characterized by impulse noise, frequency-selective fading, and in-band interference. Recall that interleaving spreads out the effect of a burst by rearranging code symbols. The average P_B was improved about two orders of magnitude over the raw (unencoded) value of nearly 10^{-2} by the use of a (63, 36) five-error-correcting BCH code interleaved 1027 times. Unfortunately, the total number of data bits necessary in this case is 1027 x 36, or about 37,000, far in excess of the 1,000 to 2,000 data bits per block in the application.

The nonbinary codes considered used symbols consisting of m binary digits each. These codes had already been extensively tested via computer simulation and actual use. One code considered had m=8, block length 2,040 binary digits and the ability to correct up to 120 binary digit errors. In 1970, the encoder for this very potent code was estimated to cost $1350 in a buy of 10 units, a figure well in excess of the allowable cost. Another code, having m=4 with k=7 and n=15 4-bit symbols, was also examined for its performance when interleaved 33 times, and for its cost. The overall interleaved block length of 924 data bits was highly compatible with the DCP message length. Its burst correcting capability at 100 bps is about 2.4 seconds of channel digits, which is very good indeed. Decoder cost was estimated at $13,000.

Sequential decoding was judged ineffective against the long bursts anticipated because of the long searches and consequent input buffer overflows. (See Chapter 9 and Section 11.2 for additional discussion.)

Diffuse threshold decoding was found to provide protection against up to three seconds of errors with rate = 1/2, constraint length 1200 to 1800 channel digits, and a guard space of about 1800 channel digits between bursts. Encoder parts cost was estimated at $100, and the decoder was available commercially off the shelf for about $5000.

Error detection and retransmission were found to provide protection against fades up to about one second, as well as against random errors. One potential drawback was the need to add retransmission logic to each of the so-called self-timed DCP's, thus increasing the cost and complexity.

On balance, the recommendation was to use either the interleaved (n, k) = (15, 7), m = 4, Zierler code or diffuse threshold decoding.

Today this same set of requirements probably could be met by a commercially available Reed-Solomon encoder/decoder combination having (n, k) = (31, 15) 5-bit symbols and the ability to correct up to 8 symbol errors. For the 1000-bit transmission, interleaving to a depth of 14 would provide an adequate number of data bits and a burst-correcting capability of 560 digits or nearly 3 seconds at 100 bits/sec.

11.2 Example #2: Satellite and Space Communication

Heller and Jacobs [51] treat not only code choice but also the choice of modulation in their analysis of satellite and space communication channels*. The channel model used happens not only to fit observed behavior very well but also to be the one most often assigned because of its analytical tractability; namely, the additive white Gaussian noise (AWGN) channel. The whiteness of the noise implies independence of noise statistics from one bit interval to the next. At the same time, the channel response to the signal is sufficiently broad-band to permit the modest bandwidth expansion required by the error-control technique.

Two algorithms are considered for this memoryless channel: Viterbi decoding and sequential decoding. You may recall that both of these algorithms were originally developed, as were many convolutional and block codes, for a memoryless channel. For a space-based system, a key constraint is the need to minimize the

*These could be between satellites, between satellite and ground, or between space probe and ground.

size and weight of the equipment, including the transmitter in particular. Heller and Jacobs also address problems caused by uncertainty in carrier phase at the demodulator and by inaccuracies in receiver AGC. However, we shall not discuss these issues any further here. (Carrier tracking has been addressed briefly in Chapter 2).

Reduction in transmitter power means a corresponding reduction in received E_B/N_o, which of course leads directly to an increase in raw, uncoded bit error probability P_B. Possible courses of action involve some combination of the following:

Accept a higher P_B.

Recoup ERP by increasing transmitting antenna gain.

Increase received power and E_B by increasing receiving antenna gain.

Seek the optimum modulation of the carrier.

Utilize an error-control scheme.

The last two alternative approaches are chosen for further analysis, with the condition that efficient, though not necessarily optimum, modulation be chosen. This turns out to be binary phase-shift keying (BPSK), sometimes called binary antipodal modulation. Three main reasons are given for this choice:

1. BPSK wave forms are easy to generate. Furthermore their amplification in a TWT amplifier makes best use of the TWT efficiency near saturation, compared to multi-level amplitude modulated waveforms.
2. BPSK is nearly optimum* in terms of E_B/N_o vs P_B (9.6 dB at $P_B = 10^{-5}$).
3. BPSK modulation of two quadrature carriers is equivalent to quadrature phase modulation of a single carrier.

Viterbi decoding was examined for both hard (0 or 1) and soft (4-level and 8-level) received digit decisions. Emphasis was on codes of rate R = 1/2 and lengths K = 3 through 8, although rates 1/3 and 2/3 were also studied. In all cases, 3-level quantization gave an added improvement of about 2 dB at $P_B = 10^{-5}$, compared with hard decisions. The price of the 0.3 to 0.5 dB improvement in rate -1/3 codes compared with rate -1/2 codes is increased bandwidth and increased difficulty in symbol (channel digit) tracking due to decreased symbol energy to noise ratio E_s/N_o, where

*Only orthogonal signaling is better.

$E_s = RE_B$. At the time this study was performed, a Viterbi decoder having R = 1/2 and K = 7 and operating at up to 2 megabits per second with 2-, 4-, or 8-level quantization was cited as being available off the shelf in a model which required a total of 356 TTL integrated circuits. This relatively simple decoder provided more than 5 dB improvement in E_B/N_o at $P_B = 10^{-5}$ compared to uncoded BPSK, and 6 dB at $P_B = 10^{-8}$, using 8-level decisions.

Heller and Jacobs [51] point out that the output P_B for either type of decoding is extremely low in the absence of bursts of errors at the decoder input. When such bursts do occur, the effect on a sequential decoder is far more serious than it is on a Viterbi decoder. In the former case, decoder output errors are likely to result not as a direct consequence of the decoder's inability to handle bursts, but rather because of the following chain of causally related events:

- Burst of decoder input errors
- Long searches for correct path
- Decoder input buffer overflow
- Loss of received data
- Undetected errors at decoder output

In the case of the Viterbi decoder, however, error bursts at the input will cause error bursts at the output of only one to three constraint lengths, with no loss of data, since the decoder produces decisions at a fixed rate independent of channel noise.

While soft decisions definitely benefit the Viterbi decoder performance with negligible impact on decoder size and processing time, this is not the case with sequential decoding. In this case, there is a formidable price, both in terms of processing time and in branch metric storage. Consequently, the use of soft decisions with sequential decoding is not recommended. As Heller and Jacobs [51] point out, the performance of the Viterbi decoder degrades gracefully with adverse channel and/or receiver conditions.

References

[1a] Glenn, A.B., "Multi-Service Communications Network for Civil Command and Control," *EASCON 76 Record*, September 26-29, 1976, pp. 24-A—24-G.

[1] Wozencraft, J.M. and I.M. Jacobs, *Principles of Communication System Engineering*, John Wiley & Sons, Inc., New York, N.Y., 1965.

[2] Carlson, A.B., *Communication Systems*, McGraw-Hill, New York, N.Y., 1968.

[3] Hancock, J.C., *An Introduction to the Principles of Communication Theory*, McGraw-Hill Book Company, New York, N.Y., 1961.

[4] Cahn, C.R., "Comparison of Phase Tracking Schemes for PSK," *Proceedings of International Telemetering Conference*, 1971, pp. 172-180.

[5] Heller, J.A., "Sequential Decoding for Channels with Time Varying Phase," Ph.D. dissertation, Massachusetts Institute of Technology, Cambridge, MA., 1967.

[6] Cahn, C.R., G.K. Huth, and C.R. Moore, "Simulation of Sequential Decoding with Phase Locked Demodulation," *Magnavox Co. Report No. MX-TM-3119-71*, 1971.

[7] Viterbi, A.J., *Principles of Coherent Communication*, McGraw-Hill, New York, N.Y., 1966.

[8] Gardner, F.M., *Phaselock Techniques*, John Wiley & Sons, Inc., New York, N.Y., 1966.

[9] Gallager, R.G., *Information Theory and Reliable Communication*, John Wiley & Sons, Inc., New York, N.Y., 1968.

[10] Abramson, N., *Information Theory and Coding*, McGraw-Hill Book Company, New York, N.Y., 1963.

[11] Peterson, W.W. and E.J. Weldon, Jr., *Error Correcting Codes*, Second Edition, John Wiley & Sons, Inc., New York, N.Y., 1972.

[12] Bose, R.C., and D.K. Ray-Chaudhuri, "On a Class of Error Correcting Binary Group Codes," *Information and Control*, vol. 3, 1960, pp. 68-79.

[13] Bose, R.C., and D.K. Ray-Chaudhuri, "Further Results on Error Correcting Binary Group Codes," *Information and Control*, vol. 3, 1960, pp. 279-290.

[14] Hocquenghem, A., "Codes Correcteurs d'Erreurs," *Chiffres*, vol. 2, 1959, pp. 147-156.

[15] Berlekamp, E.R., *Algebraic Coding Theory*, McGraw-Hill Book Company, New York, N.Y., 1968.

[16] Massey, J.L., "Shift Register Synthesis and BCH Decoding," *IEEE Transactions on Information Theory*, vol. IT-15, no. 1, January 1969, pp. 122-127.

[17] Carhoun, D.O., T.F. Roome, and E.A. Palo, "Finite Field Arithmetic with Charge Transfer Devices," *Third International Conference on the Applications of Charge-Coupled Devices*, Edinburgh, Scotland, September 28-30, 1976.

[18] Carhoun, D.O., T.F. Roome, and E.A. Palo, "Error Correction Coding with Charge Transfer Devices," *Third International Conference on the Applications of Charge-Coupled Devices*, Edinburgh, Scotland, September 28-30, 1976.

[19] Stenbit, J.P., "Tables of Generators for Bose-Chaudhuri Codes," *IEEE Transactions on Information Theory*, vol. IT-10, no. 4, October 1964, pp. 390-391.

[20] Lin, S., *An Introduction to Error-Correcting Codes*, Prentice-Hall, Inc., Englewood Cliffs, N.J., 1970.

[21] Chien, R.T., "Block-Coding Techniques for Reliable Data Transmission," *IEEE Transactions on Communication Technology*, vol. COM-10, no. 5, October 1971, pp. 743-751.

[22] Reed, I.S., and G. Solomon, "Polynomial Codes over Certain Finite Fields," *Journal of the Society for Industrial and Applied Mathematics*, vol. 8, 1960, pp. 300-304.

[23] Gorenstein, D., and N. Zierler, "A Class of Error-Correcting Codes in p^m Symbols," *Journal of the Society for Industrial and Applied Mathematics*, vol. 9, 1961, pp. 207-214.

[24] Fano, R.M., "A Heuristic Discussion of Probabilistic Decoding," *IRE Transactions on Information Theory*, vol. IT-9, no. 2., 1963, pp. 64-74.

[25] Viterbi, A.J., "Convolutional Codes and Their Performance in Communication Systems," *IEEE Transactions on Communication Technology*, vol. COM-19, no. 5, Part II, 1971, pp. 751-772.

[26] Wozencraft, J.M. and B. Reiffen, *Sequential Decoding*, M.I.T. Press, Cambridge, MA., 1961.

[27] Massey, J.L., "Shift Register Synthesis and BCH Decoding," *IEEE Transactions on Information Theory*, vol. IT-15, no. 1, January 1969, pp. 122-127.

[28] Heller, J.A., "Sequential Decoding: Short Constraint Length Convolutional Codes," Jet Propulsion Laboratory, California Institute of Technology, Pasadena, *Space Program Summary 37-54*, vol. 3, 1968, pp. 171-174.

[29] Fano, R.M., *Transmission of Information*, published jointly by The MIT Press, Cambridge, MA., and John Wiley & Sons, New York, 1961.

[30] Larsen, K.J., "Short Convolutional Codes with Maximal Free Distance for Rates 1/2, 1/3, and 1/4," *IEEE Transactions on Information Theory*, vol. IT-19, no. 3, 1973, pp. 371-372.

[31] Odenwalder, J.P., "Optimal Decoding of Convolutional Codes," Ph.D. dissertation, Department of System Sciences, School of Engineering and Applied Science, University of California at Los Angeles, 1970.

[32] Bahl, L.R., and F. Jelinek, "Rate 1/2 Convolutional Codes with Complementary Generators," *IEEE Transactions on Information Theory*, vol. IT-17, no. 6, 1971, pp. 718-727.

[33] Paaske, E., "Short Binary Convolutional Codes with Maximal Free Distance for Rates 2/3 and 3/4," *IEEE Transactions on Information Theory*, vol. IT-20, no. 5, 1974, pp. 683-689.

[34] Johannesson, R., "Robustly Optimal Rate One-Half Binary Convolutional Codes," *IEEE Transactions on Information Theory*, vol. IT-21, no. 4, 1975, pp. 464-468.

[35] Massey, J.L., *Threshold Decoding*, MIT Press, Cambridge, MA., 1963.

[36] Reed, I.S., "A Class of Multiple-Error-Correcting Codes and their Decoding Scheme," *IRE Transactions on Information Theory*, vol. PGIT-4, 1954, pp. 38-49.

[37] Robinson, J.P., "Error Propagation and Definite Decoding of Convolutional Codes," *IEEE Transactions on Information Theory*, vol. IT-14, January 1968, pp. 121-128.

[38] Massey, J.L. and M.K. Sain, "Inverses of Linear Sequential Circuits," *IEEE Transactions on Computers*, vol. C-17, no. 4, April 1968, pp. 330-337.

[39] Viterbi, A.J., "Error Bounds for Convolutional Codes and an Asymptotically Optimum Decoding Algorithm," *IEEE Transactions on Information Theory*, vol. IT-13, no. 2, 1967, pp. 260-269.

[40] Wozencraft, J.M., *Sequential Decoding for Reliable Communication*, Ph.D. thesis and Research Laboratory of Electronics Report No. 325, Massachusetts Institute of Technology, Cambridge, MA., 1957.

[41] Reiffen, B., "Sequential Decoding for Discrete Memoryless Channels," *IRE Transactions on Information Theory*, vol. IT-8, no. 2., 1962, pp. 208-220.

[42] Jelinek, F., "Fast Sequential Decoding Algorithm Using a Stack," *IBM Journal of Research and Development*, vol. 13, 1969, pp. 675-685.

[43] Zigongirov, K. Sb., "Some Sequential Decoding Procedures," *Problemy Peredachi Informatsii*, vol. I, no. 4, 1966, pp. 13-25. (English translation, *Problems of Information Transmission*, available through Plenum Publishing Corporation).

[44] Reiffen, B. and D. Wiggert, "Some Experimental Results for a Sequential Decoding Algorithm Applied to an Asymmetric Channel," *M.I.T. Lincoln Laboratory Group Report 25G-17*, 1963.

[45] Benice, R.J., and A.H. Frey, Jr., "Comparisons of Error Control Techniques," *Tenth National Communications Symposium*, Utica, N.Y., 1964.

[46] Fontaine, A.B. and R.G. Gallager, "Error Statistics and Coding for Binary Transmission over Telephone Circuits," *Proc. IRE*, vol. 49, no. 6, June 1961, pp. 1059-1065.

[47] Reiffen, B., W.G. Schmidt, and H.L. Yudkin, "The Design of an Error Free Data Transmission System for Telephone Circuits," *Transactions of the AIEE (Communications and Electronics)*, vol. 80, 1961, pp. 224-231.

[48] Fire, P., "A Class of Multiple-Error-Correcting Binary Codes for Non-Independent Errors," *Report RSL-E-2*, Sylvania Reconaissance Systems Laboratory, Mountain View, CA., 1959.

[49] Burton, H.O., "Inversionless Decoding of Binary BCH Codes," *IEEE Transactions on Information Theory*, vol. IT-17, no. 3, July 1971, pp. 464-466.

[50] Kohlenberg, A. and G.D. Forney, Jr., "Convolutional Coding for Channels with Memory," *IEEE Transactions on Information Theory*, vol. IT-14, no. 5, September 1968, pp. 618-626.

[51] Heller, J. and I.M. Jacobs, "Viterbi Decoding for Satellite and Space Communications," *IEEE Transactions on Communications Technology*, vol. COM-19, no. 5, part 2, October 1971, pp. 835-848.

[52] Burton, H.O. and D.D. Sullivan, "Errors and Error Control," *Proceedings of the IEEE*, vol. 60, no. 11, November 1972, pp. 1293-1301.

[53] Bussgang, J.J., "Some Properties of Binary Convolutional Code Generators," *IEEE Transactions on Information Theory*, vol. IT-11, no. 1, January 1965, pp. 90-100.

Problems

1-1. From your own experience, choose a communication or storage system (perferably one with error control) and draw it in block diagram form. Label each channel, modulator, encoder, multiplexer, etc.

2-1. a. Use the curves of Figure 2-5 in the text to determine, relative to uncoded PSK optimum binary, the decrease in transmitter power possible with the (24,12) augmented BCH code and with (64,32) and (96,48) sequential decoding at

$$P_B = 10^{-5}.$$

b. At $E_B/N_0 = 5$ dB, what is the improvement in P_B in going from no coding to (64,32) sequential decoding?

2-2. a. Referring to Figure 2-2 in the text, use calculus to prove that, for 0 and 1 equally likely to be sent, the decision boundary for transmission through an AWGN channel is in the optimum position for decision variable $\phi = 0$.

b. Try to generalize the result for 0 and 1 having arbitrary transmission probabilities.

3-1. Given the generator matrix

$$G = \begin{bmatrix} 1\,0\,0\,1\,1 \\ 0\,1\,0\,1\,0 \\ 0\,0\,1\,0\,1 \end{bmatrix}$$

a. Find the transmitted code word corresponding to messages $\mathbf{u}_1 = [1\ 1\ 0]$ and $\mathbf{u}_2 = [0\ 1\ 1]$.

b. Generate the entire code.

c. By inspection of the results of part b, determine the minimum distance of the code.

3-2. a. Find the parity-check matrix H for the code of Problem 3-1.

b. Do the same for the code of Examples 4-11 and 4-12. (This is the well-known (7,4) Hamming code.)

3-3. a. Find a standard array for the code of Problem 3-1. Use the array to decode the following received vectors: [0 0 0 0 1], [1 0 1 0 1], [1 1 1 1 1].

b. Use syndromes to decode the vectors of part a.

3-4. Carry out the computations of Examples 3-14, 3-15, and 3-16 for received vector $y_R = 011$.

4-1. Show that for a cyclic shift of the row vector representation of a word in an (n,k) cyclic code, the corresponding polynomial representation must be reduced modulo $t^n - 1$. (Try the one-place shift ta (t) of code word a (t).)

4-2. Prove the following statements (which are made on page 72 of the text) about cyclic codes:

a. All polynomial multiples of generator polynomial g(t), after reduction modulo $t^n - 1$, are code words of the same cyclic (n,k) code.

b. g(t) is a factor (i.e., an exact divisor) of $t^n - 1$.

c. g(t) has degree n–k.

6-1. For the doce specified by the first line of Table 6-1:

a. Find G and d_{min}, and verify the result $d_{free} = 5$. (It may be helpful to draw the code tree with the help of G.)

b. Draw the encoder shift register.

6-2. For the Code having $\upsilon = 4$ in Table 6-5:

a. Find G.

b. Verify d_{free} and d_{min}.

c. Draw the encoder.

6-3. For the first code in Table 6-8:

a. Find G.

b. Draw the code tree.

c. Find d_{min}.

d. Draw the encoder.

9-1. The search tree of Figure 9-4 was used in conjunction with an example in which the metric function was path likelihood. Suppose, instead, that the metric is Hamming distance. Still using the Fano algorithm, construct a table similar to Table 9-1 for about the first dozen moves in the search. Note: It will be necessary to postulate a second path from the base of the tree. Let this new path have a metric value between $T_o + \Delta$ and $T_o + 2\Delta$ at lengths 1 and 2.

9-2. Refer to Figure 9-5 and 9-6 of the text. Let the branches to nodes 9 and 10 have likelihood values 2 and 1, respectively, and let branches from nodes 7, 8, 9. and 10 have likelihood values 1, 2, 3, 4, 5, 6, 7, and 8, respectively.

a. Continue the little table on p. 167.

b. Produce a decoding decision.

c. Purge members of the incorrect subset.

d. Delete the effect of the decoded branch in the correct subset.

10-1. Show, by deriving detailed expressions for the syndrome digits and orthogonal parity checks, that the diffuse threshold decoder of Figure 10-5 performs as claimed in the text.

10-2. Analyze the operation of the Gallager burst decoder of Figure 10-7.

Index